HOW TO GROW
FUCHSIAS

HOW TO GROW
FUCHSIAS

Beautifully illustrated with 550 photographs showing gardening techniques and varieties

JOHN NICHOLASS

Photography by Peter Anderson

southwater

This edition is published by Southwater
an imprint of Anness Publishing Ltd
Blaby Road, Wigston
Leicestershire LE18 4SE; info@anness.com

www.southwaterbooks.com
www.annesspublishing.com

If you like the images in this book and would
like to investigate using them for publishing,
promotions or advertising, please visit
our website www.practicalpictures.com
for more information.

OCT. 1 1 2012

Publisher: Joanna Lorenz
Senior Editor: Felicity Forster
Photographer: Peter Anderson
Illustrator: Liz Pepperell
Maps: Rob Highton
Designer: Lisa Tai
Cover Design: Nigel Partridge
Production Controller: Christine Ni

ETHICAL TRADING POLICY

At Anness Publishing we believe that
business should be conducted in an ethical
and ecologically sustainable way, with
respect for the environment and a proper
regard to the replacement of the natural
resources we employ.

As a publisher, we use a lot of wood
pulp to make high-quality paper for printing,
and that wood commonly comes from
spruce trees. We are therefore currently
growing more than 750,000 trees in three
Scottish forest plantations: Berrymoss
(130 hectares/320 acres), West Touxhill
(125 hectares/305 acres) and Deveron
Forest (75 hectares/185 acres). The forests
we manage contain more than 3.5 times
the number of trees employed each
year in making paper for the books
we manufacture.

Because of this ongoing ecological
investment programme, you, as our
customer, can have the pleasure and
reassurance of knowing that a tree is
being cultivated on your behalf to naturally
replace the materials used to make the
book you are holding.

Our forestry programme is run in
accordance with the UK Woodland
Assurance Scheme (UKWAS) and will
be certified by the internationally recognized
Forest Stewardship Council (FSC). The FSC
is a non-government organization dedicated
to promoting responsible management of
the world's forests. Certification ensures
forests are managed in an environmentally
sustainable and socially responsible way.
For further information about this scheme,
go to www.annesspublishing.com/trees.

© Anness Publishing Ltd 2012

A CIP catalogue record for this book
is available from the British Library.

Previously published as part of a larger
volume, as *The Gardener's Guide to
Growing Fuchsias*

PUBLISHER'S NOTE

Although the advice and information
in this book are believed to be accurate
and true at the time of going to press,
neither the authors nor the publisher
can accept any legal responsibility or
liability for any errors or omissions that
may have been made nor for any
inaccuracies nor for any loss, harm
or injury that comes about from following
instructions or advice in this book.

CONTENTS

INTRODUCTION   6
Origins and history   8
The early hybridizers   10
Fuchsia species   12
Hybridization trends   14

THE FUCHSIA GARDEN   16
Single specimen fuchsias   18
Specimen plants as features   20
Groups of specimen plants   22
Red and white fuchsias   24
Fuchsias as summer bedding   26
Triphyllas as summer bedding   28
Upward-looking fuchsias   30
Triphylla fuchsias   32
Fuchsias in the shrub border   34
Fuchsias in the rockery   36
Pink and white fuchsias   38
Permanent fuchsia beds   40
Fuchsia beds with hedging   42
Fuchsias in cottage gardens   44
Aubergine fuchsias   46
Standard fuchsias   48
Trained fuchsias   52
Blue fuchsias   56

THE CONTAINER GARDEN   58
Large pots   60
Urns   64
Troughs and boxes   66
Hanging baskets   68
Hanging pots   72
Half baskets and wall troughs   74
Wall pots   76
Chimney pots   78
Putting containers together   80

THE INDOOR GARDEN   82
Fuchsias inside the home   84
Conservatory fuchsias   88
Varieties for a conservatory   90
Greenhouse fuchsias   92
Ventilation, shading and heating   96
Varieties for a greenhouse   98
Shadehouse fuchsias   100

GARDENING TECHNIQUES   104
Selecting and buying fuchsias   106
Composts and feeds   108
Hybridization techniques   110
Propagating fuchsias   112

Potting on   114
Multi-planting   116
Training shrub and bush fuchsias   118
Growing standard fuchsias   120
Growing pillars and pyramids   122
Growing espaliers and fans   124
Bonsais and fuchsia topiary   126
Planting in containers   128
Planting in hanging baskets   130
Planting in borders   132
Planting a hardy fuchsia bed   134
Planting a fuchsia hedge   136
Pruning fuchsias   138
Overwintering fuchsias   140
Pests and diseases   142

CALENDAR OF CARE   146
Spring care   148
Summer care   150
Autumn care   152
Winter care   154

Useful addresses   156
Index   158
Acknowledgements   160

Introduction

This is a book for anyone who loves fuchsias. It describes how to grow them, which types are best for particular positions in the garden, and how to deal with any problems that might arise in their cultivation. Fuchsias are superb summer-flowering plants. They are fast growing, come in a range of flower colours and sizes and can be used in containers, hanging baskets and as summer bedding in the garden borders. These versatile plants also have a range of growth types – some are upright and bushy, others are trailing or cascading, and some even have a rambling habit, ideal for decorating walls and fences. Fuchsias are very easy to train into different shapes, the standard fuchsia being most familiar.

IN THIS BOOK

Wild fuchsias grow mainly in warm parts of the southern hemisphere, where they enjoy the climate. The first section of this book gives a short history of the fuchsia's distribution, discovery and hybridization.

Next, a section on the fuchsia garden is packed with ideas for growing these rewarding plants, whether as temporary residents in a summer border or as

Top: The large double flower of 'Irene Sinton', with its blush-pink sepals, a full lilac-blue corolla and splashes of pink on the petals. The opening flower bud, sprinkled with raindrops, is about to reveal its inner secrets.

permanent shrubs, or even hedges. There are also tips for growing fuchsias in containers and, for those who really want to extend the growing season of these stunning plants, the book gives instructions for growing fuchsias inside the house, in the greenhouse, in a shadehouse or in a conservatory.

Then comes a section on practical gardening techniques, which explains how to select and buy fuchsia plants, how to train fuchsias into all sorts of shapes, hints on planting containers, taking cuttings, and keeping the plants alive over the winter. There is information about pests and

diseases, with tips for dealing with the most common problems that may occur.

The book concludes with a calendar of care that lists the appropriate tasks to be carried out in each season – for example, when to encourage dormant plants back into life, when to re-pot shooting plants to give them a boost, how to care for standards to make sure they will flower well from year to year, when to take cuttings, and when to plant up hanging baskets and containers.

Every gardener will be able to find something in the following pages to inspire them to experiment with some different fuchsia cultivars and planting techniques.

Left: A mixture of hardy fuchsias growing in a border next to a lawn, with dancing red and purple flowers. A fruiting clematis vine with fluffy seed heads can be seen in the background, scrambling over a fence.

Right: A hardy fuchsia growing strongly against a high stone wall, and partially covering a wrought-iron gate.

Origins and history

The fuchsia belongs to the plant family Onagraceae, a family that also includes the genus *Oenothera* (evening primrose) and the genus *Epilobium*, for example *Chamerion angustifolium* (rosebay willowherb or fireweed). The original discovery of the genus *Fuchsia* was in the southern hemisphere, and the first record of the fuchsia in Western civilization was in the early 18th century. The European explorers and plant collectors of the 18th and 19th centuries brought back many of the species fuchsias from which the range of cultivars we grow today were developed, including hardies, Triphyllas, single and double-flowered fuchsias, and those with upright trailing habits.

GEOGRAPHICAL DISTRIBUTION

There are more than 100 identified fuchsia species found mainly in the southern hemisphere of the world. The majority are originally from South America, with most of the remainder found in Central America, Tahiti and New Zealand.

The genus *Fuchsia* is divided into nine sections, covering the wide range of discovered plant forms. Most are tropical or subtropical shrubs, which vary in height.

F. excorticata from New Zealand is unusual, in that it is a tree growing up to 12–15m (39–49ft) in its native habitat.

The fuchsias from the section known as *Quelusia* originate from the colder southern parts of South America, and these plants allowed fuchsia cultivars to be developed with winter hardiness. Of these, *F. regia*, *F. magellanica* and *F. coccinea* are the most common and the best varieties for areas with cold winters.

Top left: *F. fulgens*, a species fuchsia growing wild in Central America. It has beautiful long red flowers and forms root tubers.

Below left: Many of the known fuchsia species flourish in the wild in South and Central America, where they are mainly found along the chain of the Andes mountains.

Below: Fuchsia species of the section Skinnera originate from New Zealand, where the Maoris used the blue pollen from the flowers of *F. excorticata* for body decoration.

KEY
- Sections Jimenezia, Encliandra, Fuchsia, Scufia and Ellobium
- Sections Fuchsia and Hemsleyella
- Sections Fuchsia, Pachyrrhiza and Hemsleyella
- Sections Quelusia and Kiershlegerai

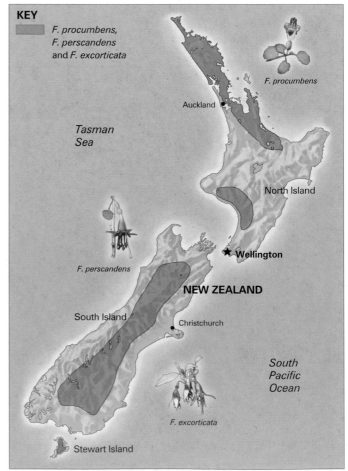

KEY
- *F. procumbens*, *F. perscandens* and *F. excorticata*

DISCOVERY OF THE FUCHSIA

Father Charles Plumier, a Jesuit priest working as a missionary in San Domingo in the Caribbean, was the first European to record this beautiful plant. He named it *Fuchsia triphylla flore coccinea* in honour of Dr Leonhard Fuchs, a noted 16th-century herbalist and professor of medicine in Germany. The fuchsia was later renamed simply *Fuchsia triphylla* according to the well-known rules developed by the Swedish naturalist Linnaeus.

It should be noted that there are two different pronunciations of the word fuchsia. In Germany, the Netherlands and other parts of Europe the pronunciation is 'fook-sya', while in the UK, USA and Australia the pronunciation is a softer 'fyew-sha'. The first version reflects more closely the fact that the word is based on the German name 'Fuchs'.

ARRIVAL IN EUROPE

It is difficult to establish the exact date when the cultivation of fuchsia species began in Europe. It is likely that Plumier brought some seeds of this exciting plant back to France with him and he would probably have given some of them to other gardeners. There is a reference to the plant *Thiles*, which is the native name of the fuchsia in southern Chile, with an illustration, published in a French botanical journal of 1725.

The first live plant to reach Europe was *F. coccinea*, brought to England by a Captain Firth and presented to Kew Gardens in 1788. James Lee, a horticulturalist and nurseryman in Hammersmith, then a village outside London, obtained a fuchsia plant and propagated it, offering the plants for sale in 1793. After this more plants and seeds quickly arrived and were developed, as we can see in the records at Kew Gardens. First *F. lycioides* arrived in 1796; then *F. arborescens* in 1824; *F. microphylla* in 1827; *F. fulgens* in 1830; *F. corymbiflora* in 1840; and in 1843–44, *F. apetala*, *F. decussata*, *F. dependens* and *F. serratifolia*. Many other species and variants have been discovered.

Above: *F. magellanica*, a profusely flowering species from which many hardy cultivars originate. It is very hardy and grows wild on the mountains of Magellan, one of the coldest parts of South America.

FIRST HYBRIDS

As early as 1825, there were attempts at hybridization between species. The first attempt was to cross *F. arborescens* with *F coccinea* and *F. arborescens* with *F. macrostemma*, but the results were unclear. Over the next 25 years, Europe saw the introduction of many new successful cultivars, several of which were confusingly similar, and also many very different ones under the same popular name, such as 'Queen Victoria'. In 1840 the first cultivar with a white tube and sepals was produced, called 'Venus Victrix'. It is still available commercially, and is reputed to be the parent of many of today's white cultivars, although some experts would dispute this. In 1848, the release of the first double-flowered cultivar, 'Duplex', was credited to William Storey, although this may have had only seven petals.

The early hybridizers

In the last half of the 19th and the first part of the 20th century, several important, prolific hybridizers introduced a tremendous range of new cultivars. Their work is the basis of the range of cultivars now available. Most of this early hybridization took place in Europe, especially in the UK and France, where Félix Porcher's book *Le Fuchsia: Son Histoire et sa Culture* reached its fourth edition by 1874. Although many of these early cultivars are now lost, some – especially the hardy ones – are still grown. However, the naming of new cultivars was then an unorganized process, with many cultivars being given identical names in various counties, while many similar cultivars were given different names.

EDWARD BANKS (ENGLAND)

Born in 1820, Banks ran a fuchsia nursery on the outskirts of Deal, in Kent, and was one of the largest producers of fuchsias in his time. He also hybridized fuchsias and introduced 111 new cultivars, many of which are still grown today, including 'Arabella', 'Blue Beauty', 'Forget-Me-Not', 'Rose of Castile' and 'Rose of Denmark'. He died aged 90, in 1910, when fuchsias were declining in popularity in the UK.

Top: 'Rose of Denmark' was hybridized by Edward Banks and introduced in 1855. It is a hardy cultivar with pink/rose-pink flowers.

Below: 'Phenomenal' is a hardy French cultivar with large double scarlet/indigo-blue flowers. It was hybridized and introduced by Victor Lemoine in 1869.

VICTOR LEMOINE (FRANCE)

One of the most prolific fuchsia hybridizers of his era, Lemoine produced around 450–500 new cultivars, as well as being famous for new varieties of other genera, including lilacs, hydrangeas, pelargoniums and weigela. He was born in Delme in 1823; his family had a long history of being nurserymen and gardeners, and from his early years he had a huge interest in horticulture. He trained with some of the finest nurserymen in Europe and later started his own nursery in Nancy. Among the many fuchsia cultivars he produced that are still widely grown today are 'Abbé Farges', 'Brutus', 'Caledonia', 'Drame', 'Emile de Wildman', 'Enfant Prodigue', 'Flocon de Neige', 'Phenomenal', 'Royal Purple' and 'Voltaire'.

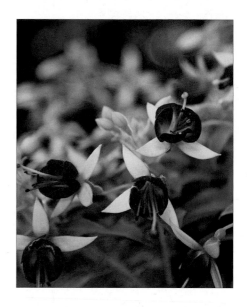

Above: 'Rose of Castile', introduced by Edward Banks in 1855, is a long-established hardy cultivar with white/red-purple flowers.

JAMES LYE (ENGLAND)

One of the best-known English fuchsia hybridizers in the 19th century was James Lye, who produced many cultivars bearing his hallmark of flowers with waxy white tubes and sepals. Born in 1830 in Market Lavington, Worcestershire, he started as a 12-year-old apprentice to the head gardener in the gardens of Clyffe Hall and actually became head gardener when he was 23.

He became interested in fuchsias in the late 1850s, and the first record of one of his fuchsia cultivars was in 1869. He went on to introduce 82 cultivars, most of which had strong, upright growth with the distinctive Lye characteristics. He became famous for growing large specimen pillars

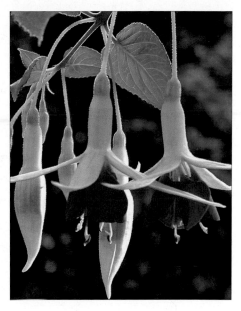

Above: This late 19th-century picture shows James Lye in front of several of his large trained fuchsias in the gardens of Clyffe Hall.

Above: 'Lye's Unique' has single flowers with a long waxy-white tube and sepals, and a beautifully contrasting salmon-orange corolla.

Above: 'Amy Lye' has medium-sized single flowers with a creamy white tube and sepals, and a coral-orange corolla. It is easy to train.

and pyramids, 2.5–3m (8–10ft) high and 1.2–1.5m (4–5ft) in diameter at the base, which had to be transported to exhibitions by horse and cart. Many of the cultivars he produced are still readily available; they include 'Amy Lye', 'Beauty of Trowbridge', 'Charming', 'Harriet Lye', 'Loveliness', 'Lye's Excelsior' and 'Lye's Unique'.

CARL BONSTEDT (GERMANY)
At the end of the 19th century and the beginning of the 20th century, Bonstedt started to produce hybrids from *F. triphylla*, including 'Bornemanns Beste', 'Mary', 'Thalia', 'Coralle', 'Gartenmeister Bonstedt', 'Göttingen' and 'Traudchen Bonstedt'.

These introductions are some of the best Triphylla hybrids available and are still widely grown today.

Born in 1866 in Naumburg, he trained as a gardener at the Pomologischen Institute in Proskau, and later spent some years in Great Britain, notably at Kew Gardens. On returning to Germany, he headed the Botanical Gardens at Rostock from 1892–1900, and then became Technical Director of the Botanical Garden in Göttingen. He was involved in the breeding of other genera, including primroses and lilies. He also wrote and lectured on horticultural subjects, and edited *Parey's Flower Garden*. Bonstedt died in 1953.

OTHER EARLY HYBRIDIZERS
In the later part of the 19th century, Cornelissen hybridized fuchsias in his Belgian nursery, and is best known for 'Madame Cornelissen', a very good hardy cultivar that is still widely available. He also introduced the variegated leaf cultivar 'Meteor', possibly still grown as 'Autumnale'. In Germany, Johan Nepomuk Twrdy produced around 40 cultivars. Among those still available are 'Europa' (1872), 'Papagena' (1870) and 'Schneeball' (1874). Other important hybridizers include Bull, Bass, Henderson, Vietch and Storey in England, and Rozain-Bouchariat and Meillez in France.

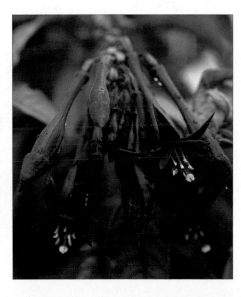

Far left: The hot flower colours of 'Gartenmeister Bonstedt', standing out among the surrounding shrubs and palms.

Left: The Triphylla 'Mary', showing its clusters of vivid red flowers and green velvety leaves, is a beautiful sight.

Fuchsia species

Many of the species fuchsias, which mainly originate from South and Central America, are unrecognizable to those who are used to modern fuchsia cultivars. Their form varies from small prostrate spreading plants with upright flowers, to shrubs with glossy leaves and panicle flower spikes, up to small trees. The species fuchsias, unlike their modern hybrid cultivar descendants, will grow true from seed, the main mechanism of their spread and survival in the wild. Categorization of the species is divided into nine separate sections, the largest of which is sub-divided into many different groups. Many of the primary species have several variants that occur naturally in the wild.

SECTION QUELUSIA

The plants in this section come from Argentina, Chile and the south-east coast of Brazil. This section is historically very important to the modern cultivars, since most winter hardiness came from hybridization of this group. It includes *F. alpestris*, *F. coccinea*, *F. glazioviana*, *F. magellanica* and *F. regia*.

   F. magellanica is a hardy shrub originating from the southern mountainous regions of South America. It has small single flowers with a red tube, deep red sepals and a purple corolla, freely produced on an upright bush with small mid- to dark green

Top: The climbing species shrub *F. boliviana* occurs naturally from southern Peru to northern Argentina, and has clusters of striking red tubular flowers.

leaves. This species is very hardy and is an ancestor of many of the fuchsias grown today. It has many natural variants, often grown as hardy garden shrubs.

SECTION FUCHSIA (EUFUCHSIA)

This is the largest section, containing 13 different subgroups of plants found in the tropical Andes, Haiti and the Dominican Republic. The fuchsias in this group are usually tender and have flowers with long tubes and short sepals, and include *F. abrupta*, *F. boliviana*, *F. decussata*, *F. denticulata*, *F. loxensis*, *F. macrophylla*, *F. pallescens*, *F. sessilifolia*, *F. tincta*, *F. triphylla*, *F. venusta* and *F. vulcanica*.

   F. boliviana is a climbing shrub with large hairy mid- to dark green red-veined leaves up to 20 x 10cm (8 x 4in) and

clusters of long red-tubed flowers. It occurs from southern Peru to northern Argentina growing at elevations up to 3,000m (10,000ft), and easily reaching 5m (16ft) in height. It also has a white-tubed variant, *F. boliviana* var. *alba*, which is synonymous with *F. corymbiflora alba*.

   F. denticulata is a very attractive species, easy for the beginner to grow. The flower has a long, light pink to red waxy tube, small pink to light red sepals turning green at the tips and an orange to scarlet corolla. The growth is upright, with large dark green spear-shaped leaves, normally 3–4 per node. It generally flowers best in the spring and autumn, the flowering becoming sparse in the summer. It originates from Peru and Colombia, where it can grow to more than 5m (16ft) in height.

Left: *F. glazioviana* is a species from the cloud forests of southern Brazil, with deep pink and mauve semi-erect flowers.

Right: *F. denticulata* is a species from Peru and Bolivia, and is an easy and rewarding species for the beginner to try. It has striking long flowers with multiple colours.

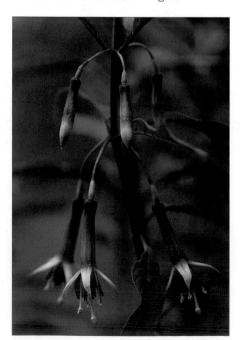

SECTION KIERSCHLEGERIA

This section, found in central Chile, has only one member, *F. lycioides*.

SECTION SKINNERA

This section is found in New Zealand and Tahiti. The fuchsias have unusual flower colours and blue pollen and include *F. x colensoi*, *F. cyrtandroides*, *F. excorticata* and *F. procumbens*.

F. procumbens is a very unusual species with its prostrate spreading growth, small green fernlike leaves, tiny yellow-green upward-facing flowers with no corolla and blue pollen, and red grapelike fruits. This species is easy to grow, but will benefit from the addition of sharp sand to the growing mix. If you grow it in an elevated position – in a pot on a kitchen stool, for example – it will trail attractively downwards. In time, the long growths can reach 1.5m (5ft).

SECTION HEMSLEYELLA

This section, found in the tropical Andes (Bolivia and Venezuela), contains 14 species, including *F. apetala*, *F. garleppiana*, *F. inflata*, *F. juntasensis*, *F. mezae*, *F. pilaloensis* and *F. salicifolia*.

SECTION SCHUFIA

Plants in this section are shrubs with flowers that are erect on the plant in a corymb-like panicle, and include *F. arborescens*, *F. paniculata* and subspecies.

F. paniculata grows like a shrub, with strong upright growth and large glossy laurel-like leaves. It has tiny pink flowers, held upright in large clusters, and later bears small dark berries. This species is an easy one for the beginner to grow and often known as the lilac fuchsia.

SECTION ENCLIANDRA

This section, which is found growing on the mountainous slopes of Central America and Mexico, has very small flowers and leaves. It includes the species *F. encliandra*, *F. microphylla*, *F. thymifolia* and their subspecies. Many of the fuchsias in this section are quite hardy.

F. encliandra is a rather hardy shrub with tiny rose-orchid to red flowers, small

Above: *F. procumbens* is a hardy prostrate spreading species with upright flowers, and comes from New Zealand.

broad ovate leaves and small black berry fruits, and will grow up to 2.4m (8ft) tall left unchecked in the wild. In cultivation, it grows well in semi-shaded positions.

SECTION JIMENEZIA

This section, found in Panama and Costa Rica, has only one member, *F. jimenezii*.

SECTION ELLOBIUM

This section is found in Central America and Mexico. The fuchsias are unusual in forming root tubers. The section contains *F. decidua*, *F. fulgens* and *F. splendens*.

Above: *F. microphylla* originates from Mexico. It is a fairly hardy shrubby species with tiny but very pretty red flowers which then produce black berries.

Right: *F. paniculata* is a stunning upright shrub originating from southern Mexico and Panama. It has glossy leaves and panicles of tiny purple-pink flowers.

Hybridization trends

Extensive fuchsia hybridization in the last 150 years has resulted in many new cultivars we can still grow today. With this rich heritage in mind, it is fascinating to look at recent hybridization trends around the world. It takes at least five years from sowing the seed that results from the hybridization cross, following a process of selection and testing for genetic stability, until a new cultivar is ready for release to the gardening public. Growing either the seedling or a tip cutting from it without stopping enables growers to assess the growth habit, to see how naturally self-branching it is and most importantly, promotes earlier flowering so that the new fuchsia's flower potential can be judged.

EFFECTS OF CLIMATE CHANGE

All gardeners, not just fuchsia growers, face new challenges from the changing climatic conditions brought on by global warming, and current predictions indicate these conditions are going to be with us for some years. This is going to make some aspects of gardening more difficult, but those living in colder latitudes will be able to grow more tender plants as winter temperatures rise, and this could greatly increase the range of viable fuchsias. There are already lists available on the internet giving details of fuchsias that tolerate the heat of the sun, and those that are more resistant to pests and diseases. Most of the fuchsias we grow today have *F. magellanica* blood in them and hybridizers are investigating other species fuchsias to introduce new characteristics.

UNITED STATES

The rapid spread of the fuchsia gall mite since its arrival in California in the early 1980s has caused the fuchsia to drop in popularity in the USA, especially since the big colourful doubles seem to be the most affected by the pest. There are now fewer active hybridizers of fuchsias than in former years, but those who are still working in the field are focusing on breeding new mite-resistant fuchsias.

Top: 'Flying Cloud' is a large double, white-flowered, lax spreading cultivar from San Francisco, typical of the flamboyant Californian cultivars. It was hybridized by Victor Reiter from San Francisco and released in 1949.

Nearly all the species are tested for mite resistance, and new cultivars have now been produced; lists of resistant fuchsias are available. You can read articles on the subject via the American Fuchsia Society website, where one author, Dr Peter Baye, has described the results obtained at Annapolis, California and is advocating a wider 'open pollination' programme from resistant varieties.

Among the hybridizers responsible for large beautiful double cultivars associated with California are Robert Castro, Raymond Hodges, Charles Kennett, Gus Niederholzer, Annabelle Stubbs, Hazard and Hazard, Tiret, Muriel Waltz and Mrs Soo Young.

Below: *F. magellanica* var. *aurea* is a golden-leaf variant of *F. magellanica*, with small red and purple single flowers. It will show the best leaf colour in a sunny position.

Above: 'Apricot Ice' is a recent single-flowered cultivar. The flowers are crisp apricot-cream and a lovely rich apricot.

AUSTRALIA

Ronald Lockerbie was the first prolific hybridizer of fuchsias in Australia, followed by Richardson, Richardson/Yandina and Southall. The preference in Australia, as in the USA, seems to be for double cultivars, and especially those that are suitable for baskets. Some of the best of these have become available in other countries, for instance 'Australia Day', 'Happy Wedding Day' and 'Marlene Gilbee'. There was a stir when a new variety named after Ronald Lockerbie was reputed to be the first yellow fuchsia, but sadly it turned out to be more of a cream colour, at least in northern European light conditions.

NEW ZEALAND

There are very different growing conditions from the southern tip of the South Island to the northern point of the North Island. The cultivars hybridized in New Zealand are a mixture of single, semi-double and double cultivars, both upright and trailing. Some well-known hybridizers are Sharpe and Proffit, who have introduced cultivars such as 'Apricot Slice' and 'Ted Sweetman', and Butcher, who has introduced a number of cultivars with the prefix 'Omar', many grown outside New Zealand.

EUROPE

In Europe there has been a revival of fuchsia hybridization, with prolific hybridizers such as Carel Roes and Herman de Graaff in the Netherlands, Marcel Michiels in Belgium, Karl Strümper in Germany, René Massé in France, and Edwin Goulding and Mick Allsop in the UK. There have been some interesting new flower colours, such as the aubergine fuchsias started by de Graaff, as well as large doubles with very long tubes, and some unusual cultivars obtained by crossing back or between the species – all produced by the efforts of these dedicated enthusiasts.

Right: 'Hazel' is a large double-flowered, lax-growing fuchsia hybridized by Richardson of Australia and released in 1985.

Above: 'Gerharda's Aubergine' is a beautiful fuchsia that has a vigorous trailing habit and looks wonderful in a hanging pot.

LOOKING FORWARD

One challenge that remains is to produce a true yellow fuchsia, which will doubtless happen at some point in the future. Hybridizers are also trying hard to develop gall mite-resistant and heat-resistant fuchsias with a bigger range of flower sizes and colours for fuchsia lovers to grow.

THE FUCHSIA GARDEN

Fuchsias flower profusely in the summer, often blooming from late spring right through to the first autumn frosts. A greenhouse can extend that flowering period even further, with plants either kept under cover all year round, or brought outside for the warmer months. This chapter will give you many ideas for using fuchsias in a garden scheme. Large hardy fuchsia cultivars look splendid alongside other evergreen and deciduous shrubs to provide some areas of the garden with colour interest all the year round. Many hardy fuchsias will make a beautiful flowering hedge as a division within a garden. Non-hardy fuchsias make excellent summer bedding plants. Grown on their own as specimen plants, cultivars such as 'Border Queen' and 'Celia Smedley' can be really striking. Triphylla hybrids such as 'Thalia' or 'Coralle', mixed with other traditional summer bedding plants, make an attractive natural border. Smaller, more compact fuchsias can be excellent edging plants for flowerbeds or for the rockery.

Left: This splendid example of the hardy cultivar 'Margaret Brown', with its pretty single flowers, is more than 1.8m (6ft) tall, and looks beautiful growing among other shrubs such as weigela and camellia.

Top left: 'Brenda White' is an attractive single-flowered cultivar which is perfect for a border edging plant or small standard. It has lightish foliage and a truly classic bell-shaped flower.

Top middle: 'Tennessee Waltz' is a beautiful hardy with large red and lilac-lavender semi-double flowers. It is excellent as a permanent planting or for use in a summer border.

Top right: 'Celia Smedley' has medium to large neyron-rose/currant-red single flowers and is excellent for a bedding plant used in the centre of a border.

Single specimen fuchsias

Large fuchsia plants can make striking, eye-catching centrepieces when grown as specimen plants. When grown in large pots using a large single plant or multi-planting placed in the centre of a terrace or patio, they will clamour for your attention. Alternatively, for a display requiring less maintenance, plant them in the ground in the main garden borders, or dominating a small border in a paved area. They can make a striking focal point when grown against the right background. For example, you can choose a flower colour that contrasts well with a ground cover of chippings or slate, or the backdrop colour when grown in front of a fence or hedge.

SELECTION AND PLACEMENT

With such a range of flower colours and sizes, and a long summer-flowering period, using fuchsias as specimen feature plants gives very satisfying results. If you are lucky enough to live in an area with mild winters, where the stems of hardy fuchsias survive, you can make them part of a permanent planting scheme. Otherwise, specimen plants need winter protection to survive. This will allow them to start into growth again in the late winter and early spring, and will ensure they look good each year. Large specimen plants can be formed from single plants trained as shrubs or bushes, or one of the trained shapes. Alternatively, to obtain a large specimen in a short time, the multi-plant technique works well.

Use these specimen plants to create a focal point on terraces or patios, in the middle of lawns, on the edges of wide steps, beside gates or doorways or on large areas of gravel or stone chippings. They also look very striking in low stone or brick walls, which have a planting area built into them, or in a square stone pot placed on top of a wide wall – as long as it is stable and cannot be knocked over or blown off by the wind. Pick the right fuchsia for the height of the wall – for a low wall, an upright-growing variety will look best, and for a medium or high wall, a more lax variety will create a flowing effect, cascading downward.

Top left: 'Thalia', a Triphylla hybrid, has racemes of long brilliant red flowers contrasting perfectly with its dark olive-green leaves, and flourishes in full sun.

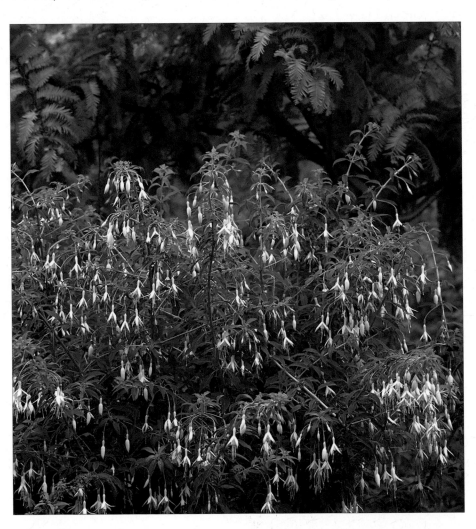

SUNNY AND HOT AREAS

Triphylla hybrids are a natural choice for sunny and hot areas, where they will reward you with continuous flowering through the summer. Grow them in the ground or in large porous clay pots to help keep the roots cool. This is one of the most important factors to ensure fuchsias do well when exposed to full sun.

Above: This striking shrub of 'Hawkshead', planted permanently in the ground, is covered with small white flowers contrasted against the small dark green leaves.

DAPPLED SHADE AREAS

Areas with dappled shade are ideal for growing most fuchsias, as they recreate the conditions where the species grows naturally in the wild. Good examples

SINGLE SPECIMENS

Plants that form a good natural shape with distinctive flowers that stand out from the foliage are superb to use as specimen plants.

Full sun: 'City of Leicester', 'Coralle', 'Falling Stars', 'Gartenmeister Bonstedt', 'Genii', 'Joan Pacey', 'Nancy Lou', 'Other Fellow', 'Tennessee Waltz', 'Thalia'

Dappled shade: 'Border Queen', 'Lady Kathleen Spence', 'Lilian', 'Misty Blue', 'Rolla'

Shady: 'Alaska', 'Constellation', 'Evensong', 'Flirtation Waltz', 'Florence Mary Abbot', 'Iceberg', 'Lady Kathleen Spence', 'Ting a Ling'

Shady against white background: 'Gruss aus dem Bodenthal', 'Haute Cuisine', 'Marin Glow', 'Ortenburger Festival', 'Roesse Blacky', 'Royal Velvet', 'Symphony'

Above: 'Richard John Carrington' is a bush cultivar and has medium-sized single flowers with bright cerise sepals and a blue-violet corolla. This compact hardy plant has light green foliage that ages to dark green.

are on the edges of the shade cast by open tree canopies, in the shade created by artificial structures, or near east- or west-facing walls.

While you can use almost any of the fuchsia cultivars in these areas, the pastel-coloured varieties look at their best in dappled shade, as their flower colours intensify.

SHADY AREAS

Fuchsias will grow well in light shade, although this can reduce the amount of growth they will make in a season. An ideal situation would be a wall that gets the early morning and the late evening sun, painted white or a light colour, so that it will reflect any available light back on to the plant. Many of the white or light pastel-coloured fuchsias will do well here, as the whites stay really white in the shade, rather than taking on pink hues, as sometimes happens when they are in bright sunlight.

Right: 'Genii' is a superb hardy cultivar whose foliage becomes a vivid yellow-green in a sunny position, contrasting beautifully with the delicate red and purple single flowers. Here, it is growing by a path together with other shrubs.

Alternatively, you can use fuchsias with very dark flower colours, as many of them have a tendency to bleach in the sun. In shadier conditions, they will maintain their deep colours without fading. The flowers will not show up as well as light-coloured ones, though, unless you give them a light background, such as a painted wall or perhaps a golden-leaved hedge.

Right: 'Other Fellow' drips continuously with waxy white and coral-pink single flowers on a vigorous plant with mid-green foliage. It is a really eye-catching fuchsia when grown as a single specimen.

Specimen plants as features

When they are given sufficient root room and encouragement, many of the more vigorous fuchsias can grow into large plants quite quickly. Placed at key locations in the garden or on the garden boundaries, they make excellent eye-catchers. The large feature fuchsias can be divided into the non-hardy and hardy kinds. In temperate climates, non-hardy ones need to be grown in large pots and moved into a greenhouse or conservatory every winter, so that they can keep growing from year to year. Hardy varieties can be left in the ground all year. In very cold areas, however, where winter temperatures may kill the wood structure back to the ground, then they should be treated like non-hardy types.

FAST-GROWING HALF-HARDY FUCHSIAS

These are best grown in large pots, either using a single plant grown over a few years, allowing it to reach a suitable size, or the multi-plant technique described later in this book. Growing fuchsias to a large size in pots requires quite a lot of watering and feeding, but the rewards are high. The plants make good eye-catchers when in flower, especially some of the Triphylla cultivars, and the pots are easy to remove and replace with a flowering or winter-berrying substitute when they stop

Top: A large specimen of the hardy fuchsia 'Riccartonii', permanently planted in the west of England. This plant is around 4m (13ft) high and is covered in flowers.

performing. Good vigorous contenders include the following:

• 'Barbara', an upright cultivar with medium-sized bell-shaped single pink flowers. As it is not very self-branching, it needs some early pinching to encourage it to form a bushy plant.

• 'Celia Smedley', with large white blushed pink and red single flowers. It makes a lot of heavy wood quickly, is a strong upright and responds well to intense feeding.

• 'Checkerboard', a strong upright with long arching branches covered with unusual, attractive single flowers with a red tube, white sepals and a deep red corolla.

• 'Kolding Perle', another strong upright producing long branches covered with medium-large white and red single flowers.

• 'Lady Isobel Barnett', a strong-growing and upright cultivar that is one of the most floriferous. It has rosy-red and rose purple flared single flowers and will be eye-catching for long periods.

• 'Phenomenal', an old, fast-growing strong upright with bushy growth. Because of the weight and size of its large double red and deep indigo blue flowers, the main branches need cane supports in the early years, to prevent them from snapping.

FAST-GROWING HARDY FUCHSIAS

Many of the hardy varieties make a significant amount of growth in a single season, and several grow 1.5m (5ft) a year. When grown in areas with milder winters, typically zone 9 and above, temperatures will not be low enough to kill the old wood down to the ground, and these fuchsias can therefore be pruned down to the main framework. Over a few years, they will make large plants, and one of the best examples concerns a 'Riccartonii'. One was planted on the island of Valentia off the south-west coast of Ireland in 1854. By 1870 it had reached a circumference of 36m (120ft) and, by 1905, it was 76m (250ft) and had reached the cliff edge. The island's climate is windswept, mild and wet. As the branches bend over in the wind and touch the ground, they root readily, making new plants and eventually forming a large thicket covered with flowers.

Left: A large hardy fuchsia is growing over an old brick wall, dripping its flowers on to the pavement outside.

Above: *F. magellanica* var. *molinae* is a fantastic hardy fuchsia with vigorous growth, whose alternative US name of 'Maiden's Blush' comes from the small white and pale pinkish-lilac flowers.

Above: The classic red and purple flowers of *F. magellanica* var. *gracilis* are delicately hanging on its beautiful arching branches. It is a wonderful fuchsia, and is seen in many gardens.

That is very unlikely to happen in your garden but, with suitable annual pruning and shaping, it is possible to obtain a substantial shrub using a hardy fuchsia. Those worth trying include:

• 'Hawkshead', with upright growth of 1.3m (4ft) a year, small white flowers and dark green foliage. The flowers remain white even in direct sun.

• *F. magellanica* var. *gracilis* or *F. m.* var. *gracilis* 'Variegata', both with spreading, arching growth of 1–1.2m (3–4ft) a year and dainty red and purple flowers, and the latter with silvery variegated leaves. It looks very good on a hill or elevated position.

• *F. magellanica* var. *molinae*, with upright growth of 1.5m (5ft) a year and small white and pale lilac flowers.

• 'Mrs Popple', a strong-growing hardy cultivar which strong upright branches and plentiful medium-sized scarlet and violet-purple single flowers. This cultivar will easily grow 1–1.2m (3–4ft) in a season.

• 'Riccartonii', which has upright growth of 1.5m (5ft) a year and small single red and purple flowers.

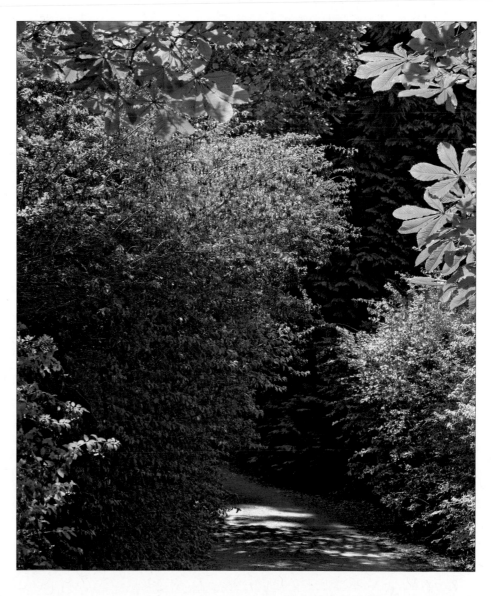

Right: These hardy fuchsias, growing under the shade of a large horse chestnut tree, are overhanging a narrow roadway and making it almost impassable.

Groups of specimen plants

Large fuchsias grouped together in pots or planted permanently in the ground look spectacular when in flower from early summer onwards. If you choose plants with contrasting flower colours and possibly different foliage colours, the impact can be even greater; on the other hand, if you use several plants of the same variety, you can create the effect of a single, much larger specimen. In milder climates, typically Zone 9 and above, groups of hardy fuchsias can be trained into large shrubs to form a large, easy centrepiece needing minimal attention. Groups of pot-grown fuchsias can also be effective, especially when arranged in tiers, one above the other, making them easily visible from a distance.

GROUPS OF HARDY FUCHSIAS

Here are some suggestions for groups of three hardy fuchsias to place close together – either planted out permanently or in pots – with a choice of different sizes, depending on how much space is available.

For a group of large plants, place 'Riccartonii' at the back, which has upright growth of 1.5m (5ft) a year, with small single red and purple flowers, and *F. magellanica* var. *molinae* beside it; it will reach the same height and give small white and pale lilac flowers. In front of these two,

Top: 'Beacon Rosa' is a lovely hardy fuchsia with self pink flared single flowers that contrast well against the dark green leaves, which have a serrated edge.

the lower-growing *F. magellanica* var. *gracilis* 'Variegata' looks very attractive, with spreading arching growth of 1–1.2m (3–4ft) a year and dainty red and purple flowers and silvery variegated leaves.

A group of medium-sized hardy fuchsias could include 'Hawkshead' at the back; it has upright growth of 1.2m (4ft) a year and small white flowers with dark green foliage. Grow it beside the upright 'Margaret', which puts on 90cm (3ft) a year, and has small single rose-pink and light rose-coloured flowers and light green foliage. 'Genii' goes in front, making an attractive domed bush to a height of 70cm (28in), with golden-green foliage and delicate cerise and violet flowers.

If you only have space for small plants, 'Beacon' is a good choice for the back, with its upright growth of 60cm (2ft) a year, darkish green serrated foliage and deep pink and mauve-pink single flowers. 'Santa Cruz' grows to the same height and has bronze-green foliage and red and reddish-purple semi-double flowers. Use 'Lady

Below left: This pair of 'Mrs Popple' hardy fuchsias, covered with a mass of red and purple flowers, has been planted either side of a flight of steps, guarding the ascent to the rear garden above.

Below: 'Riccartonii' growing in front of the *Canna* 'Tchad'. This is a hardy fuchsia; it is strong growing and often found naturalized in hedgerows.

Thumb' to the front, with its natural mound-forming, bushy compact growth of 40cm (16in) a year, small dark green foliage and red and white semi-double flowers.

GROUPS OF FAST-GROWING NON-HARDY FUCHSIAS

When creating groups of pots, using three again works very well, with two at the back and a third at the front or vice-versa. For a bigger feature, with more height, try a large, raised pot with one or more cascading or upright plants, surrounded by several pots on the ground. You could also use a half or full standard, or a trained shape such as a pillar, in the middle of a group.

For the first possible trio, try 'Celia Smedley' at the back with its large pinkish-white and red flowers and mid-green leaves, contrasting well with 'Phenomenal', an old fast-growing cultivar with large double red and deep indigo-blue flowers. 'Happy Wedding Day' to the front has good strong arching growth and large flared double white flowers.

Another effective group could use the upright 'Royal Velvet' at the back with light to mid-green foliage, crimson red and deep purple double flowers, joined by 'Nancy Lou' with full pink and white double flowers and dark green foliage. 'Annabel',

in front, has lax upright growth, pale green foliage and medium to large white double flowers.

A final suggestion, with all upright, bushy and erect-flowered single cultivars, involves 'WAI 7 Jubelteen' with light green foliage, pink and pinkish-orange single flowers alongside 'Pink Fantasia' with its dark green foliage and red and violet single flowers. In front, 'Dawn Fantasia' has cream and green variegated foliage and single pale pink and pink flowers.

Above left: A tremendous and highly colourful group of hardy cultivars, including 'Joan Smith', 'Rufus', 'Rose of Castile', 'Genii' and 'Rose of Denmark', planted on a sloping border.

Above: These established plants of the hardy cultivar 'Tom Thumb', forming a compact mound, are covered in flower at the front of a herbaceous border.

Below: This superb mixture of hardy fuchsias planted in a long bed surrounding a sculpted grass area with another island bed in the centre is just coming into flower.

Red and white fuchsias

The dancing flowers of red and white fuchsias stand out waving in the breeze, especially in the dawn or evening. A wide choice of red and white fuchsias is available, with single, semi-double or double flowers, in upright or trailing growth habits. Most have red sepals and a white corolla, though there are some with the colours reversed. The colours show up well, since red complements green, and the white makes a good contrast. Cultivars with red sepals and a white corolla were among the first hybridized cultivars. Some that are still cultivated today include 'Madame Cornelissen', introduced in 1860, and 'Snowcap', introduced in 1888. Fuchsias with white sepals and a red corolla include *F. boliviana* var. *alba*, a species with these characteristics, plus 'Waternymph' from 1859, 'Beauty

△ **'Brookwood Belle'** A sturdy, upright, short-jointed cultivar with medium-sized double flowers with cerise sepals and a pink corolla flushed white with red veining on the petals. It makes a good pot plant. This fuchsia was hybridized by Gilbert in the UK in 1988.

△ **'Toby Foreman'** A new cultivar introduced in 2007, hybridized by Peter Waving. It is a small single-flowered fuchsia with deep rose sepals and a white corolla. It has vigorous, short-jointed and bushy growth and is likely to prove a popular cultivar.

△ **'Frosted Flame'** A lovely lax fuchsia with single flowers with white sepals and a barrel-shaped flame-red corolla with white patches at the petal base. It is excellent grown in a half basket and may also be trained as a weeping standard.

△ **'Sir Matt Busby'** This is a trailing fuchsia with small to medium double flowers with red sepals and a flared white corolla with red veins, rather like a smaller version of 'Swingtime'. It grows very well in mixed baskets and containers.

△ **'Snowcap'** This fuchsia is an old hardy cultivar which has proved very adaptable over the years. It has medium-sized semi-double flowers with red sepals and a white corolla with red veins. It can be trained into most shapes, or left to grow as a shrub.

of Trowbridge' from 1879 and 'Lye's Elegance' from 1884. Some fuchsias with white sepals, such as 'Celia Smedley', acquire a pink blush with more direct sunlight. There are some superb showy red and white fuchsias. 'Swingtime', the big American trailing double, is very popular and well worth growing, and other trailing cultivars include 'Princessita', 'Frosted Flame', 'Land van Beveren' and 'Sylvia Barker'. Introductions such as 'Nellie Nuttall', 'Ernie' and 'John Bartlett' are very floriferous singles. Growing red and white-flowered cultivars as large structures works well because of the way the flowers stand out, showing up well from quite a distance. A fan shape of 'Swingtime' or a pyramid of 'Snowcap' will look stunning in the garden with their flowers moving in the wind.

△ **'Lancashire Lad'** This is an upright double-flowered cultivar with red sepals and a red-veined white corolla, with a pretty frill at the edges of the petals. The flowers stand out against the dark green foliage and it grows well in containers or borders.

△ **'Swingtime'** This is perhaps the most popular of all the red and white trailing fuchsias. It has large, full, fluffy double flowers and medium-sized mid- to dark green foliage. It looks superb in a basket or as a weeping full or half standard.

▷ **'Sylvia Barker'** This is a floriferous single-flowered cultivar with small to medium flowers with a long waxy white tube and white sepals, and a smoky red short corolla. The growth is lax but quite vigorous, so this fuchsia is very good for baskets, half baskets and hanging containers or pots.

△ **'Nellie Nuttall'** A compact self-branching plant, quite slow-growing, with beautiful semi-erect single flowers with red sepals and a white corolla. This fuchsia is superb grown as a small standard, as a compact bedding plant or in small containers.

Fuchsias as summer bedding

Many gardeners use a variety of plant types and sizes within summer bedding schemes and fuchsias can be very useful as part of these schemes. The best fuchsias for summer bedding are those that tolerate being in full sun and display their flowers well. There is quite a choice of available colours, both in flower and in foliage. The summer garden border is the ideal spot for fuchsias of different growth sizes, leaf colour, and flower sizes and shapes. They will suit all sorts of bedding schemes, from mass planting to more informal arrangements. A useful tool in planning summer bedding schemes is the colour wheel, which gives a guide to complementary colours.

MASS PLANTING SCHEMES

Formal schemes for large areas require compact and uniform plants so that the edges in the design remain clearly defined, and several fuchsia cultivars fit these requirements. The raisings by Tabraham, including the Seven Dwarfs series and the Thumbs, are ideal as they are very small and compact. Use them as edging plants in their own right, or interplant them with other

Top: 'Pink Fantasia' is a floriferous single with masses of upward-facing pinkish-red and violet mauve flowers. It is an excellent choice for bedding.

suitable bedding subjects for edging. Alternatively you could plant them in blocks in a background of edging or ground-cover plants, which will contrast well against the fuchsia's foliage and flowers. The effect can look quite spectacular with the small fuchsia flowers moving in the breeze and sparkling in the sun, or lighter colours and whites standing out in the dusk. Avoid over-feeding these small cultivars to keep their dwarf and compact growth.

Fuchsias with variegated foliage are also worth using as formal summer bedding plants, since the leaf colours intensify in the bright light of the sun, and the growth becomes sturdier. Some cultivars worth trying are 'Autumnale', 'Sunray' and 'Tom West' (which is almost hardy). These have some of the best foliage colours, but they are not quite as compact, so are not suitable for edging. A newer one that is more compact is 'Baby Thumb'.

PLANTS FOR MIXED BEDDING

Use fuchsias that grow to larger sizes in mixed bedding schemes, either as single plants or in groups. The best cultivars are those that have upright and self-branching growth, display their flowers well and are happy in a sunny position. Some of the darker-coloured blooms bleach and fade with strong sunlight and many whites change to shades of pink, so bear this in

Left: 'Tom Thumb' is a compact hardy cultivar from France, introduced in 1850. It is seen here flourishing at the front of a border, contrasting beautifully with the perennial *Kalimeris incisa* 'Charlotte'.

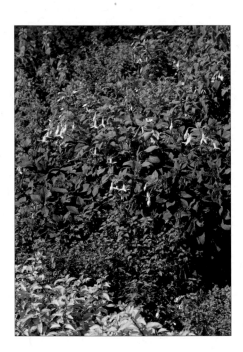

Above: Planted with a mixture of fuchsias, this pale foliage cultivar cleverly delineates the edge of the border.

mind when choosing cultivars. The leaf colours of many fuchsias are mid-green, but some cultivars have quite pale or dark green leaves, so consider this too while planning combinations of colour.

There are plenty of beautiful fuchsias to try in mixed schemes. 'Mickey Goult' is a good small pink single, vigorous and upright, covered in small semi-erect pink single flowers over a long period. 'Bow Bells' is a strong-growing single cultivar with white sepals and a magenta corolla that is an excellent summer bedder. 'Lye's Unique' has waxy white sepals and a salmon-orange corolla; 'Other Fellow' is

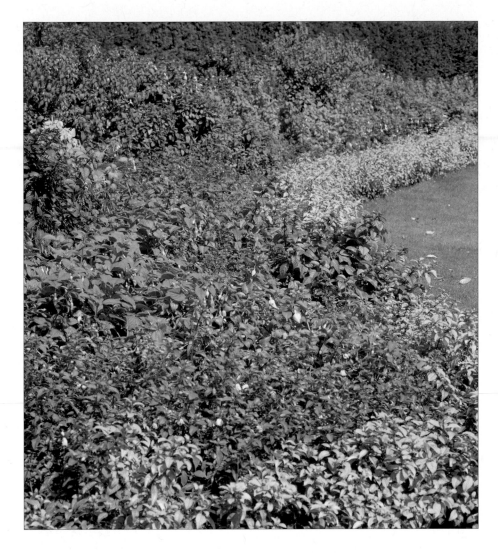

VARIETIES FOR SUMMER BEDDING

The following are suggestions for fuchsias that are suitable for single-season use as a summer bedding plant for mass or single planting.

Edging or mass planting: 'Alwin', 'Bambini', 'Baroness van Dedem', 'Bashful', 'Ben Jammin', 'Doc', 'Dopey', 'Geoffrey Smith', 'Grumpy', 'Happy', 'Lady Thumb', 'Mischief', 'Sleepy', 'Sneezy', 'Son of Thumb', 'Tom Thumb', 'Tsjiep', 'Vobeglo'

Group or single planting: 'Bon Accord', 'Border Queen', 'Coralle', 'Dawn Fantasia', 'Jack Siverns', 'Nellie Nuttall', 'Nice 'n' Easy', 'Olive Smith', 'Pink Fantasia', 'Rose Fantasia', 'Rose Quartet', 'Snowcap', 'Thalia', 'Thamar', 'Tom West', 'Upward Look', 'Variegated Pink Fantasia', 'WALZ Jubelteen'

Single planting: 'Alan Titchmarsh', 'Celia Smedley', *F. boliviana* and *F. boliviana* var. *alba*, 'Mrs Lovell Swisher', 'Other Fellow', 'Sharpitor'

Above: A fuchsia border, including 'Genii', 'Thalia' and 'Checkerboard', giving an impressive, flower-filled overall effect.

a lovely pink and white single; 'Jack Siverns' is a new vigorous bush with aubergine flowers that should make a very nice bedding plant; and 'Snowcap' is a semi-double with red sepals and white corolla. The Triphyllas are excellent for summer bedding, and some suggestions are: 'Thalia', with dark foliage and orange flowers; 'Coralle', with sage-green foliage and orange flowers; 'Andenken an Heinrich Henkel', with dark green to purplish-red foliage and pinkish-orange flowers; or how about trying 'Firecracker', the variegated-leaf sport from 'Thalia'.

PLANTS FOR SINGLE PLANTING

Some fuchsia plants grow quickly into large spreading shrubs, and therefore they are excellent for planting as single specimens in the border or any other space that needs filling with summer colour. Some examples are 'Celia Smedley', 'Checkerboard', most of the larger *F. magellanica* variants and the larger Triphylla hybrids.

Far left: 'Autumnale' has beautiful yellow and green foliage when young, which matures to red and salmon with yellow. The single flowers are red and purple.

Left: 'WALZ Jubelteen' is a vigorous upright with masses of pale pink and pinkish-orange upward-facing single flowers. It is excellent for bedding.

Triphyllas as summer bedding

The long tubular flame-red and orange flower clusters of the Triphyllas standing out against the backdrop of their large dark velvety leaves are a superb sight in a summer border. Their tolerance of sun and continuous flowering with vivid colours are the reasons that many professional gardeners use Triphylla cultivars in parks and public gardens, planting them in summer borders. These fuchsias blend happily with many other hot-coloured bedding plants such as red zonal pelargoniums, vivid red salvias or yellow and orange marigolds, complemented by the cooler blues and whites of edging plants such as ageratum, alyssum and lobelia.

USING TRIPHYLLAS

Once they start to flower, the terminal clusters of flowers last a long time and, when they finish, side shoots from below the main clusters carry on the show. This means that once they start flowering they do not let up until the first frosts, or until their removal to make way for planting the spring bedding schemes.

When used in summer bedding they can be treated as annuals and either left in the ground until they are killed by the frost or removed and discarded. If you want to save them for next year, they need to be lifted before the first frost. Pot them up into fairly dry compost (soil mix), prune them once and keep them at a minimum of 4–5°C (39–41°F). In spring, water them and spray lightly to bring them back into growth.

RANGE OF COLOURS

While the majority of the terminal-flowering Triphyllas are different shades of red, pink and orange, other colours are available if you include the Triphylla types that have Triphylla-shaped flowers which are also axial-flowering. For notably different

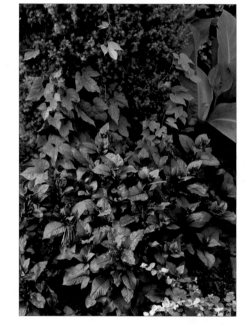

Top: The Triphylla cultivar 'Mary' is a beautiful slightly lax-growing plant with long green velvety leaves and large clusters of vivid red flowers.

Right: This Triphylla cultivar 'Thalia' has been used as a bedding plant in front of shrubs and climbers, and is just starting to come into flower.

colours try 'Roger de Cooker' with a white tube and sepals and a rose corolla, 'Jaspers Triphywhite' with a rose-white flower, 'Pabbe's Torreldöve' with a magenta-purple flower and 'Our Ted' with a white flower. In addition, there are cultivars with different flower sizes. Smaller-flowered cultivars include 'Adinda' with small pink flowers, 'Anja Robbens' in magenta-rose, 'Bessie Kimberly' (red), 'Boy Marc' (orange-red), 'Eruption' (magenta-pink), 'Pan' (purple-red-rose) and 'Sparky' (red-purple). Medium-sized cultivars include 'Billy Green' (salmon pink), 'Coralle' (orange-red), 'Gartenmeister

Left: This 'Gartenmeister Bonstedt' is growing with *Corynocarpus laevigatus* 'Picturatus', *Metrosideros mexicana*, *Iresine lindenii* (bloodleaf) and *Justicia brandegeana* (shrimp plant).

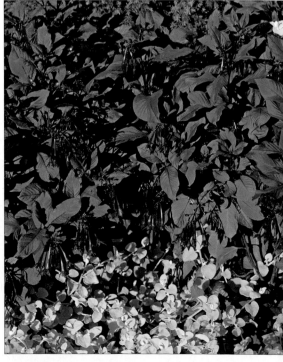

white or pastel blue petunias or white zonal pelargoniums. For a cool border choose the white or pink-flowered Triphyllas or Triphylla types, again mixing them with white and blue bedding plants. Useful Triphyllas include 'Adinda', 'Billy Green', 'Roger de Cooker', 'Fulpila', 'Phaidra' and 'Orient Express'.

Finally, try spot planting using large Triphylla fuchsias in a summer bedding scheme creating focal points to catch the eye, with the quick-growing, free-flowering 'Thalia' and 'Coralle' being high on the list. In a sunny border, they will thrive for the whole summer in a riot of colour. Also, quarter standards grown from Triphylla cultivars are excellent for creating differences in height along a summer bedding scheme and, again, will flower continuously from midsummer on, but remember that they will need heated winter protection if you wish to keep them for next year.

Bonstedt' (orange), 'Insulinde' (red-orange), 'Mary' (brilliant red) and 'Thalia' (orange-red). 'Orient Express' is an unusual Triphylla type that has very long flowers with pinkish-white sepals and a rose corolla.

VIVID BORDERS

An excellent way of using these Triphylla fuchsias is in groups or blocks with other similarly hot-coloured bedding plants. For example, the brilliant yellows and oranges of French or African marigolds go perfectly with the flame oranges and reds of the Triphylla fuchsias to create a vivid border.

Red-hot salvias can also be used in this way, and why not try orange-flowered Triphyllas such as 'Gartenmeister Bonstedt' or 'Coralle' with blocks of yellow rudbeckia or tagetes? Zonal pelargoniums, including the bi- and tri-colour leaf types, with intense red flowers will also happily sit in blocks alongside the Triphylla fuchsias.

COOL AND MIXED BORDERS

Alternatively create a border with alternate patches of hot and cold, mixing blocks of red and orange Triphyllas with cooler plants such as blue ageratums, white impatiens,

Upward-looking fuchsias

Traditional fuchsias hang delicately down from the leaf axils, hence the origin of their common nickname, 'ladies' eardrop'. In recent years, hybridizers have produced many more fuchsias with semi-erect and erect flowers ('upward-looking'). Semi-erect means the plants hold flowers horizontally, and erect means they hold flowers upwards so that you look down from above into the corolla. This gives the plants a surprisingly different character, even though the flower forms are the same as the hanging varieties. They are excellent used as half-hardy bedding plants in groups or individually, mixed with bedding plants that are more traditional.

FIRST UPWARD-LOOKING FUCHSIAS

The first recorded cultivar of this type, 'Bon Accord', was hybridized and introduced in 1861 in France by the grower Crousse, and is still widely cultivated. It is not naturally self-branching and needs frequent pinching in the early stages of growth. Sent from France to the USA, it then later reappeared in England as a new introduction under the name 'Erecta Novelty'. This name still appears in hybridization parent lists today. It was not until 1968, over 100 years after the first upward-looking fuchsia was created, that the next significant introduction appeared – 'Upward Look',

with carmine and rose-purple flowers, hybridized by Cliff Gadsby using 'Bon Accord' as one of the parents.

CURRENT RANGE OF CULTIVARS

Nowadays, one can choose from an extensive range, including small to medium single or semi-double-flowered cultivars. Quite recently, the first semi-erect small double-flowered cultivars have appeared, but no fully erect ones yet, although it can only be a matter of time. It will have to be a

Top left: 'Minirose' is a small free-flowering cultivar with semi-erect single flowers of very pale pink and cyclamen-purple. It flowers continuously for long periods.

Left: 'Bon Accord' is the first recorded cultivar with truly erect flowers. Its small single flowers, with their white tube, white sepals flushed pink and pale purple corolla, look really stunning in a low border.

Above: 'Alison Patricia' has small semi-erect single or semi-double flowers with dark pink sepals and a violet corolla. It is an upright, compact and very floriferous fuchsia.

small double, or the weight of the flowers will pull the flower head downward.

'Pink Fantasia' was first introduced in 1989, and has been used extensively both as an exhibition plant and for summer bedding. It has thrown a number of sports, including 'Rose Fantasia', which fits its parent's name more aptly, and variegated forms such as 'Variegated Pink Fantasia', 'Colne Fantasy' and 'Dawn Fantasia'. Plant them together in blocks to form part of your bedding schemes, using different varieties for colour contrast.

The erect-flowering cultivars are all upright growers that are not especially self-branching and will grow to 60–72cm

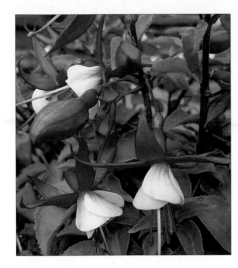

Left: 'John Bartlett' is a floriferous upright fuchsia with semi-erect red and white single flowers, often producing three flowers from each leaf axil.

means you are sure to find one that complements the rest of the planting scheme. 'Vobeglo', a Dutch dwarf erect-flowering cultivar, works well as an edging plant or a spot plant in the rockery. Many of the dwarf varieties also make excellent small standards, which are good for planting in bedding schemes.

Semi-erect types can also be used to great effect. They are not upward-looking, but they do hold their flowers out well from the foliage, which makes them excellent for planters and bedding out in the garden. You will also find a more varied choice of colours and flower sizes in this group.

The list in the panel gives suggestions for both erect-flowering and semi-erect fuchsias that have a range of colours and sizes, which you might consider for use in your own bedding schemes.

Below: 'WALZ Jubelteen' is a bushy cultivar with small erect pink to pinkish orange single flowers that seem to sparkle in the sun.

(24–30in) from a 15cm (6in) tall plant bedded out in the late spring. Try mixing them with traditional bedding plants, choosing ones that grow to similar heights and give good colour contrasts. Consider petunia, impatiens, salvia (but be careful with the colours), nicotiana, antirrhinum, godetia, verbena or dianthus as a starting point, but let your creativity put your own personal mark on the border.

You can also use them as spot plants in bedding schemes to make focal points in the border, and the large range of colours

UPWARD-LOOKING CULTIVARS

The range of erect-flowering cultivars is increasing year on year. The lists below contain some of the current fuchsias of this group that grow well.

ERECT-FLOWERING TYPES
'Bon Accord'
'Estelle Marie'
'Ivana van Amsterdam'
'Joan Goy'
'Pink Fantasia'
'Rose Fantasia'
'Thamar'
'Upward Look'
'Variegated Pink Fantasia'
'Vobeglo'
'WALZ Jubelteen'

SEMI-ERECT-FLOWERING TYPES
'Alison Patricia'
'Black Country 21'
'Bob Pacey'
'Brookwood Lady'
'Harvey's Reward'
'John Bartlett'
'Mickey Goult'
'Minirose'
'Nellie Nuttall'
'Nicis Findling'
'Pabbe's Kirrevaalk'
'Roesse Tethys'
'Sparky'
'Superstar'
'Susan Skeen'

'Pink Fantasia'

Triphylla fuchsias

The fuchsia cultivars that make up the Triphylla Group should be in everybody's collection because of their graceful foliage and striking racemes of flowers. They make very good summer bedding plants, as they will happily tolerate full sun, and while not being the quickest fuchsia to flower in early summer, once they start they will continue blooming right up to the first frosts. This group of fuchsias also does very well planted in pots or large containers. The plants have large, long and narrow leaves which are often velvety in texture and range in colour from a bronzy green to a rich purple-green colour. The flowers have long tubes and grow in terminal racemes or clusters. Although each cluster of flowers lasts quite a long time, that stem cannot grow any further, since this is a terminal

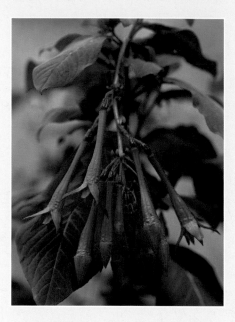

△ **'Thalia'** This is probably the Triphylla cultivar that most people will recognize. The long racemes of orange-red flowers contrast beautifully with its dark olive-green foliage. This fuchsia is really superb as a summer bedder and will also make a good standard.

△ **'Whiteknights Cheeky'** This plant is a Triphylla-type fuchsia, with flowers in the leaf axils and not just in terminal racemes. The flowers are long, Tyrian purple in colour and carried erect. It is an unusual plant with an interesting flower colour.

△ **'Coralle'** Also known as 'Koralle', this is a striking fuchsia with racemes of long orange flowers that contrast beautifully with the large sage-green leaves. This cultivar is slightly more tolerant of cold temperatures in the winter than other Triphyllas.

△ **'Billy Green'** This is a lovely Triphylla-type fuchsia with long salmon-pink flowers and velvety light olive-green leaves. It is so vigorous in growth that it quickly makes a large specimen plant. It is easy to grow and highly recommended.

△ **'Insulinde'** A newer Dutch Triphylla hybrid by Herman de Graaff, introduced in 1991. It is a very striking fuchsia, with vivid orange racemes of flowers and very dark bronze-green foliage. It grows vigorously in full sun, making it very good for bedding schemes.

point. Fortunately, side shoots produced a little further down the stem quickly form new flower clusters, often taking over before the first flush is finished, giving almost continuous blooms throughout the summer and into late autumn. The flower colours are mainly self-colours of reds, oranges and pinks, but a few new colours like whites and aubergines and even multiple colours, for example 'Orient Express', with a pink corolla and pinkish-white and red sepals, have been commercially produced. They need careful feeding and watering and seem to respond very well to a high-nitrogen feed, which helps to prevent the yellowing of lower leaves. This class of fuchsias is frost tender – most varieties need a minimum winter temperature of 5°C (41°F).

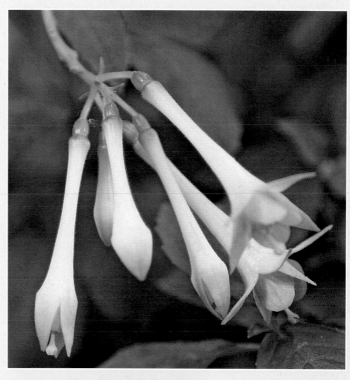

△ **'Sparky'** An unusual fuchsia with smallish semi-erect Triphylla-type flowers of deep red, with small bronzy-green, red-veined foliage. It is very useful for small mixed planters, being slightly smaller and more compact in growth than the traditional Triphyllas.

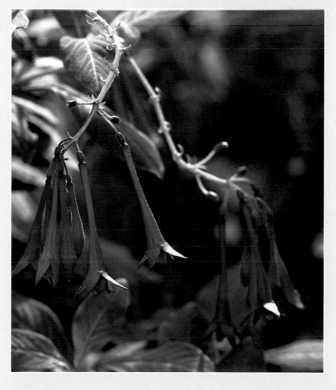

∧ **'Our Ted'** This is the first truly white Triphylla cultivar, hybridized by Edwin Goulding. It has racemes of creamy white flowers and rather dark green glossy foliage. This is not an easy cultivar to grow and it hates being overwatered, so it is one for the experts.

◁ **'Gartenmeister Bonstedt'** One of the beautiful Triphylla hybrids introduced by Carl Bonstedt in 1905. It is very similar to 'Thalia', the main difference being a pronounced bulge in the orange-red tube. It is excellent as a summer bedder.

△ **'Mary'** This is a superb Triphylla raised by Carl Bonstedt as far back as 1897. It has racemes of vivid bright crimson flowers and velvety sage-green foliage. It is not the easiest plant to grow, but can make a very nice standard or a spectacular specimen.

Fuchsias in the shrub border

If you are fortunate enough to have a large garden, you are likely to have a shrub border, or at least some area of the garden planted with shrubs. These can be extremely interesting areas, with so many shapes and sizes of shrubs, different leaf textures and colours, evergreen and deciduous plants, and some kinds of flowers at most times of the year. Hardy fuchsias grown as part of a permanent planting scheme behave like deciduous shrubs or herbaceous perennials, depending on the winter temperatures. They are useful grown among spring-flowering and autumn-flowering shrubs to give some blooms and colour in the summer months. They also show up well against dark evergreen shrubs such as camellias.

FUCHSIAS AND SHRUBS

The height and spread of shrubs can vary tremendously, even within the same genus of plants, and it is quite an art to arrange them so that they complement each other and are all clearly visible. When established, they have the advantage of being quite low-maintenance, needing only annual pruning and mulching, and the ground beneath them remains reasonably weed-free because of the amount of shade, with perhaps species like ground ivy being the major problems. Large fuchsias as shrubs can add an extra dimension, providing extra pockets of colour, especially with winter- and spring-flowering shrubs.

Top: This fuchsia species *F. arborescens* is growing happily in a border, showing off its large, glossy green leaves. The flower heads are in various stages of development, from panicles of pink flowers to ripe berries.

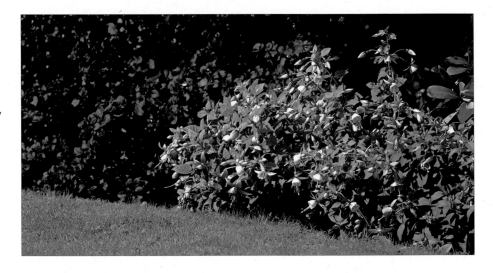

CHOOSING THE RIGHT FUCHSIAS

In areas of the shrub border with plant heights of up to 2m (6ft), grow fuchsias to add vibrant pockets of summer colour and interest, especially among spring-, autumn- and winter-flowering shrubs.

Above: Fuchsias 'Katie Susan', 'Brenda White' and 'Love's Reward' used as edging plants for a shrub border, contrasting with a purple-foliaged berberis.

In parts of the world where the frost will not kill fuchsias down to the ground in the winter, you can use vigorous-growing hardy fuchsias such as *F. magellanica* var. *molinae* or 'Riccartonii' in taller parts of the border, where they can reach heights of 3–4m (10–13ft). This may work in fairly cold areas too, since shielding from the evergreen shrubs will give some extra frost protection, allowing more growth than in the open.

While the larger hardy fuchsias are the easiest to grow, since they become a permanent part of the shrubbery, it can also be interesting to grow some of the large

Left: The hardy cultivar 'Garden News', with its rose-pink and magenta-rose double flowers, is seen here growing among other flowering plants and shrubs in a border.

tender species as temporary residents, such as *F. boliviana* or *F. boliviana* var. *alba,* both of which grow as a climbing shrub. Alternatively, *F. arborescens* or *F. paniculata,* with their upright racemes of tiny pink-purple flowers, large glossy leaves and clusters of berries later in the season, merge beautifully into the shrub border, adding extra interest for many months.

FUCHSIAS AS EDGING

Another way to use fuchsias in the shrub border is to grow them as dot plants along the edges, between the shrubs and a lawn or a paved or gravelled area. This can give nice spots of colour against the background of the leaves and structure of the shrubs. Use the larger-growing varieties in gaps in the border toward the front, and more compact-growing ones right along the edges. When growing them in this situation, it is better to treat them as bedding plants.

TEMPORARY RESIDENTS

Plant out fuchsias, especially those trained as standards or pillars, as temporary residents in the summer in the shrub border. This works especially well in a spring-flowering shrub border with plants such as rhododendrons, camellias, azaleas and other similar evergreen shrubs. Usually pruning of these takes place in the late spring or early summer, and in the created spaces fuchsia standards of an appropriate

height can give excellent patches of summer and autumn flower in an otherwise green border. Full or half standards of red and white flowered cultivars such as 'Snowcap' and 'Celia Smedley', or red flowered such as 'Rufus' or 'Olive Smith', are very effective. Pillars of cultivars such as 'Phyllis' or 'Kolding Perle' can also be effective. With pillars, a space where the plant is visible almost down to the ground will give the best results.

Below: This striking hardy species variant *F. magellanica* var. *gracilis* 'Tricolor' is displaying its variegated foliage to perfection here, planted among a selection of other flowering plants and shrubs.

Above: An unusual use of the species fuchsia *F. denticulata* as a tall edging plant, with its pretty pink, red, green and orange-red long tubed flowers along the edge of border.

HARDY FUCHSIAS AND COMPANION SHRUBS

The following tall-growing hardy fuchsias and companion shrubs can be used together to create some interesting shrub border designs.

LARGE HARDY FUCHSIAS

F. magellanica var. *molinae,*
F. magellanica var. *versicolor,*
'Hawkshead', 'Margaret',
'Margaret Brown', 'Mrs Popple',
'Mrs W.P. Wood', 'Riccartonii',
'Sharpitor', 'Waldfee'

COMPANION SHRUBS

Deciduous, spring-flowering:
Cornus, Forsythia, Genista, Lonicera, Ribes, Sambucus, Spiraea, Syringa, Viburnum, Weigela
Evergreen, spring-flowering:
Brachyglottis, Camellia, Ceanothus, Choisya, Daphne, Garrya, Ilex, Magnolia, Mahonia, Osmanthus, Pieris, Pittosporum, Prunus, Rhododendron, Skimmia, Tamarix, Viburnum

Fuchsias in the rockery

Many of the smaller hardy or half-hardy fuchsias can be used to great effect in the rockery. A number of cultivars will only grow to 45cm (18in) in a season if you cut them back hard at the start of the season. This type usually has quite small flowers, which are in proportion and keeping with other rockery plants. A rockery may include many of the low-growing and smaller-flowered plants commonly available, with alpines such as *Armeria juniperifolia*, *Aurinia saxatilis*, *Dianthus alpinus*, *Draba aizoides*, *Gentiana acaulis* and *G. septemfida*, *Primula marginata*, *Saxifraga*, small conifers, miniature shrubs and heathers or other small plants or your choice.

ROCKERY PLANTING

The smaller fuchsias can do very well in these situations, enjoying the good drainage conditions in most rockeries and contrasting well with the green foliage of the heathers or small conifers. Use the hardy varieties as a permanent planting, and the less hardy ones as a spot planting, but be careful not to plant hardy varieties in a soil-filled depression in a rock, which will fill with water when it rains. The resulting waterlogging will certainly kill them over the winter.

Top: 'La Campanella', with its stiff trailing growth and smallish leaves, is excellent for growing over low rocks. It has round buds and semi-double flowers, with white sepals flushed pink and an imperial purple corolla.

SMALL-FLOWERED HARDY FUCHSIAS

The prostrate-growing New Zealand species *F. procumbens* is an interesting choice, as its fern-like foliage will creep and spread over rocks. It is medium hardy and you can use it as a permanent planting. The flowers are very small, upright with a yellow-green tube, green sepals but no corolla, and blue pollen on the anthers. It forms grape-like fruits, which turn pink-red when ripe.

The Thumb varieties – 'Tom Thumb', 'Lady Thumb', and the variegated 'Baby Thumb' and 'Son of Thumb' – are good rockery plants, along with the series hybridized by Tabraham, named after the seven dwarfs: 'Bashful', 'Doc', 'Dopey', 'Grumpy', 'Happy', 'Sleepy' and 'Sneezy', which all have annual

Above: 'Sharonelle' is a compact bush cultivar with semi-erect single flowers. It is ideal for use in the rockery.

growth of only 22–45cm (9–18in). The Seven Dwarfs fuchsias are often planted alongside the cultivar 'Snow White', but this is a larger double white trailer, not suitable for the rockery.

Two very hardy varieties, *F. magellanica* var. *pumila* and 'David', are excellent choices, with small foliage and flowers, and these also only grow to 45cm (18in). 'Papoose' is a low-growing, spreading, hardy cultivar, which can also be encouraged to trail over rocks.

Others worth considering are 'Alice Hoffman', 'Bouquet', 'Elf', 'Forget-Me-Not', 'Liebriez', 'Red Imp', 'Thornley's Hardy', which has a trailing habit, and 'Tinker Bell' (note that this is the cultivar raised by Tabraham, not the one with the same name raised by Hodges).

Left: This selection of small-flowered fuchsias is growing with a variety of companion plants in a multi-levelled rockery. Note how the foliage of the variegated cultivar 'Tom West' stands out in the sun.

DWARF HARDY FUCHSIAS

The following are some recommendations for compact, hardy and half-hardy small-flowered varieties that are excellent for use in a rockery.

Hardy: 'Alice Hoffman', 'Bashful', 'David', 'Doc', 'Dopey', 'Geoffrey Smith', 'Grumpy', 'Happy', 'Lady Thumb', *F. magellanica* var. *pumila*, 'Papoose', *F. procumbens*, 'Sleepy', 'Sneezy', 'Son of Thumb', 'Tom Thumb', 'Thornley's Hardy'

Half hardy: 'Andrew Hadfield', 'Auntie Jinks', 'Ben Jammin', 'Harry Grey', 'La Campanella', 'My Little Cracker', 'Nellie Nuttall', 'Pink Rain', 'Postiljon', 'Sophie Louise', 'Sharonelle', 'Superstar', 'Tom West', 'Twinny', 'Westminster Chimes', 'Vobeglo'

Above: Ferns, small conifers, miniature campanulas and other rockery plants accompany fuchsias in this steep rockery.

SMALL-FLOWERED HALF-HARDY FUCHSIAS

Use these as spot plantings in the rockery over the summer. If you are in a very mild area they may survive the winter, but cut them back hard in the late winter or early spring to keep them small. The best plants for this situation are the low-growing types with small flowers, especially the ones that throw their flowers outward. The types used for showing at exhibitions grown in 9cm (3½in) pots are a very good choice for spot planting in a rockery.

Some cultivars to consider are 'Andrew Hadfield', 'My Little Cracker', 'Nellie Nuttall', 'Sophie Louise', 'Sharon Leslie', 'Sharonelle', 'Superstar' and 'Twinny'. Try also some of the smaller growing Encliandra types, but beware, some of them are strong growers. Try *F. hemsleyana*, variegated 'Lottie Hobby', 'Miniature Jewels', *F. microphylla* and its subspecies. You can also consider growing the smaller cascading types, to trail over the rocks. Some suitable cultivars are 'Auntie Jinks', 'Harry Grey', 'Pink Rain' and 'Westminster Chimes'.

Left: This bright collection of fuchsia cultivars is thriving on a warm rockery slope, giving an interesting combination of textures and shapes.

Above: *F. procumbens* is a hardy prostrate-growing species from New Zealand. It is excellent for a rockery because it scrambles energetically over the rocks.

Pink and white fuchsias

There are many fuchsias with pink and white flowers, and those with darker foliage show up the pale flowers especially well. The pink shade softens the hardness of the white and gives a warmer feeling. These fuchsias can be a great way to create a transition between cool and hot colours in the garden. There are many varieties in this colour range to choose from, bearing both white sepals with a pink corolla and pink sepals with a white corolla, but one point to remember is that the shades of both pink and white may change in the sun. Many white varieties keep their pure white only in the shade, turning to pink in full sun, and pink shades may become deeper in the sun. Some examples of cultivars which do this are 'Shelford', 'Katrina Thompsen' and 'Trudi Davro'. If you

△ **'Shelford'** This is a superb single-flowered cultivar that is very adaptable and possible to grow in most forms. Although white in the shade, the medium-sized single flowers become pink in the sun.

△ **'Margarite Dawson'** This is a borderline hardy cultivar with strong upright growth and quite large mid-green leaves. The medium double flowers have rose-pink sepals and a pink-veined white corolla.

△ **'Miss California'** This is a spreading semi-lax, semi-double-flowered cultivar with pink sepals and a white corolla. Grown as a bush it will need some support, and in a basket, weights to pull down the branches.

△ **'Camcon'** This is a single-flowered cultivar, making an upright, bushy and very floriferous plant, with attractive sparkling flowers. The flowers have white sepals flushed with pink and a deep pink corolla. It makes a good small pot plant or a smaller standard.

△ **'Harlow Carr'** This is a very pretty cultivar with lovely single flowers having pink sepals and a flared white corolla. It is excellent to grow as a standard and as a trained shape. The dark green foliage enhances the flower display, allowing them to stand out.

want to grow a pink and white in a shady area, make sure it is a variety that has natural pink colours that will not fade. One of the best double-flowered bush fuchsias with pink sepals and a white corolla is 'Nancy Lou', hybridized by Annabelle Stubbs and almost discarded because it did not have the trailing habit she believed was commercially necessary. 'Miss California' and 'Harlow Carr' also have pink sepals and a white corolla, while 'Margarite Dawson' is a double with similar colours. 'Other Fellow' is a cultivar with lovely white sepals and a pink corolla, and 'Flirtation Waltz' is a superb double with similar colours. 'Puts Folly' is a trailing single cultivar with white sepals and a deep pink corolla, while 'Impala' is a double with the same characteristics.

▷ **'Other Fellow'** This is a very floriferous single-flowered cultivar with a longish waxy white tube, waxy white sepals and a coral-pink corolla. It thrives in direct sun and makes an excellent bedding plant.

▽ **'Trudi Davro'** This is a trailing cultivar, excellent for hanging baskets or pots. It has small to medium double flowers with pale pink sepals and a fluffy white corolla. The flower is almost white in the shade, but the sepals gradually gain pink shades with exposure to the sun. The flowers stand out against the dark green leaves.

△ **'Countess of Aberdeen'** This is an old cultivar first introduced in 1888. It has a beautiful small single flower with a longish ivory-white tube, white sepals and a corolla which is almost white in the shade, but gradually becomes pink with exposure to the sun. It dislikes overwatering.

△ **'Sophisticated Lady'** This is a lax-growing large-flowered double American cultivar with a pale pink tube and sepals, and a white corolla. It is an excellent cultivar for use in baskets and containers.

Permanent fuchsia beds

Hardy fuchsias can form the basis of fantastic low-maintenance beds, giving colour in the garden for much of the year. They flower continuously from early summer to the first autumn frosts – much longer than most shrubs and perennials. In some temperate areas, especially on the west and south-west coasts of Europe touched by the Gulf Stream, it is possible to grow half-hardy varieties as permanent plantings right through the milder winters. In warmer areas that have entire frost-free growing seasons, it is even possible to grow almost all fuchsia types permanently, although they might need some shading during the hotter months, and pruning in the cooler months.

CHOOSING SUITABLE HARDIES

This section focuses on fuchsias that are recognized hardy types when grown in a climate with hard winters, typically around USA Zone 7, which will remove all the leaves and kill the growth down to ground level. It is always a good idea to look at local public gardens to see which hardy fuchsias grow well in your area.

You can choose hardy fuchsias in a wonderful range of heights, flower sizes, types and colours, varying from small, dwarf singles, through medium-sized doubles and semi-doubles, up to the large, rapid-growing *magellanica* hybrids, thanks to the efforts of many different hybridizers since the early 19th century. The growth made from ground level during the season ranges from a modest 13cm (5in) in the case of the spreading *F. procumbens*, up to 1.2m (4ft) for *F. magellanica* var. *molinae* and 'Margaret'.

PERMANENT BED DESIGNS

When planning a hardy fuchsia bed, do as much research as possible and get advice from your local fuchsia specialist nursery, as well as from neighbours or your local gardening society. You also need to check the different flower colours and typical annual growth of the plants before deciding how to lay out your border. Although most hardy fuchsias have mid or dark green foliage, there are some cultivars with pale green, golden or variegated leaves. Use these as eye-catching individuals or groups to create extra interest.

The easiest plans are for borders backing on to a high wall, fence or hedge, where the aim is to create an increase in height from the front to the back of the border, with some differences or undulations in height

Top: A single flower of *F. magellanica*, with its red sepals and purple corolla. This hardy shrub is commonly found in gardens, where it thrives with little attention. It also makes a good hedging plant.

Right: A group of hardy fuchsias growing and flowering together as permanent plantings, carefully protected by a windbreak of small trees and shrubs.

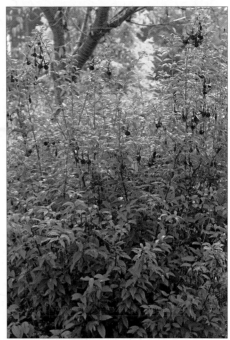

Above: *F. magellanica* var. *variegata* is a single-flowered hardy fuchsia that makes an attractive low bush. The crimson-red sepals and purple corolla contrast well with the pale green foliage, which is edged with cream.

Right: 'Empress of Prussia' is an old and very floriferous hardy cultivar with scarlet and magenta flowers. It was almost lost from cultivation, but luckily found again.

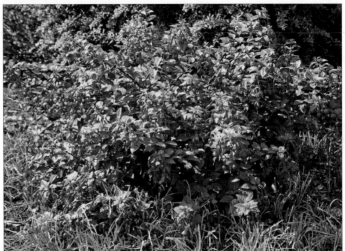

Above: 'Purple Splendour' is a strong, upright, hardy cultivar growing to 60cm (2ft), and was introduced by Sunningdale Nurseries in 1975. The lovely single flowers have crimson sepals and a blue-purple corolla.

along the length of the scheme. These borders can be different shapes – rectangular, square, semi-circular or with an uneven scalloped edge – with the colour of the backdrop chosen to enhance the fuchsia display.

A more elaborate design involves surrounding a bed by a path on all sides, or placing the bed in the middle of a lawn. Such designs are more common in public or botanical gardens, where there is space to create large beds that are best viewed from all sides. Make sure that the larger plants are in the middle, with the smaller ones at the edges and a gradation in size between the extremes. Surrounding the border with low hedges, grown from a dense, evergreen plant such as box, helps to shelter the fuchsias from the worst of the cold winter winds.

The choice of hardy fuchsias is very subjective, but if you select carefully you will have a beautiful show of colour right through summer and autumn.

RELIABLE HARDY FUCHSIAS

This list contains some high-quality fuchsias recommended for permanent fuchsia beds, arranged by the height of their seasonal growth.

Small: 'Abbé Farges', 'Alice Hoffman', 'Baby Thumb', 'Beacon Rosa', 'Beranger', 'Bouquet', 'Carmen', 'Constance', 'David', 'Dollar Prinzessin', 'Elfin Glade', 'Happy', 'Heidi Ann', 'Lady Thumb', 'Liebriez', *F. magellanica* var. *pumila*, 'Papoose', 'Son of Thumb', 'Thornley's Hardy', 'Tom Thumb'

Medium: 'Achievement', 'Ariel', 'Beacon', 'Blue Gown', 'Brutus', 'C.J. Howlett', 'Chillerton Beauty', 'Garden News', 'Glow', 'Herald', 'Howlett's Hardy', 'Lady Bacon', 'Mauve Lace', 'Phyrne', 'Prosperity', 'Red Ace', 'Rose of Castile', 'Rufus', 'Snowcap', 'Tennessee Waltz', 'W.P. Wood', 'White Pixie'

Large: 'Abundance', 'Army Nurse', 'Charming', 'Diana Wright', 'Empress of Prussia', 'Enfante Prodigue', 'Exmoor Gold', 'Graf Witte', 'Greatham Mill', 'Hawkshead', *F. magellanica* var. *molinae*, 'Madame Cornelissen', 'Margaret', 'Margaret Brown', 'Mrs Popple', 'Waldfee', 'Whiteknights Amethyst'

Fuchsia beds with hedging

Beds of fuchsias defined and protected by low hedges are a very attractive addition to a formal garden, with the colours of the fuchsia flowers contrasting with the greens of the hedging. There are two main advantages to using hedging around a fuchsia bed. The first is practical: closely growing dense evergreen hedging will give protection on exposed, windswept sites from the added wind chill in the coldest months, enabling you to grow fuchsias where it might not otherwise be possible. The second is aesthetic: you can create a striking feature by dividing a bed into different areas, with each section containing either a group or a single specimen fuchsia, or just have one small bed surrounded by a hedge.

HEDGING PLANS

Taking a hedging plan to its limit by including coloured gravel pathways to divide the fuchsia beds and intricate designs of hedges and edging, a hedged fuchsia garden could approach a knot garden or even a parterre. Although this extreme needs a large, flat space with a suitable vantage point so that it can be viewed from above, it is possible to apply the techniques and principles to smaller areas. For example, a garden could include a central paved area with several paths radiating outwards and a circular path around the outside. Each segment of the circle could be defined by dwarf box hedges enclosing a single variety of fuchsia. This would be

an excellent way to display individual fuchsias without the plants intermingling, as they often will in hardy beds with continuing growth later in the season.

The plants can be set out in single or double rows, depending on the width of the desired hedge. It will take a few years before it reaches its final size and density, after which it needs maintaining at that size and shape. For larger boundary hedges, especially those where you require a strong windbreak, yew (*Taxus baccata*) is perfect. Clip it to below its final height at first, to encourage dense growth all the way from the ground up. Different varieties are available with colours ranging from golden-yellow to the traditional dark green.

When planning a hedge, large or small, always make sure that you have easy access for clipping a few times each year.

Also note that taller hedges can be used to make an attractive backdrop for the fuchsias. When the background is dark opt for bright flower colours, and when it is pale yellow or green choose darker flowers, to make sure that they really stand out.

Top left: 'String of Pearls' is an upright fuchsia with long growths covered in pretty single or semi-double flowers coloured China-rose and rose purple.

Below: An arrangement of fuchsias in a bed divided into compartments with low hedging. Other large fuchsias are visible in the background, along with agaves in large pots.

Above left: This bed of mixed hardy fuchsias is flowering happily in the summer, and will be well protected during the winter months with a low evergreen hedge on two sides.

Above: This tall hardy fuchsia covered in flowers is starting to envelop the fountain statue of a cherub on a dolphin. The fuchsia is large because of the hedge protection.

SUITABLE FUCHSIAS TO USE AGAINST HEDGING

White, pink or red fuchsias display well against green hedging.

White: 'Alaska', 'Annabel' (hardy), 'Flying Cloud', 'Happy Wedding Day', 'Hawkshead', 'Sleigh Bells', 'White Joy'
White and pink: 'Baby Love', 'Countess of Aberdeen', 'Grandma Sinton', 'Hidcote Beauty', 'Micky Goult', 'Other Fellow'
White and lavender: 'Alberttina', 'British Stirling', 'Doreen Redfern', 'Eden Lady', 'Lady Kathleen Spence', 'Lilian', 'Violet Bassett-Burr'
White and red: 'Beauty of Trowbridge', 'Celia Smedley', 'Checkerboard', 'Hiawatha', 'Nellie Nuttall', 'Snowcap' (hardy)
White and purple: 'Bon Accord', 'City of Leicester', 'David Lockyer', 'Estelle Marie', 'Kegworth Carnival', 'Lena' (hardy), 'Marin Glow', 'Preston Guild', 'Quasar', 'Rose of Castile Improved' (hardy), 'Stanley Cash'
Pink: 'Barbara', 'Beacon Rosa' (hardy), 'Cotton Candy', 'Elfriede Ott', 'Leonora', 'Margaret Brown' (hardy), 'Pink Bon Accord', 'Regal' (hardy), 'Rose of Denmark' (hardy), 'String of Pearls'
Red: 'Achievement', 'Caledonia' (hardy), 'Kwintet', 'Mephisto', 'Nettala', 'Phyllis' (hardy), 'Rufus'

TYPES OF HEDGING

There are a number of plants that will make good hedges, but for the low formal kind different varieties of box (*Buxus*) are the most suitable. The following list includes those for different hedge sizes. The best range is available from specialist nurseries.

	TYPE	HEIGHT	LEAF
Buxus microphylla	Low	82cm (32in)	Small, dark green
Buxus microphylla 'Faulkner'	Medium	1.5m (5ft)	Green; red/bronze in winter
Buxus sempervirens 'Blauer Heinz'	Dwarf	30cm (12in)	Small, bluish-green
Buxus sempervirens 'Elegantissima'	Medium	1.5m (5ft)	Green and cream variegation
Buxus sempervirens 'Green Gem'	Low	82cm (32in)	Bright green
Buxus sempervirens 'Suffruticosa'	Low	82cm (32in)	Bright green

Buxus microphylla

Buxus microphylla 'Faulkner'

Buxus sempervirens 'Elegantissima'

Buxus sempervirens 'Suffruticosa'

Fuchsias in cottage gardens

The words 'cottage garden' summon up a vision of a chocolate-box picture: a thatched cottage with white walls and a wonderful garden with all kinds of annual and perennial flowering plants growing by a weaving path in informal beds and borders. Stone walls around the boundaries will have cascading and rambling plants all over them, covered in flowers. Hardy fuchsias are one of the components of this image and a cottage garden would be incomplete without them. The cottage garden is particularly associated with old dwellings in the countryside in England, but it is perfectly possible to create a cottage-style garden in a town or city.

PLANTS FOR COTTAGE GARDENS

Cottage gardens always have many different plants crammed into a small space, yet they are quite low-maintenance, with many perennial and self-seeding annual plants. A vegetable and herb garden would also be part of the traditional theme. The pathways are an integral part of these gardens, usually made of flagstones or cobbles, with a main path leading to the front door, and other paths snaking off to encourage exploration of other parts of the garden. All these paths help to break the garden up into separate areas, leading you from one to another.

Typical examples of cottage garden plants are achillea, alliums, buddleia, Canterbury bells, carnations, columbines, cornflowers, delphiniums, echinacea, euphorbia, foxgloves, gladioli, hollyhocks, lilies, hardy pelargoinums, phlox, poppies, rudbeckia, snapdragons, stocks, sweet Williams, and of course the spring-flowering bulbs such as crocuses, daffodils and tulips. The list would not be complete without roses, especially the old-fashioned scented varieties and climbing or rambling roses. Other climbing plants often found in this setting are clematis and honeysuckle. All the climbing plants grow up walls, pergolas and trees, or just scramble where they will, through the other plants.

SUITABLE COTTAGE FUCHSIAS

In the 19th century, fuchsias were not part of a cottage garden, as people considered them to be tender plants. Once it was realized that many were hardy, gardeners enthusiastically adopted them as another

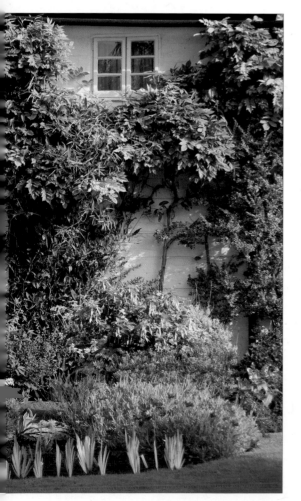

Top left: A hardy fuchsia growing among a clump of hosta plants. The small red and purple flowers stand out beautifully against the pale green of the hosta leaves.

Left: A large double-flowered fuchsia growing in a pot by a pond, surrounded by other plants. It looks beautiful set against the contrasting background of a white wall covered with wisteria and pyracantha.

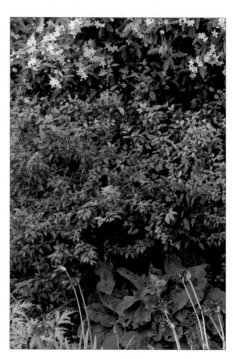

Above: A cottage garden hardy fuchsia growing among flowering shrubs, with a white-flowering *Choisya* (Mexican orange blossom) shrub in the background.

hardy perennial in their planting schemes. Since the 20th century, extensive use has been made of many of the *F. magellanica* varieties, along with many of the early hardy single-flowered cultivars. *F. magellanica* var. *molinae* is an excellent choice, with its white and pale lilac flowers on long stems, which will reach 1.5m (5ft) or more in a single year. In a sunny spot, the ideal fuchsias would be *F. magellanica* var. *aurea*, with its elegant growth and golden yellow foliage, *F. magellanica* var. *riccartonii*, or *F. magellanica* var. *gracilis* 'Tricolor' (or 'Variegata') with its variegated foliage.

There is a lovely story that illustrates how these cottage gardens can be repositories for older plants. The fuchsia cultivar 'Empress of Prussia' was introduced by Hoppe in 1868, but the plant became lost from commercial cultivation for many years. In 1957, a London fuchsia enthusiast was on holiday in Devon and noticed a large fuchsia growing in a cottage garden. The owners did not know the name of the cultivar, but they were sure that the plant had been growing there for at least 50 years. Subsequent identification proved it was the long-lost 'Empress of Prussia', and it was reintroduced by the grower Bernard Rawlins. 'Empress of Prussia' is a good hardy plant with a medium to large single flower, with a vivid scarlet tube and sepals and a reddish-magenta corolla. It is very floriferous, having as many as eight blooms on each pair of leaf axils, and will grow to 90cm (36in) in one season.

COTTAGE-STYLE CONTAINERS

Another important feature in cottage gardens is the use of unusual containers. Different shapes and sizes can work well,

Below: Two large hardy fuchsias, both in full flower, growing either side of shallow steps in front of a cottage wall, surrounded by other cottage garden plants.

as long as they look old, and preferably might have been part of the original cottage inventory. Remember that they should have enough drainage holes, and beware of using metal containers, which can become very hot in the sun. There are many possibilities, such as weathered terracotta (clay) pots, chimney pots, terracotta drainpipes placed vertically with the top full of plants, stone sinks, buckets or watering cans. Filling these with fuchsias, especially the older single cultivars, creates a splendid display. Suitable cultivars include 'Blue Beauty', 'Corallina', 'Countess

Above: The hardy fuchsia 'Army Nurse' growing among *Sorbus* 'Sunshine', hibiscus and *Potentilla fruticosa* 'Elizabeth'. 'Army Nurse' is a strong cultivar, with semi-double flowers with red sepals and a mauve-blue corolla.

of Aberdeen', 'Drame', 'Mauve Lace', 'Rose of Castile', 'Snowcap' and 'Tom Thumb'. Light-coloured or variegated-leaf cultivars such as 'Old Somerset', 'Sunray' or 'Tom West' are also valuable, as they will stand out well in darker corners or against dark green foliage.

Aubergine fuchsias

Fuchsias with different shades of purple in the corolla have been in commerce for many years. As a further refinement of this colour, hybridizers started to release fuchsias in aubergine shades in the mid-1980s. The Dutch hybridizers, especially Herman de Graaff, introduced some beautiful and vivid aubergine cultivars, including 'Aubergine', 'Gerharda's Aubergine' and 'Haute Cuisine'. There is quite a choice of aubergine fuchsias with flowers of different sizes from small singles to large doubles, and habits of growth from trailing to strongly upright. New aubergine-coloured cultivars are still being released every year. The photographs on these pages give an idea of some of the cultivars that are available. An excellent way to grow them is as standards or in hanging baskets, so you can see

△ **'Black Country 21'** This is a single-flowered cultivar with a tube and sepals of deep magenta and a violet to aubergine corolla. The erect blooms stand out on a compact and bushy plant with small mid-green leaves. Released in 2007, it makes a nice small standard.

△ **'Gerharda's Aubergine'** This trailing fuchsia has small to medium single flowers with a deep red/aubergine tube and sepals and an aubergine corolla. It has mid- to dark green leaves and is excellent for baskets. It was hybridized by Herman de Graaff of the Netherlands and released in 1989.

△ **'President George Bartlett'** A semi-double cultivar with a burgundy-red tube and sepals and a deep aubergine corolla. It is excellent when trained as a standard, with its slightly lax growth habit. It was hybridized by Bielby/Oxtoby and named after a former British Fuchsia Society president.

△ **'Ben Jammin'** A small, compact plant, borderline hardy, superb for growing as a mini standard or a small pot plant. It has small to medium single flowers with pale pink sepals flushed aubergine and a dark aubergine corolla, and mid- to dark green foliage.

△ **'Jessica Reynolds'** A floriferous medium-sized single-flowered cultivar with beautiful white sepals flushed with aubergine and an aubergine corolla. It has neat, compact self-branching growth, excellent for growing standards, with mid-green leaves.

the beauty of the flowers at eye level. They will also contrast well with pastel and white-flowered cultivars in mixed baskets, containers or planting arrangements. There are two aubergine fuchsias which are listed as hardy: 'Ben Jammin', a small compact-growing single, and 'Dorothy Handley', a vigorously upright semi-double that will grow 75cm (30in) in one season. A fuchsia that is good for summer bedding is 'President George Bartlett'. Lax types for baskets include 'Art Deco', 'Haute Cuisine' and 'Ratatouille'. An attractive Triphylla type named 'Pabbe's Torreldöve' has aubergine-blue flowers. 'Whiteknights Amethyst' is an unusual hardy fuchsia with blue pollen, hybridized from *F. excorticata*, and is in the parentage of many aubergine fuchsias.

△ **'Tarra Valley'** This fuchsia resulted from an interspecies hybridization cross and has very unusual single flowers with a long light greenish-yellow tube, short greenish-white sepals and an unusually coloured dark red/aubergine/purple corolla.

△ **'Haute Cuisine'** A superb double-flowered cultivar with dark red sepals and a deep aubergine corolla, contrasting beautifully with its light to mid-green leaves. It has a vigorous but stiff trailing habit, and is excellent for baskets and patio containers.

▷ **'Jack Siverns'** This cultivar has a vigorous and bushy growth habit, and is excellent grown as a specimen plant or a standard. The flowers are single and medium in size with aubergine sepals blushed with pink and an aubergine corolla.

Standard fuchsias

One of the best ways to display fuchsias is by growing them as standards of different heights, making vibrant focal points around the garden. They look like small trees covered in flowers and, from a distance, attract the eye to different parts of the garden, standing out against fences and hedges. There are many places in most gardens that are ideal for standard fuchsias, where they will greatly enhance the view. Excellent places include either side of an entrance gate, next to a doorway, by a fence, against a non-flowering evergreen background, such as a conifer hedge, and in the hardy fuchsia border, where they give extra height and colour. Also try growing them in groups of identical standards in a more formal border.

SMALL STANDARDS

The smaller standards look wonderful on the edges of steps, around a patio or pond, and you can even use miniature standards in rockeries. Where it is impossible to set any of these plants in the ground, they will need some kind of support to keep the pot and standard upright, especially in windy conditions. Quarter standards, often referred to as table standards, will make an attractive display on a garden table.

Top: 'Royal Velvet' is a strong double cultivar with red and violet flowers. It makes a superb half standard, but tie the head in well as the weight of the flowers can break branches.

GATEWAYS, WALLS AND CORNERS

Large standards grown to either side of a gateway are very striking, especially when the gate is in a low boundary wall or fence about 1–1.5m (3–5ft) high. In addition, the wall or fence gives a good anchoring point and supports the standards while also giving them some protection. Standards can be equally effective to either side of a front door, creating a beautiful entrance and a good topic of conversation.

Below: Two attractive wrought iron planters either side of an archway planted with standards of the double flowered fuchsia 'Annabel', finished with bedding plants.

Above: A standard of the hardy cultivar 'Lady Thumb' growing among ferns by a doorway, carefully placed to stand out against a white wall. The small flowers and compact growth habit are excellent for a smaller standard.

Full and half standards are very impressive against taller walls, when combined with half baskets and wall pots to brighten up the background. Choose plants with flower colours that will complement the brickwork. If the wall is a dark colour, pastel shades or lighter coloured flowers are best, while a rendered wall painted with a light colour needs darker flowers. In both cases avoid using the hottest, sunniest brick walls because in the middle of summer it

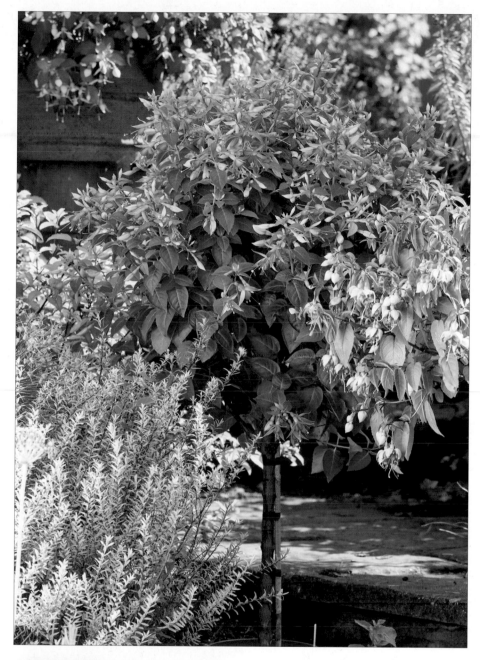

Left: 'This quarter standard of 'WALZ Jubelteen' is growing by a path with its pot set into the soil. Covered with prolific pale-pink and pinkish-orange single flowers, it is a wonderful sight.

CREATING EXTRA HEIGHT

Standard fuchsias are excellent for raising the height and increasing the impact of other displays. For instance, in a group of pots of different sizes and heights, adding one or more standards at the back can create a much more impressive effect. Similarly, you can place a standard at the back of a border, against a hedge or fence, when extra height is required and there is a need for a focal point to draw the eye upward. Standards with white or lighter pastel-coloured flowers look splendid against dark fences and hedges, and deeper-coloured cultivars are best against light walls or golden-yellow hedges. Red and white flowers stand out well against mid-green hedges, while standards grown from variegated cultivars make excellent eye-catchers anywhere, with the best foliage colours developing in bright conditions. Use the same technique in the hardy fuchsia border, adding variations in height with standards and even some spectacular early colour if the standards are already in flower, forced into growth, early in the year, in the protective warmth of a greenhouse.

Below: The cultivar 'Miss California' grown as a quarter standard. It has a wiry and slightly lax habit of growth, giving a weeping effect with pink and white flowers.

will probably be too hot for the fuchsias. If you do use a standard in a hot spot, ensure it is a sun-tolerant type, and in any case protect the pot (and the plant's roots) with shading or sink it into the ground.

Weeping standards are ideal for an internal corner, with the profusion of flowers filling up what might otherwise be an awkward space. Periodically turn the standard 45 degrees so that you get a fully rounded shape, otherwise it will produce all its growth towards the light.

Left: 'Cambridge Louie' is a strong-growing single-flowered cultivar, which makes a very good quarter or half standard. When grown in plenty of sun, its growth is stronger and harder.

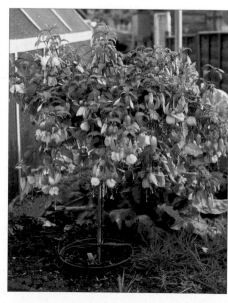

STEPS, PATHS AND BORDERS

Putting half or quarter standards at the edge of garden steps creates a terrific effect. The standards help define the edges and simultaneously soften the transition between the steps and garden. Similarly, position them along the edge of a path – provided it is wide enough – and they will help delineate the outline. Quarter standards are also excellent in summer bedding borders, especially when surrounded by many low-growing plants. This technique is commonly, and very effectively, used in parks, botanical gardens and other public displays.

Standard fuchsias again make excellent specimen plants, and placing a full standard in a small, circular bed in the centre of a lawn creates a brilliant focal point. Plant the remainder of the circular bed with other bedding plants to complement the standard's height and colour. A weeping standard grown in such a scheme will often be a spectacular sight with its masses of flowers raining down on its cascading branches.

Below: A half standard with pink and white flowers, growing in an attractive pot. Standing on paving close to a gate, it makes a really eye-catching feature.

TERRACES AND PATIOS

Another exciting way of using standard fuchsias is along the edge of a terrace or patio. If you are constructing a new terrace or patio, sink some large pots into the ground around the edges for placing the standards in over the summer. This technique will help keep the plants' roots cool and the stems upright. You can use these same pots for bulbs and spring-flowering plants, until the time comes to bring out the standards in summer.

Fuchsias grown in this way help define the edge of a patio, and create lovely bursts of colour. In the case of patios surrounded

Top: Four standards planted in the ground above a mass of bedding plants, including alyssum, lobelia, marigolds and pelargoniums at the back of a semi-circular border.

Left: A full standard of the hardy 'Margaret' growing against an evergreen background, close to a bench seat and surrounded by colourful containers of ageratum, begonias and pelargoniums.

by a low border wall, create some planting areas within the wall, hollowing out the centre along the top, and plant the standards here. Half or full standards placed close to bench seats against light-coloured walls can also look very pleasing and make the seat a little more of a private place.

PONDS

Just as paths can be defined and dramatically brightened by standard fuchsias, so too can ponds. Use larger standards to create spot features, placing them in the line of sight, while smaller standards are ideal for highlighting the outline. The fuchsias thrive on the humidity of the air and soil near the pond, but do not place them so close to the edge that the falling flowers drop into the water, spoiling the effect.

PERGOLAS

When using the standards to soften hard landscaping, try placing them around the outside of pergolas, arches and other similar structures to help hide the sharp edges of the vertical posts. The posts, in turn, provide additional support for the standard, preventing them from being blown over. If you have extra standards, position some inside large pergolas to complement the other plants, hanging baskets and containers, to create extra focal points.

CHOOSING STANDARDS

The following cultivars are suggestions for growing different types of standard. The measurements show the length of clear stem between the surface of the soil and the lowest branch of the head. The measurements are for classification guidance only, and the actual dimensions and size very much depend on you. It is possible to grow standards with even longer stems, perhaps up to 1.8m (6ft), although handling and overwintering them will be very difficult.

Miniature standard 13–25cm (5–10in): 'Baby Bright', 'Marilyn Olsen', 'Nellie Nuttall', 'Sophie Louise', 'Tom Thumb'
Quarter or table standard 25–46cm (10–18in): 'Chang, 'Estelle Marie', 'Genii', 'Katrina Thompsen', 'Paula Jane', 'Rose Fantasia'
Half standard 46–76cm (18–30in): 'Annabel', 'Border Queen', 'Checkerboard', 'Garden News', 'Olive Smith', 'WALZ Jubelteen'
Full standard 76–107cm (30–42in): 'Achievement', 'Amy Lye', 'Barbara', 'Celia Smedley', 'Mrs Lovell Swisher', 'Snowcap'
Weeping standard 46–107cm (18–42in): 'Brutus', 'Ernie Bromley', 'Eva Boerg', 'Falling Stars', 'Jack Shahan', 'Swingtime'

Left: A miniature standard of 'Midwinter' covered in white single flowers. This size of this standard makes it suitable for a table decoration, or you can use it in the rockery.

Above: Full standards of 'Snowcap' and 'Celia Smedley' with their pots sunk into the ground either side of an entrance gate. They are wired to the wall and ground for support.

Trained fuchsias

A well-grown fuchsia trained into a shape like a pyramid or a fan can be a stunning sight and can make a real focal point in a garden. A pyramid or pillar can make a striking freestanding display in the middle of a lawn, while a trained fan or an espalier can cover a large area of a wall or fence. Before embarking on growing large trained fuchsias for display as specimens in the garden, it is important to consider how they will be stored for the winter, as they are best kept ticking over in green leaf. It is easier if you live in an area without frosts, where leaving them outside all year without winter protection is possible, but most growers will need heated protection big enough to overwinter these structures.

PYRAMIDS

Large pyramid shapes will grow more than 3m (10ft) over a few years with the right care and growing conditions, but smaller specimens of 1m (3ft) or more in height may be grown in a single season and still make a very impressive show. As the plants

Top: A young pyramid in its first full year of growth, in flower against a background of Japanese anemones and *Fatsia japonica*.

age, the wood becomes harder and stronger, and they are better able to stand the ravages of strong winds and heavy rains, but during the first year when green growth is maturing to wood, some extra protection and support is needed. It is therefore important to make sure the centre stake or cane is in good condition and strong enough, especially the part that stands in the compost (soil mix), which is more prone to rotting. The best time to

change the cane is when you cut back the plant in the autumn. Use ties such as PVC tape, and check the tightness as the stem thickens. Tying the top of the cane to an overhead support helps to stabilize the structure and will reduce the chances of it blowing over in strong winds.

PILLARS

This form of training develops an attractive column of flowers, with the diameter of growth being very similar at the top and bottom of the structure. When a pillar is in full flower, it makes a very attractive and eye-catching sight, which is sure to raise many comments. This type of structure is ideal to place either side of a doorway or gateway, as the girth at the base does not restrict placement.

CONICALS

The conical form of training is intermediate between the pyramid and the pillar. It is trained in a similar way to a pyramid, but has a narrower base, forming a slimmer, tapered shape compared to a pyramid. The end result resembles an elegant tree. Conicals are easy to use in similar ways to both pyramids and pillars, but during winter storage they do not take up quite as much floor area as pyramids.

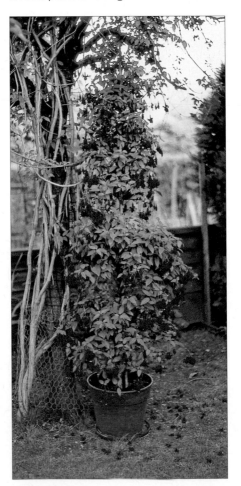

Far left and left: A trained shape of 'Brutus', dripping with red and purple flowers and growing with the top of the cane tied up to a pear tree. In the earlier picture (far left), the plant training was toward a pyramid. In the later picture (near left), pruning the base of the plant produced a narrower conical shape.

Above: A small-scale trained pyramid of the cultivar 'Midwinter', flowering for the first time with its white single flowers.

Above: A small pillar of the cultivar 'London 2000', trained up to the desired height. Next, the side growth will be filled out.

You may use all of the forms above in a similar way to large standards, but they look especially impressive when placed either side of a doorway, or at the edges of a patio or yard where they will help to highlight the corners and edges. They will also stand out beautifully as a feature in the centre of a lawn or as a centrepiece in an arrangement of pots.

Right: A young conical of the cultivar 'Little Beauty', grown to a height of 2m (6ft), flowering for the first time. As the plant gets older, the growth will thicken up.

FANS AND ESPALIERS

The usual way to grow fans and espaliers is against a wall, where they can benefit from the shelter and warmth (especially if it is a house wall) and an easy means of supporting them. Choose a wall that receives a reasonable amount of sun, but ideally not full sun all day.

If you don't have a suitable wall, you can also train fuchsias against a wire fence where you can see them from both sides, provided the fence is strong enough. In both cases, be aware that these shapes,

especially the fan shape, will have a large frontal surface area. A specimen measuring 2m (6ft) high and wide can present a surface area of $1-1.5m^2$ (1.2–1.8sq yd) to the wind, resulting in a huge pressure on the structure . Therefore, it is important to secure it well against the wall or fence, ideally by ties between the wall or fence and the top of the frame, to prevent the wind from damaging it. If there is a border along the wall or fence, try to sink the pot partially or completely in the ground to help keep the roots cool. You may also plant the specimen in the soil but it will be tricky removing it at the end of the season.

When in full flower, such plants can be breathtaking, making superb focal points. A double cultivar, such as 'Annabel', 'Lillian Annetts' or 'Swingtime', will look truly spectacular when grown as a fan, and it will be well worth moving it to a warm place every winter, enabling it to grow to an impressive size.

Top left: A magnificent fuchsia fan grown from the cultivar 'Lillian Annetts'. This structure measures more than 2m (6ft) high and wide, and was grown by Chris Woolston.

Top right: This small fan of 'Waveney Gem' has been grown in a 13cm (5in) pot. Placed on a lawn against a stone wall, it is displaying its flowers forward.

Left: A young espalier of the red and white double-flowered cultivar 'Swingtime', being grown on a framework of green canes.

OTHER TRAINED SHAPES

Topiary shapes can be very successful if you position them where they will catch the eye, for example on low walls, perched on top of entrance pillars or even on purpose-built stands. Ensure that you fix the pots securely so they cannot blow off, and they will be sure to create a lot of interest. There are so many different wire-framed shapes now available that you could even create a tableau of different animal images along the top of a wall. You can also create individual letters and numbers, and even

Above: A topiary cat shape grown from a vigorous Encliandra cultivar inside a wire mesh former. Note how the ears have filled but the feet and tail need more growth.

a living message along the top of a wall. If you use the Encliandra types, let them flower, just clipping off any long growths to keep them tidy and maintain the shape of the basic framework. Use miniaturized versions of rings, fans, pyramids and other trained shapes to enhance walls, pillars, porchways and steps.

CLIMBING FUCHSIAS

Some fuchsias have such vigorous, rampant growth that they are very difficult to train in a conventional way. While they might not be true climbers, since they do not twist around supports like a vine, and they do not have tendrils or leaves that curl around and attach the plant to supports, such as a clematis, some do make

excellent clambering plants. You can grow them permanently in a greenhouse or against a fence, a pergola or a simple post by using large plants started into vigorous growth in the greenhouse.

Good candidates include the species *F. boliviana*, *F. regia* and the cultivars 'Giant Cascade', 'Lady Boothby', 'Pride of the West', 'Royal Purple' and 'Wisteria'. In recent years, some large companies have promoted 'Lady Boothby' especially for this purpose. When left to grow unstopped, this cultivar makes long, extended upright growths with minimal side shoots until it starts to flower, with attractive cerise and dark purple small single flowers near the growing tips. Removing the growing tips will promote branching.

Fuchsias grown in this way need tying to supports, just as you would secure a climbing rose, to prevent the supple growth from being broken off. Both *F. regia* and 'Lady Boothby' are hardy and therefore may be planted permanently, and will shoot from the base again if killed down to the ground in winter. The other mentioned cultivars need winter protection or should be grown outside only in milder, frost-free climates.

Below left: This climbing fuchsia cultivar of 'Lady Boothby' has been planted against the wall of a house, trained and supported on a wire mesh secured to the wall.

Below: This vigorous and well established hardy fuchsia looks quite at ease climbing naturally up a fence, covered in wild columbine and other creeping and trailing plants.

THE CONTAINER GARDEN

Fuchsias are an ideal choice for growing in containers, both on their own and as companion plants in mixed plantings. There is a tremendous range of colours to blend with every colour scheme, from the traditional red and purple through whites, pinks, blues, aubergines, indigos and violets. Stately standard fuchsias stand to attention, demanding respect and displaying their flowers proudly, while fans or pyramids make striking architectural features. Large double-flowered trailing fuchsias, such as 'Swingtime' or 'Haute Cuisine', display their flowers at the ideal eye level in hanging baskets, demanding a closer look. Variegated-leaf cultivars such as 'Golden Marinka' in hanging containers, or 'Firecracker', 'Tom West' and 'Sunray' in freestanding containers, can add some variation of leaf colour. This chapter contains examples of different types of containers to use, tips on caring for the plants, and ideas for placing and grouping them into eye-catching displays, even co-ordinating the colours to create different moods within the garden.

Left: This trailing fuchsia has been planted in an old wooden wheelbarrow, along with different coloured lobelias, catmint and other bedding plants.

Top left: 'Cambridge Louie' is a vigorous and bushy single-flowered cultivar that thrives in containers placed in sunny positions around the garden.

Top middle: 'Cloth of Gold' has beautifully coloured foliage that looks wonderful in hanging containers, where the colours can be appreciated at eye level.

Top right: The beautiful double-flowered cultivar 'Walsingham' works beautifully when used in either planters or hanging containers.

Large pots

Grown alone as specimen plants or mixed with other plants, fuchsias make an excellent show in large pots around the garden. They make pleasing focal points on terraces, steps and patios. By using different varieties, you should find one to suit every part of the garden – most fuchsias do best in partial shade, where a lot of other flowering shrubs would be less happy, but in sunny positions the Triphylla hybrids are ideal. For a specimen, it is best to start with a large single plant, or multiple plants (at least three) of the same variety. For a mixed pot, try different fuchsias with contrasting flower colours, or mix fuchsias with begonias, busy Lizzies, pelargoniums and foliage plants.

TYPES OF POT

There are many different shapes, sizes and finishes of pot, including colour-glazed and unglazed types, manufactured from many materials such as stone, cast concrete, plastic and fired clay. The unglazed terracotta (clay) type is the best choice for fuchsias, as the pots breathe and help to cool the root ball by evaporation. The glazed type can also work well and is a good choice if you want a particular colour scheme. Try to avoid pots with very narrow necks, as it is often difficult to remove large plants at the end of the season. An alternative is to grow the plant in a separate smaller pot, which then sits in the neck of a

large pot. Do not choose a container with a narrow base in a position exposed to wind, as it could blow over – wide-based pots are more stable. You can stand pots on clay pot feet to improve drainage.

SINGLE-SPECIMEN FUCHSIAS

In pots up to 30cm (12in), you can achieve a good effect by using a large fuchsia plant brought into growth early in the year, or three or more smaller plants of the same variety. Preferably, plant it up in the early spring, so the plant can establish itself in the pot. Pinch out the growing tips until early to mid-spring and then let it grow on and it will be in flower in early summer. Double-flowered and Triphylla hybrids need a little longer to come into flower, so stop the pinching out a few weeks earlier. Grouping some of these large specimen plants together in a large garden can also be very effective. Try using a large Triphylla fuchsia with hot red-orange flowers such as 'Thalia' or 'Gartenmeister Bonstedt' at the back of a display, and in front, place two pots with slightly more lax white-flowered cultivars such as 'Annabel' or 'Shelford'.

Top left: Multiple plants of the cultivar 'John Bartlett' grown in a glazed black pot placed in the middle of a lawn.

Above right: This large blue pot has been multi-planted with the cultivar 'Shelford', and placed on the edge of a flight of steps.

Left: The hardy cultivar 'Tom Thumb' has small red and purple flowers. This example, grown in an aged terracotta pot standing on a terrace, is just coming into flower.

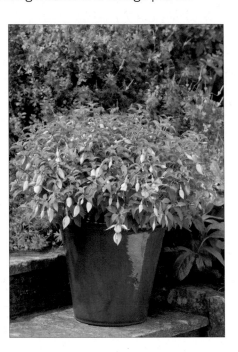

RECOMMENDED TRIPHYLLA CULTIVARS

Many of the cultivars hybridized by Carl Bonstedt, including 'Bornemann's Beste', 'Coralle', 'Gartenmeister Bonstedt' and 'Thalia', are strong growers that will quickly form a large plant. 'Traudchen Bonstedt' is trickier to grow but has beautiful salmon-pink flowers and dark foliage, while 'Mary' will always make a spectacular, eye-catching plant with its vivid red flowers and attractive green leaves and slightly more lax growth, which creates a large, arching shape. Grow it in a dark glazed pot to contrast strongly with the vivid flowers. Other older cultivars worth trying are 'Obergartner Koch', hybridized by Sauer in 1912, with bright orange flowers and dark foliage, and 'Leverkusen', hybridized by Rehnelt in

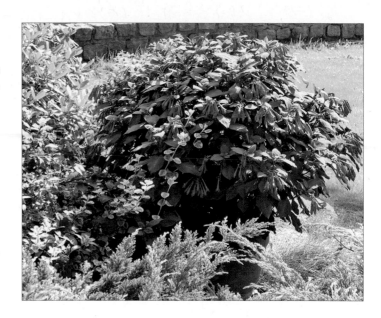

Left: 'Chantry Park' is one of the more lax-growing Triphylla types, with long scarlet flowers. It is excellent for planting around the edge of a large pot.

Right: This large multi-planted pot of the Triphylla 'Coralle' is in full flower, fringed with conifers and standing on smooth granite rock in full sun in a front garden in Sweden.

FUCHSIAS FOR LARGE POTS

Many of the wide range of beautiful fuchsias will look superb in large pots. Below is a list to consider.

Triphyllas: 'Billy Green', 'Coralle', 'Gartenmeister Bonstedt', 'Georg Bornemann', 'Mary', 'Thalia'
Single-flowered: 'Cambridge Louie', 'Celia Smedley', 'Joy Patmore', 'Lady Isobel Barnett', 'Lenora', 'Other Fellow', 'Shelford'
Semi-double-flowered: 'Delta's Sara', 'Miss California', 'President George Bartlett'
Double-flowered: 'Annabel', 'Blue Waves', 'Garden News', 'Royal Velvet'
Foliage: 'Autumnal', 'Cloth of Gold', 'Golden Marinka', 'Popsie Girl', 'Sunray', 'Tom West'

'Joy Patmore'

Right: This Triphylla fuchsia in a large terracotta pot basking in the sunshine is covered from top to bottom with racemes of long-tubed orange-red flowers.

1928, with rose-cerise flowers produced very freely. Of the more recent cultivars, 'Firecracker' (the variegated leaf sport from 'Thalia') is well worth growing, but do not overwater it. 'Brian Kimberley' has very long, pale orange flowers and light sage-green foliage, 'Insulinde' has bright orange flowers and very dark, slightly shiny leaves,

'Len Beilby' has scarlet-red flowers and very vigorous growth, and the free-flowering 'Roos Breytenbach' has a pinkish-red tube and sepals, and an orange-red corolla with vigorous growth. One newer, unusual cultivar is 'Pabbe's Torreldöve' with purple-magenta flowers, hybridized by Tielko Koerts in 1996.

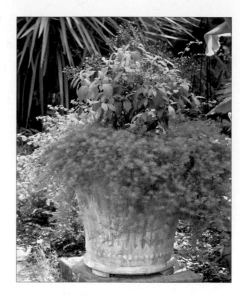

You can also mix in different companion plants such as begonias or pelargoniums. The Pendula begonias and ivy-leaf pelargoniums look particularly good around the edges of a pot. Zonal pelargoniums are excellent in the centre, especially the bi- and tricolour leaf types such as 'Frank Headley' and 'Mrs Pollock'. Try using a striking foliage plant like a canna with a white or pale pink-flowered fuchsia. Other foliage plants such as *Helichrysum petiolare* 'Limelight' or 'Variegatum' are useful as fillers. Make use of some of the variegated leaf fuchsias such as 'Tom West', 'Sunray' or 'Golden Marinka', as these have both beautiful foliage colours and flowers. These mixed pots will look lovely with a few edging plants such as lobelia, the small blue trailing campanula or *Bacopa* 'Snowflake' around the sides. Fuchsias combine well with many different plant species, so it is worth experimenting with some of your own favourites.

With a minimal amount of care, adequate watering and feeding through the summer, these pots will give months of colour and pleasure.

Above: A large white stone pot filled with *F. arborescens* and trailing plants *Lotus berthelotii* and *Iresine lindenii*.

Right: An attractive blue-glazed pot planted with a standard of 'Tom West' and some trailing ivy, set against an aged blue fence.

Below: A terracotta bell pot, standing on the edge of steps, filled with fuchsias, including 'Thalia', 'Cotton Candy' and 'Auntie Jinks', as well as zonal pelargoniums and other companion plants.

Above: A large terracotta flowerpot, planted with multiple plants of 'Thalia', placed at the top of steps by a lawn. The plant is just coming into flower in midsummer.

There are also Triphylla-type cultivars that are worth considering because of their vigour or unusual flower colours. These cultivars have Triphylla-shaped flowers, and tend to be more axial- than terminal-flowering. Look out for the vigorous and free-flowering 'Billy Green' with pink self flowers and 'Efried Ott' with plenty of salmon-pink flowers, 'Orient Express' (one of a series of cultivars named after famous trains by Goulding), with a pretty pink and white flower, and 'Roger de Cooker', with white and rose flowers.

MIXED CONTAINERS

It is a good idea to use different fuchsias with contrasting flower colours, but similar growth habits. An example of a good mix of double-flowered types is 'Royal Velvet' with 'Alaska', or 'Annabel' with 'Haute Cuisine'. Try planting upright types in the centre and more lax or trailing types on the outside.

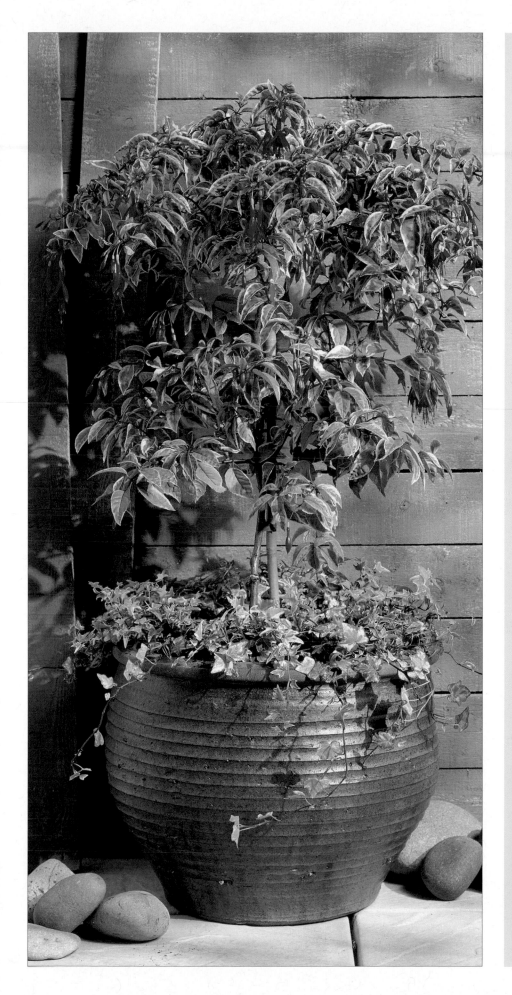

COMPANION PLANTS FOR LARGE POTS

The following are ideal companions for fuchsias in mixed pots.

Larger flowering plants: *Begonia*, *Calibrachoa* (million bells), *Dahlia* (dwarf varieties), *Dianthus*, *Gazania*, *Impatiens*, *Matthiola* (stock), *Nicotiana*, *Osteospermum*, *Pelargonium* (angel, ivy-leaf, scented-leaf and zonal), *Penstemon*, *Petunia*, *Salvia*, *Verbena*
Larger foliage plants: *Canna*, *Coleus*, *Helichrysum*, *Nemesia*
Compact edging plants: *Ageratum*, *Alyssum*, *Bacopa*, *Campanula*, *Diascia*, *Hedera* (compact ivies), *Lobelia*

Dianthus

Helichrysum

Lobelia

Urns

Fuchsias, especially those with a lax shape, make a very attractive picture when grown in an elegant urn on a patio or flight of steps. Usually an urn is in the shape of a large vase, and sits on a pedestal or feet. Such containers are available in many different shapes, finishes and colours, and are made from materials including cast iron, plastic, terracotta (clay), GRP (glass-reinforced plastic) and carved or reconstituted stone. Shapes vary from the tall, slim and elegant, such as the Venetian urn, to the Versailles type and the larger bowl-shaped urns (the Regency type), which are usually placed on a pedestal and base. Often they have surface decoration with elegant relief patterns that add to the attraction.

URN PLANTING IDEAS

The smaller, narrower type of container is best suited to growing a single fuchsia cultivar, either a group or a single plant. The best varieties have lax or semi-trailing compact growth so that they trail over the edge of the container but do not completely cascade or they will hide its beauty. Alternatively, plant it with a fuchsia that grows in the shape of a compact dome, leaving the urn completely visible. Hardy cultivars often exhibit these characteristics and good examples include 'Dollar Prinzessin', 'Genii' and 'Lady Thumb'.

The large pot or bowl-shaped containers are better suited to mixed fuchsia cultivars or a mixed planting. Use smaller trailing fuchsias around the edge and an upright bushier plant in the middle for a really striking effect. Alternatively, use a large-flowered cultivar with arching growth that will easily fill a large container. Good varieties include 'Annabel', 'Celia Smedley', 'Checkerboard' and 'Royal Velvet'. Always choose cultivars whose flower and leaf colours will complement or contrast with the container. An urn made from light coloured stone, such as the creamy pale yellow Bath stone, is best with a darker flowered cultivar.

Top: This small blue urn, planted with the cultivar 'Martin's Umbrella', is standing on a patio in front of larger pots containing cannas and hostas.

Right: This embellished lead urn looks impressive and dramatic, planted with 'Marinka', a red single-flowered trailing fuchsia, around the edges, and the Triphylla cultivar 'Thalla' in the centre.

Conversely, a dark cast-iron container, or a clay container glazed with a dark colour, may look better with a cultivar with a white or pale-coloured flower.

Using a mixture of plant types, with fuchsias as just one component of the whole display, is also an inspiring way of using these containers, especially the bowl-shaped kind. There are many suitable companion plants but zonal pelargoniums, especially the single-flowered types that tolerate the rain or those with variegated

Left: This attractive embossed terracotta urn is standing on a brick paved patio, and is planted with the hardy fuchsia 'Tom Thumb'. Other fuchsias and plants provide a background of contrasting textures and colours.

foliage, such as the bi-color leaved 'Frank Headly' or the tricolor leaved 'Mrs Pollack', are excellent choices. Ivy-leaf pelargoniums are also effective, offering a tremendous choice of colours and trailing-cascading growth. Good single varieties include 'Crocodile', 'Surcouf', 'Sugar Baby' and the red or pink 'Mini Cascade'. Variegated leaf varieties include 'Hederinum Variegated',

Below: A terracotta strawberry pot planted with many different fuchsia cultivars, including 'Roesse Blacky', 'Waveney Gem', 'Emma Louise' and 'Land van Beveren'.

'Jips Twink', 'L'Elégante' and 'Pac Ekva'. If planting the urn with mainly upright plants, then compact lobelia, campanula or alyssum can be used to trail around the edge of the container.

An attractive way of positioning urns planted with fuchsias is by placing a matching pair either side of a doorway with a wide set of steps leading up to them. They are also excellent as a single feature on a patio or terrace, or in multiple groups around the edges or in corners where a wall gives a lovely backdrop.

Finally, try planting fuchsias in urn-shaped containers with planting pockets on the side designed for growing herbs or strawberries. Use the smaller trailing varieties such as 'Auntie Jinks', 'Harry Grey', 'La Campanella' or 'Gordon Thorley' around the edges and a more vigorous cultivar in the top, and it will reward you with a mound of colour throughout summer.

Below: A large blue urn planted with a Triphylla and other fuchsias and trailing plants, standing on paving in front of a white painted brick wall.

Troughs and boxes

Fuchsias grown in troughs and boxes are marvellous for brightening many areas of the garden, such as low walls, roof patios and paved areas. They are also probably the best way to grow fuchsias if you have no garden – they can sit on a broad windowsill, or on the ground next to the house wall. There are many different types of trough made of various materials, including terracotta (clay), wood, plastic, stone, concrete and metal. It is best to avoid metal ones, as the roots can become very hot in the sun. Some have feet to stand on; some have a tray to stand in; yet others are made to hang on a wall. Troughs standing on windowsills, walls or roofs must be fixed down securely.

WALL TROUGHS

These containers, usually made from metal strips in a framework, are hung on a wall. They need lining with moss, plastic or a suitable bespoke liner before planting. Several different shapes are available, such as wall-mounted hay feeders. Ensure the wall fixings are strong enough to support the weight, as these containers can often be very heavy when fully planted. Try planting these with trailing fuchsias along the front edge and more compact upright varieties behind, or mixed with other companion plants such as begonias and pelargoniums.

Top: An attractive square black pot made of glass-reinforced plastic, with a mixed planting of fuchsias, lobelia, nepeta and petunias, standing on paving in front of a raised bed.

Below: A small terracotta trough planted with compact fuchsias, upright at the back and trailing at the front, including 'Love's Reward', 'Emma Louise' and 'La Campanella'.

Left: An elegant trough made of plastic, planted with the fuchsia 'Dollar Prinzessin' and companion plants.

TROUGHS FOR LOW WALLS

When placing troughs on top of low walls, make sure that the wall is sufficiently thick for the container to stand firmly on it, again fixing it down well. The best walls for fuchsia troughs are typically up to 1.5m (5ft) so that it is easy to access them for watering and maintenance. Trailing fuchsias, especially really prolific varieties such as 'Cascade', 'Put's Folly' and 'President Margaret Slater',

look wonderful cascading down the wall. If the trough is wide enough, plant some compact upright cultivars along the centre as well. Try using small standards as another way of lifting the centre of the trough and creating some extra interest.

FREE-STANDING TROUGHS

Troughs of various sizes can be used around the garden as stand-alone features or as part of larger container displays. Placing them around the edges of terraces, decks or patios to help define the edges can be very useful, both as a decoration and as a safety aid. Larger containers of stone, such as old drinking troughs, are often very impressive, especially if they have an aged look with lichen and moss growing on the stone and in the crevices.

Plant these types of containers with fuchsias, or fuchsias mixed with other plants, and they will make a colourful display for the whole summer. Use standards or other trained shapes such as pyramids, pillars or conicals in bigger troughs, ensuring the size of the plants fits the scale of the trough.

Right: A plastic square pot planted with a standard bay tree. The companion plants in the pot are *Fuchsia* 'Pink Fantasia', an erect-flowered fuchsia with red and mauve flowers, and *Cineraria maritima* 'Silverdust'.

WINDOW BOXES

Where the windowsills on a house are big enough, window boxes can look very attractive planted with fuchsias and companion plants. The best type are those with a flat base which will sit firmly on the windowsill; they must also be fixed or clamped in some way to prevent them falling off. Plant them in a similar way to the wall troughs described earlier, with trailing fuchsias at the front edge for those viewing from outside, and compact upright cultivars for viewing from both inside and outside, but make sure that the whole display does not obstruct the view out of the window.

PLANTING BOXES

Square boxes for planting made of plastic or hardwood can be very attractive, and are excellent homes for a tall centre plant with smaller edging or cascading plants surrounding them. They will look splendid with a standard fuchsia in the middle and trailing fuchsias around the edges. Alternatively, you can grow another tall plant such as a conifer or a standard bay, and add trailing fuchsias in the base.

Below: A cast concrete trough planted with red and white single fuchsias and white flowered bacopa as an edging plant, standing on the edge of decking.

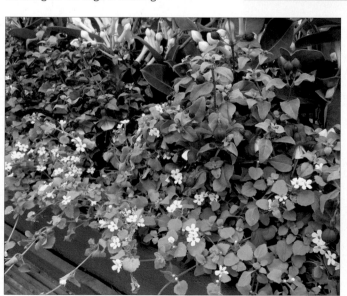

FUCHSIAS FOR TROUGHS AND BOXES

There are a great many fuchsias that will work well in troughs and boxes. Listed below are some of the most suitable lax and upright cultivars.

Lax and cascading types: 'Auntie Jinks', 'Cascade', 'Devonshire Dumpling', 'Emma Louise', 'Eva Boerg', 'Golden Marinka', 'Harry Grey', 'Haute Cuisine', 'Land van Beveren', 'President Margaret Slater', 'Seventh Heaven', 'Susan Green', 'Swingtime', 'Waveney Gem'
Upright types: 'Alison Patricia', 'Annabel', 'Border Queen', 'Dollar Prinzessin', 'Maria Landy', 'Mickey Goult', 'Millennium', 'Minirose', 'Miss California', 'Paula Jane', 'Pink Fantasia', 'Thamar', 'Twinny'

Hanging baskets

Hanging baskets are an excellent way of showing off the beauty of fuchsia flowers because you have to look up into them. There are many different trailing fuchsia cultivars, ideal for baskets. You can fill a basket with several plants of one particular cultivar, a mixture of different kinds, or fuchsias with companion plants – all look very impressive. Good growth habits for hanging baskets vary from the lax or spreading upright growers, to the stiff trailers and those that cascade over the sides of a basket. Some of the large double cultivars used in baskets do not trail very much until the flowers start to open, when the weight of the flowers drags the branches downward.

THE BEST SITES

You can use fuchsia-based hanging baskets in many places around the house and garden. They are commonly found suspended from strong brackets on the side or corners of the house, and beside doorways. You could try hanging them from tree branches, especially spreading trees with strong boughs such as Bramley Seedling apple trees. You can also hang them from the eaves of the roof if they have sufficient overhang, or even within the arch of a pergola if it is high enough. You can also use baskets to enliven

Top: The lovely lax cultivar 'Wendy's Beauty' has a double flower with white tube and sepals and an unusual pale violet-purple corolla, and works well in hanging baskets.

garages, sheds and other outbuildings, or any corners that look dull and need brightening in summer.

A further option involves using tiered baskets, which perch on top of each other using special support stands, or using those built around a single support pole. Ensure that the base of these is wide enough or weighted down to prevent it from blowing over in the wind. Baskets

Above: This basket planted with fuchsias, impatiens and begonias is in full flower, and stands out beautifully against a white wall.

Left: A plastic container hanging from a tree branch, planted with 'Susan Green'. This vigorous fuchsia cultivar has beautiful, classically shaped single flowers with green-tipped, pale pink sepals and a coral-pink corolla.

can even be placed on pedestals, chimney pots or special metal basket stands to create a lovely display.

Where fuchsias outscore many other plants is in creating a showy and long-lasting display in a shady position, where it might be too dull for many traditional colourful bedding plants, such as pelargoniums and verbena, to perform well. Choose cultivars with white or light-coloured flowers, or at least those with pale sepals, because they will stand out better in shady conditions.

SINGLE-CULTIVAR BASKETS

Baskets planted with a single cultivar produce a mass of flowers of the same colour, and invariably make a strong impact. Another effective tactic is using two baskets – with similar-shaped flowers but in contrasting colours – say, to either side of a door. For example, you could use 'Janice Ann' in one basket and 'Harry Grey' in the other. Use at least four plants, each in a 9cm (3½in) pot, in a 30cm (12in) basket, or at least seven in a 40cm (16in) basket. When making the final pinching out, stop all the growing tips at the same time so that all the plants flower simultaneously.

Above: A lovely hanging basket planted with the fuchsias 'Cascade', 'Marinka', 'Seventh Heaven', 'Sir Matt Busby' and 'Veenlust', together with pretty lobelia, ivy-leaf pelargoniums and begonias.

In a dark corner, where a white or pastel-coloured cultivar is the best choice, use fuchsias such as 'Devonshire Dumpling', 'Harry Grey', 'Natasha Sinton' or 'Walsingham'. In a brighter area, a more strongly coloured cultivar will stand out even better, with a double-flowered red and white, such as 'Swingtime', or a pink and red, such as 'Seventh Heaven', being excellent choices. Strongly coloured single-flowered fuchsias (such as 'Caradella', 'Marinka' or 'Postiljon') also work very well. Cultivars with vigorous, cascading growth, such as 'Cascade', 'President Margaret Slater' or 'Put's Folly', are less suitable for single-cultivar baskets because they flower at the end of long branches, and you will end up with no flowers in the middle. It is better to use these cultivars in mixed baskets.

Above: 'Rocket Fire' growing in a wicker hanging basket. The double flowers of this fuchsia have an unusual frilled corolla with pink outer petals and purple inner petals.

Different foliage colours can also make quite an impact, and cultivars with variegated foliage, such as 'Alton Water', 'Arcadia Gold', 'Barbara Norton', 'Golden Lena', 'Golden Marinka', 'Rosemarie Higham' and ''t Voske' (a variegated sport from 'Auntie Jinks'), are ideal. Alternatively, use fuchsias with a distinctive leaf colour adding to the display. Suitable examples include 'Autumnale' (young leaves start green and yellow but mature to red and salmon with splashes of yellow), 'Ernie Bromley' (bright yellow-green), 'Golden Anniversary' (large double, light green new foliage) and 'Tropic Sunset' (double, red-bronze foliage).

MIXED FUCHSIA BASKETS

Baskets planted with a mixture of different kinds of fuchsia can be extremely effective. Use either several plants of just a few different cultivars to a predetermined colour plan or a random mix of several different cultivars. Try to use a short-jointed, slightly lax cultivar in the centre of the basket with the more trailing, cascading types around the outside and this will ensure a superb, all-over coverage of flowers. Intermixing doubles and singles will ensure plenty of flowers over the whole basket. The large double flowers are impressive, but not always as freely produced as the single flowers. Using alternate cascading and lax cultivars around the edges gives an interesting variety of the depth of trailing growth and flowers.

When deciding how to arrange multiple plants of just a few cultivars, there are several different approaches. One is to mix plants with similar growth habits but contrasting flower colours. So, use 'Auntie Jinks' and 'Harry Grey' alternately around the edges with a slightly lax cultivar, such as the white single-flowered 'Shelford' or the double 'Ruth King', in the centre.

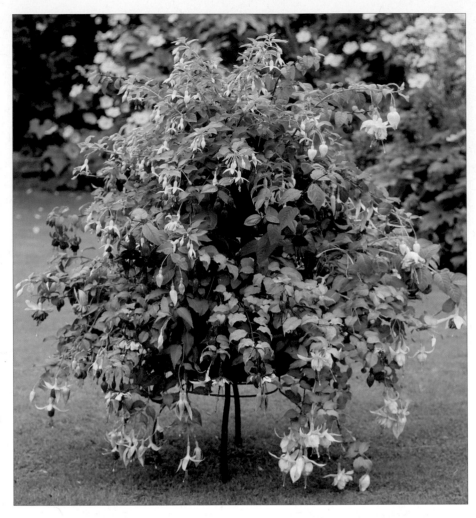

Above: Tiered baskets with stands are an excellent way to display fuchsias. This twin basket has been planted with many cultivars in front of Japanese anemones.

COMPANION PLANTS FOR MIXED BASKETS

Creating mixed summer baskets using fuchsias opens a whole world of different combinations. There are masses of possible companion plants. Some gardeners like to insert plants through the sides of the basket to obtain the full cascading effect quite quickly, but this is probably unnecessary with a mixed fuchsia basket. Instead, use cultivars that are fairly stiff and semi-upright, such as 'Annabel' or 'Ruth King', in the centre of the scheme surrounded by a ring of lax types, such as 'Seventh Heaven' or 'Millennium', and trailing or cascading cultivars around the edges, such as 'Cascade' or 'Auntie Jinks'. Contrasts of foliage and flower colour help to create a basket that is attractive from every side.

Inter-planting with ivy-leaf pelargoniums, such as 'Balkonvit' (white), 'Mauve Beauty' (freely produced deep mauve flowers), 'Sugar Baby' (miniature ivy-leaf and pink flowers) and 'Pak Ekva' (small, variegated leaves and pink flowers), generates extra interest. Pendula begonias, which grow from corms or seed, come in a range of colours including red, orange, yellow and pink, and create a wonderful cascade of colour. Their foliage comes in different colours, varying from light green to dark reddish-green. They grow big and bushy, with large leaves, so take care that they do not crowd out the other plants – use no more than one or two in a large basket.

Left: A hanging basket planted with fuchsias, attached to a wall bracket by a door. Other plants in the basket include zonal and ivy-leaf pelargoniums, ivy, *Glechoma hederacea* 'Variegata' (catmint), trailing lobelia and *Calibrachoa*. Beneath the basket are some colourful upright begonias.

Above: A mixed hanging basket planted with the fuchsias 'Deep Purple', 'Herman de Graaff', 'Ruby Wedding' and 'Auntie Jinks' with begonias and pelargoniums.

Smaller flowering plants can be used to fill gaps between the larger plants, and improve the stunning effect. Good possibilities include cascading lobelia, bacopa, small trailing campanula, diascia, busy Lizzie, surfinia, trailing viola and verbena, all of which mix really well with fuchsias in a basket. Trailing foliage plants, such as *Glechoma hederacea* 'Variegata' (catmint) and variegated ivies, add long, dangling stems and beautiful, variegated leaves, giving extra depth to the display.

Above: A hanging basket planted with bright pink fuchsias and yellow Pendula begonias decorating a building. Note the convenient watering system.

FUCHSIAS FOR HANGING BASKETS

There are far too many suitable fuchsias to list, but these are some of the best. They include a wide range of colours, with different growth habits and flower sizes. Note that while the largest doubles look spectacular, others produce more flowers.

STIFF CULTIVARS

'Haute Cuisine'	Double
'Janice Ann'	Single
'La Campanella'	Semi-double
'Rigoletto'	Double
'Swingtime'	Double
'Waveney Gem'	Single

LAX CULTIVARS

'Annabelle Stubbs'	Double
'Cecile'	Double
'Chantry Park'	Triphylla type
'Deep Purple'	Double
'Golden Anniversary'	Double
'Postiljon'	Single
'Purple Rain'	Single
'Seventh Heaven'	Double
'Trudi Davro'	Double
'Walsingham'	Double
'WALZ Citer'	Single
'Wendy's Beauty'	Double

TRAILING CULTIVARS

'Ashley and Isobel'	Single
'Auntie Jinks'	Single
'Emma Louise'	Double
'Eva Boerg'	Semi-double
'Golden Marinka'	Single
'Harry Grey'	Double
'Hermiena'	Single
'Kon Tiki'	Double
'Land van Beveren'	Single
'Marinka'	Single
'Pinch Me'	Double
'Red Spider'	Single
'University of Liverpool'	Single
'Vanessa Jackson'	Single

CASCADING CULTIVARS

'Cascade'	Single
'Pink Rain'	Single
'President Margaret Slater'	Single
'Trailing King'	Single
'Trailing Queen'	Single

'Cascade'

'Cecile'

'Haute Cuisine'

'Marinka'

Hanging pots

Fuchsias grown in hanging pots are a tremendously flexible way to brighten many a dull corner. Hang them from tree branches, pergolas, under storm porches or any other places that need a floral lift. The cascading and long-lasting flowering habit of trailing fuchsias planted in hanging pots will bring a lot of pleasure throughout the entire summer. A hanging pot is usually made of plastic, with plastic detachable hangers and a detachable watering tray measuring up to 26cm (10in) in diameter in colours of black, green or terracotta. When buying this type of pot, pay particular attention to the quality of the plastic hangers as this is the part most likely to fail.

PLANTING HANGING POTS

Plant up small pots (up to 20cm [8in]) with a trailing fuchsia cultivar, using up to five plants depending on the pot size. Plant larger pots with a mixture of fuchsia cultivars or mixed plantings, according to your preference. After the short time needed to establish themselves, these will grow rapidly and start to flower, and from then on they will need regular watering and feeding. On very hot, windy days, water them until the lower tray fills and the compost is saturated. The plants will soon use up the water in the lower tray, which acts as an extra reservoir.

Above: A hanging pot planted with the fuchsia cultivar 'Trudi Davro', with its double white flowers. The sepals are white in the shade but become pink when placed in the sun.

PLACING HANGING POTS

Hanging pots are ideal to brighten up all sorts of odd places and neglected corners in the garden. They have the advantage of being lighter than hanging baskets, and do not need such strong supports. Suspending them in the lower branches of trees works very well, since they add extra colour and the tree provides them with dappled shade from the sun in the hottest parts of the day. Hang them directly on smaller branches, using the plastic hook that came with the pot, or make some heavy wire hooks to fit over thicker branches, but remember to put some protection over the branch to prevent the wire cutting into the bark of the tree.

Another excellent way to display these pots is hanging from a large post, which has crosspieces placed horizontally and at right angles to each other at intervals up the post. Other good places for hanging are from pergolas, from overhanging roof eaves, or on small brackets attached to walls, sheds or fence posts. Even in a small garden, using a bit of thought will reveal a number of places where hanging pots will add interesting colour.

Top left: 'Golden Marinka' is a beautiful variegated leaf sport from 'Marinka'. It has yellow-cream, green variegated leaves with bright red flowers, and looks lovely when grown in a hanging pot.

Left: A hanging pot of 'Waveney Gem' in full flower hung from a maple tree looks beautiful against the foliage.

VARIETIES FOR HANGING POTS

Most trailing or cascading fuchsia cultivars will work very well in hanging pots, but the best ones are those with compact and self-branching growth, especially for the smaller pot sizes, as they will make a more dense mass of flowers and foliage. In hanging pots with mixed plantings, the compact growth of the fuchsia is less important, as the other plants will fill the spaces. Double-flowered fuchsias work very well – the smaller double types such as 'Emma Louise', 'Kon Tiki' or 'Ratatouille' are ideal. In larger pots the bigger American doubles such as 'Holly's Beauty' also work well.

Above: This aged 'Bramley' apple tree is giving superb dappled shade to several hanging pots and baskets of fuchsias.

Below: 'Princessita' is an excellent cultivar for hanging pots or baskets, with its long-lasting white and red single flowers.

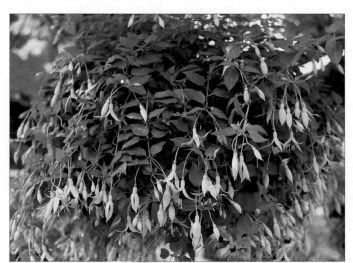

FUCHSIAS FOR HANGING POTS

Cascading or trailing fuchsia cultivars look superb in hanging pots. The list below suggests some suitable fuchsia cultivars for different-sized pots.

SMALLER POTS
'Ashley and Isobel'
'Auntie Jinks'
'Caradella'
'Chantry Park'
'Emma Louise'
'Golden Marinka'
'Harry Grey'
'Hermiena'
'La Campanella'
'Princessita'
'Susan Green'
'Trudi Davro'

'Harry Grey'

LARGER POTS
'Annabelle Stubbs'
'Cecile'
'Golden Anniversary'
'Holly's Beauty'
'Irene Sinton'
'Pink Marshmallow'
'Seventh Heaven'
'Wendy's Beauty'

'Irene Sinton'

Half baskets and wall troughs

Fuchsias planted in half baskets or wall troughs attached to walls or fences are superb ways of creating splashes of colour around the garden. A half basket, as the name suggests, is a container of a demi-hemispherical shape usually constructed of PVC-covered or galvanized heavy wire mesh. The flat side sits against the wall with the hanging points at the back of the basket suspended on screws or hooks. A variation of this is a three-quarter hemispherical shape, designed to sit neatly on an outside corner wall, looking rather unusual and eye-catching. A wall trough is typically made of flat metal strips with a flat back, curved base and rounded ends, and can be much longer than a half basket.

ADVANTAGES

Hanging from screws or hooks fixed into a wall or a strong fence, all these containers are less prone to wind damage than hanging baskets that swing when blown around. The plants also benefit from the warmth of the wall, especially if it is a house wall, as protection from frost at the beginning and end of the season. The planting scheme is very much a personal choice, but here are some suggestions.

Top: A colourful half basket, planted with fuchsias, Pendula begonias, impatiens and a small-leaved trailing ivy.

Below: This half basket, lined with sphagnum moss and planted with double fuchsias, is mounted on a white brick wall.

PLANTING WITH THE SAME CULTIVAR

This is best for the half basket and, normally, five to six plants will be sufficient to make a stunning display. Consider the site and choose a cultivar that will tolerate these conditions. If you are using an open sunny wall, make sure that a heat-tolerant cultivar is used, for example one of the lax Triphylla types such as 'Chantry Park' or 'Mantilla'. Also consider the background colour of the wall or fence. A dark surface, such as brick, is better suited to the lighter coloured cultivars such as 'Shelford' and 'Harry Grey' and some of the red and whites like 'Swingtime', 'Sir Matt Busby' and 'Wilson's Pearls' because the flowers will stand out. Conversely, lighter surfaces need darker coloured flowers such as 'Haute Cuisine', 'Millennium', 'Ruby Wedding' or 'Janice Ann'.

PLANTING WITH MIXED FUCHSIAS

Both half baskets and wall troughs suit mixed cultivars and can give a superb show. For the former, try fuchsias with colours that complement each other and, if possible, have similar flower sizes, although this is less important for large troughs. Also use cultivars with a cascading habit at the front of the container and those with stiffer, more upright growth at the

Below: This half basket of 'Shelford' is of exhibition quality, grown by Steve Andrews. He grows these baskets outdoors on a fence in the west of England.

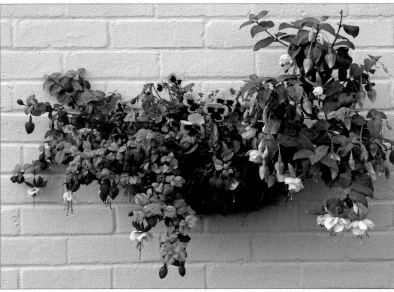

Above: This trough, suspended from balcony railings in a wire cage, has been planted with the Triphylla cultivar 'Professor Henkel' and a variegated ivy, *Hedera helix* 'Golden Cecile'.

Above: Bright yellow, black-eyed pansies, planted together with the fuchsia cultivars 'Swingtime' and 'Nancy Lou', show up well against this plain white-painted brick wall.

back. Good cascading cultivars include 'Auntie Jinks', 'Cascade', 'Kon Tiki', 'Marinka, 'President Margaret Slater' and 'Susan Green'. Those with more of a stiff lax habit include 'Annabel', 'Cecile', 'Haute Cuisine', 'Land van Beveren', 'Ruby Wedding' and 'University of Liverpool'. One of the advantages of using mixed cultivars is that some will be flowering while others are forming their second flush of buds, so there will always be some colour and interest.

MIXED PLANTING

Wall troughs are big enough to combine trailing fuchsias with other trailing and cascading plants, with ivy-leaf pelargoniums and Pendula begonias being two of the most reliable. Both flower over a long period, with many flower colours. Other possibilities include bacopa, diascia, helichrysum, impatiens, lobelia, nepeta, petunia or surfinia, verbena and viola. Remember, however, that most of these need more sun than fuchsias – for partial shade, choose begonias, impatiens, lobelia or some violas.

Also choose trailing fuchsias with complementary flower colours, both small single and large double-flowered types.

Right: A perfectly co-ordinated stone trough on a stone wall, planted with the white double-flowered cultivar 'Annabel'.

Fuchsias with different coloured or variegated foliage give added interest, with 'Ernie Bromley', 'Golden Marinka', 'Tom West' and 'Popsie Girl' being good choices. Companion plants can also be chosen for similar characteristics, with two lively possibilities being 'Pac Ekva',

a small variegated leaf ivy-leaf pelargonium with single red flowers, and *Bacopa* 'Golden Leaves' with its small golden leaves and lilac-blue flowers. For variegated foliage only, try *Glechoma hederacea* 'Variegata' or some of the excellent variegated ivies.

Wall pots

Fuchsias give a stunning display of colour for several months in wall pots. They are ideal for an individual 'spot' of colour or for arranging in groups on a wall, fence or other strong structures. There is a tremendous range of shapes and materials, varying from what might be called a half pot with a flat back but rounded front, to a wall planter that is something between a half hanging pot and half basket, to ornate wall pots with a decorative back plate. For hot, sunny walls the unglazed terracotta kind is best, because of the cooling effect from water evaporating through the porous surface. However, they will dry out very quickly, so use larger pots for these situations and be prepared for frequent waterings.

WALL POT TYPES

Available shapes include the deep-tapered kind that comes down almost to a point, half-tapered pots that are shallower with a flat base, pots with a scalloped rim, traditional wall pots with a larger body and wall urns with a completely circular rim. Another has the body of an urn sliced through at 45 degrees giving the result of a flat back on the cut side. This gives an inclined complete circular rim so the plants are leaning outwards, helping them to trail down the wall.

PLANTING WALL POTS

As wall pots are usually smaller than other containers, they tend to work best with a few plants of just one type of fuchsia, or perhaps two in a larger wall pot. Two or three small plants in 8cm (3in) pots or a single plant in a 12cm (4in) pot should be sufficient for the smaller pots, while larger ones may require more plants, depending on their size. Typically, five small plants or two to three larger plants will suffice.

SUITABLE CULTIVARS

For pale coloured singles and semi-doubles try 'Bertha Gadsby', 'Jean Dawes', 'Ostfriesland', 'Pink Rain', 'Postiljon' and 'WALZ Citer'. Paler coloured doubles include 'Claudia', 'Frank Unsworth', 'Harry Grey' and 'Powder Puff'. Darker coloured singles and semi-doubles include 'Auntie Jinks', 'Cascade', 'Derby Imp', 'Fiona Jane',

Top: A small wall pot, tapered almost to a point, planted with a flared single-flowered fuchsia hanging on a red brick wall.

'Forest King', 'Hermiena', 'La Campanella', 'Marinka', 'President Margaret Slater', 'Thornley's Hardy' and 'Trailing Queen'.

Darker coloured doubles include 'Emma Louise' and 'Kon Tiki'. Triphylla types include 'Chantry Park', 'Daisy Bell' and 'Mantilla'. Variegated foliage types include 'Autumnale' and 'Golden Marinka'. An unusual choice to try is *F. procumbens*, which makes a good trailing plant for a wall

pot. Although the flowers are rather small, they hold themselves off the fern-like foliage, showing their blue pollen; after flowering later in the season, grape-like fruits are produced.

Below: This ornate terracotta wall pot, hung on a brick wall in a gap created in the climbing vine, has been planted with the fuchsia 'Daisy Bell', which carries small orange and vermilion single flowers.

Above: The Triphylla-type 'Chantry Park' is an excellent fuchsia for wall pots because of its long-tubed red flowers and its ability to tolerate direct sunlight.

Above right: This double-flowered cultivar 'Bella Rosella', grown in a standard terracotta pot, is sitting in a heavy metal holder fixed to a white wall.

DISPLAYING WALL POTS

Use flower colours to contrast with the colour of the wall, for example growing the dark flowers of 'Janice Ann' against a white wall or the white flowers of 'Harry Grey' against red brick.

Consider how the colour of the pot and the finish will work with the flower and wall colours. Arrange groups of hanging pots to fill up a large wall space. Arranging three pots in a triangle with one pot at the highest position or a stretched triangle with the bottom two pots at different levels can be very attractive, as can diamond arrangements of four pots or star displays of five pots. Finally, note that hanging pots tend to dry out quickly and that you should use water-retaining gels to tackle the problem, and slow-release fertilizers to keep the plants growing well.

Right: This old wall-mounted basin has been adapted for garden use, planted with fuchsias and hung on a white brick wall.

Chimney pots

Chimney pots salvaged from house demolitions and rebuilding work make excellent containers for growing fuchsias, or as stands for fuchsia pots and baskets. Many are quite tall and will lift the fuchsia flowers up closer to eye level or when used in groups of pots and containers will raise part of the overall exhibit. Planted with a trailing fuchsia, they can look spectacular with a cascade of flowers tumbling down the body of the pot. Groups of planted chimney pots of different heights and styles can also be used to great effect. They are tremendous containers for planting fuchsias or fuchsias mixed with other plants, and come in a wide range of sizes, colours and styles.

TYPES OF CHIMNEY POT

There is a tremendous range of chimney pots in different shapes and sizes, to use for planting, or grouped together to form displays. The tall type is excellent as a stand-alone feature or placed at the back of a display or group of plants to raise the height. Other shorter chimney pots can be grouped together with more traditional pots to form a spectacular display with different heights, shapes and textures.

Chimney pots in different colours or with exciting and attractive surface decoration add another dimension to aid the creation of interesting displays and designs.

Look out for the 'Bishop'-type pots, which have a tall column and a wider triangular castellated cowl at the top, with 'Halifax Little Bishop' and 'Halifax Big Bishop' making dramatic containers for fuchsias or fuchsias mixed with other plants. Some have a wider square base that improves the stability. The body of the chimney can be round, square or octagonal (as with the medium 'Pittsburgh Octagonal'), and is often enhanced by a surface pattern, being finished as natural terracotta or in a coloured glaze. Another good contender, with a wider planting area at the top, is the

Top: The 'Bishop' type of chimney pot has a wider castellated area at the top, which is ideal for planting up with fuchsias.

Right: A Bishop-type chimney pot planted with the cultivars 'Canny Bob', 'Lady Isobel Barnet' and 'Daniel Reynolds' against a background of lavender and *Aucuba japonica* (Japanese spotted laurel).

'Captain's Pot'. It has a long slender body, often decorated with patterns and flowers on a polygonal base, with a wider square castellated cowl at the top, usually finished in a cream glaze. Any of these pots look excellent planted with trailing fuchsias or uprights with a trailing edging plant.

Use the shorter chimney pots up to 30cm (12in) tall as a pot, filling them with potting compost (soil mix) while standing them on the ground, before planting the fuchsias and companion plants. Leave them undisturbed until the roots have filled the pot and hold the potting compost together.

CHIMNEY POTS AS STANDS

Use other tall tapering chimney pots such as the simple rolled top, 'Cannon Head' or 'Beehive' pots, by planting fuchsias in a plant pot that sits neatly in the top of the chimney, or use them as a stand for a basket planted with fuchsias. Using the thinner rolled-top pots as a stand for a basket also works extremely well, with the basket being less likely to be damaged by the wind than if suspended on chains, when it might hit the wall while being blown about. It also makes a nice feature with fuchsias gently cascading down the side of the pot.

Another interesting variation of the chimney pot is the H-pot, formed in the shape of a letter 'H'. The pot has a central pipe linked by horizontal tubes into the outside clay tubes forming the vertical sides

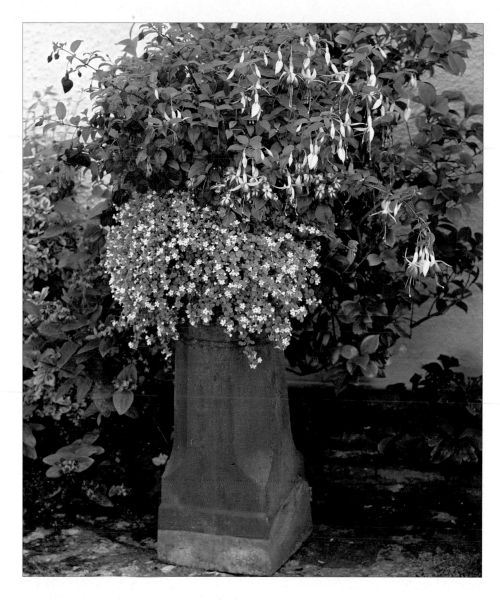

Below: A collection of reclaimed chimney pots, with the roll-top type in the foreground, some Bishop-type pots immediately behind them, and other designs in the background.

Above: A chimney pot planted with the fuchsias 'Royal Velvet' and 'Carmel Blue'. *Bacopa* 'Snowflake' has been planted with them, and is trailing over the edges of the pot.

of the H. These vertical tubes are excellent for placing suitable sized pots planted with fuchsias into the necks of the outside tubes.

SUCCESSIVE PLANTINGS

One advantage of using chimney pots to hold a planted basket or a pot inserted in the top is that you can raise a succession of plantings, placing each in the chimney when it is looking at its best. You could begin with winter pansies, heathers and spring bulbs, then bring some fuchsias into early flowering in the greenhouse, and finally put out your main planting of fuchsias when they are in full flower, to remain until the end of summer.

Putting containers together

A collection of containers containing fuchsias alone or with other plants can be a superb sight at the peak of their flowering season. Any arrangement of containers with fuchsias in flower will look beautiful and be very good value for money, flowering continuously for a long period, attracting bees and other beneficial insects. Planning your containers and flower colours beforehand is really worthwhile. Try some of the following ideas for displaying fuchsias in containers, planted out in the borders, and trained into different shapes. You may well find yourself in a fuchsia paradise, with waves of flowering fuchsias descending in tiers from each corner of your garden.

CREATIVE CONTAINERS

Use lots of different kinds of fuchsias with co-ordinating companion plants. Grow them in containers of various shapes, sizes and colours, creating different moods, using mauve, blue and white to give a cool, relaxing mood, or yellow, orange and red flowers to give an impression of warmth and cheerfulness.

ARRANGING CONTAINERS

For arrangements in corners with walls or other backdrops, create some tiers to increase the impression of height and show all the plants off really well. This can be a permanent structure, or a temporary one

with stacks of breezeblocks, block pillars or slabs, but do ensure it is strong enough to support the containers safely. Start with simple small pots at the front and larger pots or containers behind, then add more containers on the tiers behind this. Setting a standard fuchsia at the back will raise the height still further.

For a free-standing display in the centre of an area of lawn or paving, follow a similar design, but check that you have considered the full 360-degree aspect to give an equally good view from any side. These central displays can look very effective in paved areas or on surfaces covered with decorative chippings.

PLACING POTS

Tiered staging set against a wall is a good way to display pot fuchsias, especially bonsai fuchsias. Another excellent way to show them off is on a post set in the ground, with crosspieces alternating at 90 degrees to each other, all the way up the post. On the end of each crosspiece fix a plastic pot, and then drop in fuchsias in pots of the same size to create a pillar of fuchsia flowers. If you keep some spare plants in the same-sized pots, you can exchange any fuchsias that are not flowering well.

Several types of commercial pot stands are available, varying from the simplest wire ring stand on a single leg that pushes into the soil, through those with three legs and a base, to more ornate cast iron versions, including semi-circular étagères. For specimen plants, you can obtain stone or cast concrete pillars or stands with matching pots that really display the plant well. These look splendid topped with specimen fuchsias on either side of a gate. There are also ornate cast iron pot stands that attach

Top left: A lovely weathered terracotta pot planted with the hardy fuchsia cultivar 'Alice Hoffman'. The semi-double to double flower has dark cerise sepals and a cerise-veined, fluffy white corolla, and the foliage – especially at the growing tips – is an attractive bronzy green. Regal and zonal pelargoniums are growing around it.

Left: An inspired collection of containers arranged together to create a beautiful garden vista. This grouping of containers and baskets consists of fuchsias, busy Lizzies and a colourful range of other summer bedding plants.

Above: An eye-catching arrangement of summer-flowering containers on a patio, including fuchsias and pelargoniums accompanied by cool hostas.

to a wall, or you can fix pot supports to a trellis or wood framework and fill them with fuchsias to make a wonderful display.

DISPLAYING HANGING BASKETS
Apart from fixing hanging baskets or pots to tree branches or wall brackets, an excellent way of displaying them is from a pergola, which allows you to walk underneath and see the beauty of the flowers from the best angle. This is especially good for the large double-flowered fuchsias. The other advantage of a pergola is that it is easy to add shade netting over the top of the pergola in very hot spells of weather, creating the additional shade that fuchsias love. Try placing standards and pots within the pergola, all along the edges, to create the visual effect of a tunnel of fuchsias.

You can also buy stands that allow you to place baskets of decreasing sizes on top of one another, and when planted with trailing fuchsias, begonias and pelargoniums these can look superb, forming a cascading fountain of colour.

Left: Pots of the fuchsia 'WALZ Jubelteen', a dark-leaved zonal pelargonium and dianthus enhance summer-flowering bedding plants by a gravel path.

Below: An antique mangle stand forms the framework for an attractive display against an old brick wall. Mixed containers filled with fuchsias, begonias, lobelia and other flowering plants are enveloping and trailing over the framework to give a wonderful cascade of colour.

THE INDOOR GARDEN

Fuchsias grown inside the house can be striking and beautiful flowering plants, although special care is necessary to adapt and protect them from the dry atmosphere in centrally heated modern homes. Tips are given in this chapter on how to raise indoor fuchsias, from the choice of varieties to their care and treatment.

A conservatory or sun room is an excellent place to grow fuchsias intermingled with other tender plants grown for their flowers, scent and foliage, creating an enjoyable spot in which to sit and relax in the winter sunshine. A greenhouse, an important resource for any serious gardener, is ideal for growing and propagating fuchsias, though they will always benefit from a spell growing outside in the summer. When growing standards and the larger trained structures, a greenhouse is essential to protect them through the winter in temperate climates. In areas of the world that have very hot and dry summer conditions, a shade or lath house is almost a requirement in order to maintain the cooler, more humid conditions that fuchsias love and thrive in.

Left: A display of many different fuchsia cultivars in a greenhouse on a staging table. Note the arrangement of heights of the different plants, giving a tiered effect.

Top left: The beautiful flared single flower of the fuchsia 'Caroline' is eye-catching, and this cultivar grows well in the greenhouse.

Top middle: The species *F. glazioviana* has unusual glossy foliage and pink/violet flowers, and is ideal to grow in a shadehouse.

Top right: 'Laura' is a strong-growing, spreading single-flowered fuchsia with a light orange tube and sepals, and a reddish-orange corolla.

Fuchsias inside the home

During the latter half of the 19th century, when the fuchsia was first imported to Britain from South America, species such as *F. coccinea* were commonly grown as houseplants. At that time, fuchsias were very expensive and therefore only available to the wealthiest households. Just before the start of the 20th century, most houses might have been cold and damp for the owners, but fuchsias thrived in these conditions. Modern houses are often double-glazed, centrally heated and rather dry inside, and not particularly fuchsia-friendly. However, if you provide the right conditions and acclimatize plants while they are small, it is possible to grow fuchsias successfully indoors.

HUMIDITY AND LIGHT

The first major requirement for growing fuchsias indoors is a boost in the immediate humidity levels. The easiest way to achieve this is to stand the pots on a tray of gravel, small pebbles, coarse sand or vermiculite, with water in the bottom of the tray but not touching the pots. Keep the water replenished, but it must never reach the level of the pots. They will still need to be watered in the usual way to keep the compost (soil mix) moist. Make sure that the trays are impervious and cannot leak, to prevent water damage to furnishings. Additionally, regularly mist the leaves with a small hand sprayer during the early parts of the day to help maintain the required humidity. Avoid growing the fuchsias too close to any heat source such as a radiator, as this will reduce the local humidity, causing leaf drop.

The second major requirement for indoor fuchsias is light. Fuchsias need good light to grow well, but not too much direct sunlight when grown indoors. Choose a windowsill that receives only early or late sun, and do not forget to turn the plants frequently. During winter, at latitudes more than 40 degrees north or south, move the plants to where they will receive as much sunlight as possible because of the shorter days and lower intensity of the sun.

GROWING FUCHSIAS INDOORS

One method involves rooting a cutting in a small propagator on a light windowsill that is out of direct sun. A pot propagator with a tall clear plastic cover is ideal. When the cutting has rooted – look for the fresh green growth at the tip – move the pot on to a gravel tray and gradually acclimatize the cutting to indoor conditions by slowly opening and then removing the cover over a few weeks to increase the amount of

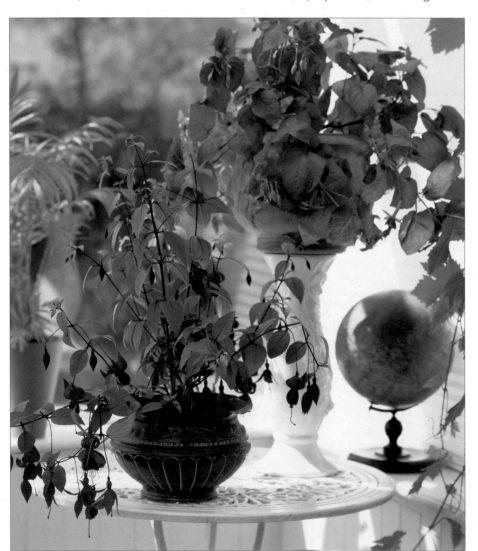

Top left: The hardy cultivar 'Heidi Ann' has attractive cerise and lilac double flowers, and is a good one to try growing indoors.

Left: The fuchsias 'Bland's New Striped' (foreground) and 'Clair de Lune' can be grown successfully as colourful houseplants.

ventilation. Grow on the rooted fuchsia cutting, potting it on to a larger pot size as and when it needs it, training the growing plant into a shrub or a bush shape. It is very important to turn the plants frequently – ideally a quarter of a turn every day, to compensate for the one-directional light on the windowsill and keep the plant growing into a nice symmetric shape.

A second method involves moving a plant that has been growing in an outdoor pot into the house. Choose a small plant that is not in flower, or is just coming into bud, and keep it growing on the dry side by watering sparsely. Grow it in a shady position that is not too high in humidity for two to three weeks to help prepare the plant for the transition. Move the plant indoors, place it on a tray of wet gravel on a windowsill and mist it frequently with water in the first week indoors, while gradually increasing the watering. After a period of about two weeks, the plant will have adjusted to its new conditions.

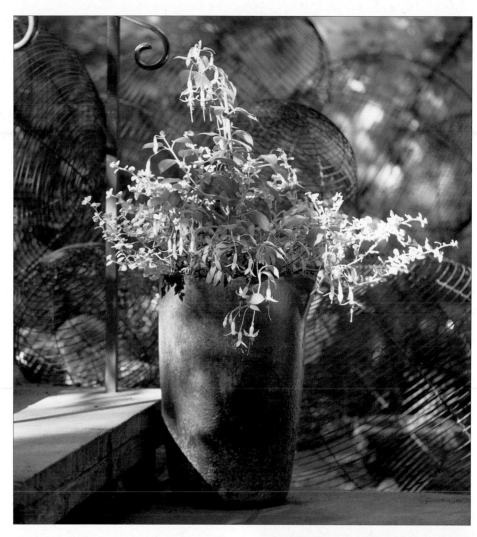

Right: Planted in an unusual smelting pot together with a golden-leafed helichrysum, 'Kolding Perle' is a single-flowered fuchsia with waxy white sepals and a pink cerise corolla. This cultivar originated from Denmark.

Above: This group of young fuchsia plants, growing on a windowsill on a tray of wet gravel to provide extra humidity, will adapt to the drier conditions inside a house.

Right: Inside the house around the Christmas tree, this fuchsia 'Alice Hoffman' is sitting in a wicker basket decorated as a special gift, grouped among the other Christmas presents.

Left: A group of fuchsias standing on a tray of wet gravel on a windowsill, not exposed to direct sun. The variegated-foliage fuchsias at either end add interest with their leaf colour.

GROWING ON INDOORS

Once the plants are growing normally indoors and you have trained them to produce the desired shape and number of flowering shoots, keep them in the same size pot and let them flower. Containing the root system makes the plant feel threatened and causes it to produce more flowers. Continue to mist daily and feed twice a week, alternating between a general-purpose fertilizer and a high-potash one (such as tomato feed), to keep the plant healthy and encourage flowering while preventing it from putting on a lot of growth. Remember that restricting the roots in a small pot means it can dry out very quickly, so you should be extra careful to water it regularly.

TRAINED SHAPES INDOORS

As well as bush plants, some trained shapes can work well indoors. The best ones to grow in miniaturized form are a standard, conical or fan.

To grow a standard, take an indoor cutting using a short-jointed small-flowered cultivar. Grow the stem of the standard up a small split cane as a support and pinch out the growing tip when it is approximately 26–30cm (10–12in) tall. Leave the top three sets of side shoots, pinching them out at two pairs of leaves, and then twice again at one pair of leaves. At this point, leave the plant in the same-size pot, normally a 9cm (3½in) or 10cm (4in) container, because being rootbound will encourage it to bloom quickly and copiously.

A conical shape can be grown in a similar way, by rooting a cutting indoors, then growing it without removing any side shoots. When the cutting is about 13cm (5in) high, remove the growing tip and then remove the weaker of the two resulting side shoots, growing the strongest as the new leader with a split cane for support. When this is 5cm (2in) long, stop all the side shoots on the main stem at the growing tips and tie in the main stem. Continue this alternate stopping of the side shoots and the leader until the desired height is reached, then let the plant flower.

Left: A tray of small fuchsia plants growing in good light on wet gravel in front of French doors, next to a *Clivia miniata* (South African bush lily), with its clusters of bright orange flowers.

Right: This fuchsia, trained as a small standard, is growing indoors, placed inside an attractive ceramic pot holder.

Above: 'Tom West' is a fuchsia grown for its beautiful green-cream and cerise foliage. This example is growing well indoors, but it needs plenty of light to keep the variegated colouring of the leaves.

Right: The attractive red and mauve flowers of the hardy cultivar 'Tom Thumb'. With its small leaves and compact bushy growth, this type of fuchsia is well worth trying to grow as an indoor plant.

For a fan shape, grow on a single stem as described later in the book, supporting the plant on a frame of small split canes. The main side branch leaders will need stopping more frequently to obtain dense growth. Turn this structure so that the front or the back of the fan faces the window.

WHICH PLANTS TO CHOOSE?

Choose short-jointed self-branching varieties if possible because the lower light levels indoors will cause an increase in the internodal stem length. In general, hardy fuchsias seem to tolerate indoor conditions quite well, and single-flowered varieties manage better than doubles. If you would like to try a double, use a small-flowered one because it has more chance of keeping its flowers than a large-flowered one.

When growing a group of plants together, try to vary the sizes and heights to create interest or use a smaller trained shape, such as a miniature standard, fan or pillar. Use varieties that give an interesting

variation in flower colour, and those with variegated foliage, such as 'Tom West', to add different colours.

If you have a large picture window, or French or patio doors not used for access in the winter, then it is possible to grow some different fuchsias on stands of varying heights to create an interesting display, as they will continue to flower through the winter indoors. You can

also grow trailing fuchsias in pots on tall stands to add extra interest. Additionally, other foliage plants, such as *Tradescantia fluminensis* (wandering Jew), *Chlorophytum comosum* (spider plant), *Maranta leuconeura* (prayer plant) or even flowering orchids, such as *Phalaenopsis* (moth orchid), or perhaps *Paphiopedilum* (slipper orchid), can be mixed in to create an eye-catching display.

FUCHSIAS FOR GROWING INDOORS

The following is a list of cultivars noted as being suitable for growing indoors.

'April'	'Dollar Prinzessin'
'Baby Chang'	'Happy'
'Bambini'	'Heidi Ann'
'Beacon Rosa'	'Little Beauty'
'Chang'	'Minirose'
'Christmas Elf'	'Sandboy'
'Display'	'Tom West'

'Dollar Prinzessin'

Conservatory fuchsias

A conservatory is an area of transition between the house and the garden. Often used as both an extension of the living room and a space for growing plants, it is ideal for growing new fuchsias and for overwintering fuchsias and other plants, creating a warm and light atmosphere where it is very enjoyable to sit and relax on a cold day. The word 'conservatory' originates from the Italian *conservato* ('stored' or 'preserved') combined with the Latin suffix -ory ('a place for'), and originally meant a place for storing food. Wealthy gardeners who wished to grow the exotic and unusual specimens discovered in warmer regions by plant hunters first built conservatories as we know them today.

MODERN CONSERVATORIES

The costs of glass and winter heating originally made them prohibitive for all but the wealthiest families, but the production of cheaper glass and other materials gradually made them more accessible. In the modern age, construction in steel-reinforced PVC or hardwood, with double-glazed glass units, combined with advances such as solar reflecting and self-cleaning glass and under-floor heating, has made the conservatory a comfortable extension to the living space. Fuchsias will grow very well there providing you can keep up sufficient local humidity and make sure the inside is cool enough in the summer. If you feel comfortable in the conservatory, the fuchsias will probably be comfortable as well.

CONDITIONS IN THE CONSERVATORY

The humidity of the atmosphere is very important. It will be beneficial to use waterproof trays containing wet gravel, expanded clay beads or similar media on the floor and underneath the plants, combined with spray misting. Therefore, it is obviously a good idea to use robust furnishings and to keep anything easily spoiled by water away from the fuchsias. Similarly, the floor around them should be easy to clean as some dead leaves and flowers are bound to fall on it.

Top: Multiple plants of 'Eva Boerg' planted in a flower tower, growing in a conservatory. 'Eva Boerg' is a trailing fuchsia with semi-double flowers with pink-white sepals and a pinkish-purple corolla.

GROWING CONSERVATORY FUCHSIAS

There are two big advantages to growing fuchsias in a conservatory. The flowering period will be much longer, and it is possible to have fuchsias in flower for most of the year. Also, while most fuchsias would either be killed by winter frost, or die back to the ground, in the conservatory they can grow on from year to year, sometimes making very large, spectacular plants.

Fuchsias combined with other plants in the conservatory can extend the season of interest even further. Some good

Below: This conservatory is filled with tropical foliage plants and different varieties of fuchsia in terracotta pots supported by an ornamental plant stand.

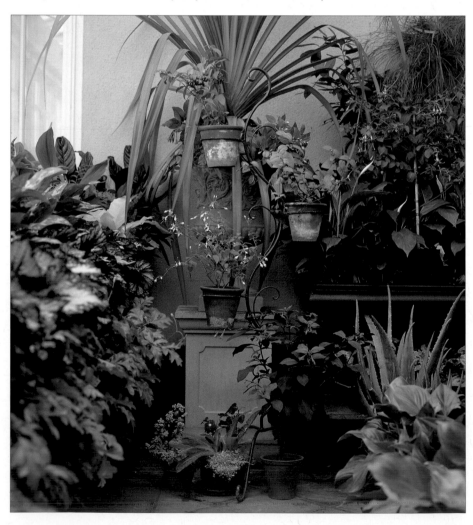

companion plants are climbers such as *Jasminum polyanthum*, bougainvillea and plumbago, or shrubs such as *Hoya carnosa* (wax plant), *Gardenia jasminoides* and citrus. Use a mixture of fuchsias – singles, doubles, trailing and trained shapes like standards – to fit in with the surrounding plants. If the conservatory is very sunny, it will need blinds and good ventilation to prevent it becoming too hot in the summer; indeed, in any continuous hot spells of weather, it is worth giving the tenderest of plants a breather outside in a shady position.

CARING FOR CONSERVATORY FUCHSIAS

In a conservatory, the aim is to keep plants flowering throughout the year, so prune fuchsias in a similar way to plants growing in frost-free equatorial or tropical regions. Conservatory fuchsias need more gentle and partial pruning than those outdoors, mainly to shape and tidy them, leaving budding shoots intact to maintain flowering.

Above: 'Autumnale' growing in a moss-lined basket hanging in a conservatory. This is a spreading fuchsia that is grown mainly for its beautiful dark red, salmon and yellow-splashed foliage.

Unglazed terracotta (clay) pots are the best to use since they allow the compost (soil mix) to breathe, helping to cool the roots. This also helps to create more humidity.

Introduce plants into the conservatory in the autumn or winter so that they have a chance to acclimatize to the conditions before the stress of the summer heat. Fuchsias can usually be moved from the greenhouse to the conservatory directly, as the growing conditions are similar. You can put both new young plants and pruned old plants in the conservatory, but ensure you eradicate any pests and diseases before moving them in. Avoid using insecticides in the house. Turn the plants every so often to prevent them leaning over toward the light, and feed them regularly or use a slow-release fertilizer in the compost.

Left: 'Happy Wedding Day' is an Australian white double-flowered cultivar with lax growth. It is seen here growing with busy Lizzies among ferns in a conservatory.

Varieties for a conservatory

The choice of positioning of conservatories is normally where it catches the best of the sun and the maximum amount of winter light. Providing the conservatory atmosphere is maintained with a high humidity, growing fuchsias is easy, with heat-tolerant varieties being the top choice. Conservatories vary greatly in size and shape, and have different maximum temperatures depending on the amount of shading and ventilation they are given. When growing fuchsias in a conservatory, they are best intermingled with other plants for a display of foliage and flowers, stood on tables or plant stands and hung from the walls or roof bars in suitable containers.

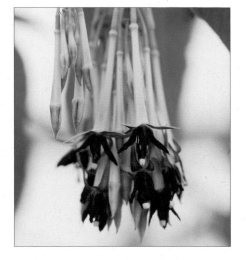

SUITABLE TRIPHYLLAS

Fuchsias that can tolerate hot conditions thrive in conservatories, so Triphyllas are an obvious choice. Larger cultivars such as 'Coralle', 'Thalia' and 'Traudchen Bonstedt' are worth trying. 'Mary' excels on a pedestal because of its arching growth, velvety green leaves and clusters of brilliant red flowers. A similar but much smaller-growing Triphylla cultivar suitable for smaller conservatories is 'Bessie Kimberly', while others are 'Adinda' and 'Sparky'. 'Mantilla' and 'Chantry Park' are excellent for hanging or wall containers.

SUITABLE SPECIES

Some of the species fuchsias are also a good choice for the conservatory, and they include *F. boliviana* or *F. boliviana* var. *alba* with their tropical appearance, large velvety green leaves and enormous clusters of red flowers for the former or white and red flowers for the latter. *F. arborescens* has leathery glossy leaves and upright panicles with first hundreds of tiny pink and mauve flowers, then later beautiful glossy blue-black berries. Try also *F. glazioviana*, *F. fulgens* and *F. lycioides*, which are recommended as heat-tolerant species.

Above: The beautiful species *F. boliviana* var. *alba* has clusters of long-tubed white and red flowers. It makes a large and very impressive conservatory plant.

DOUBLE-FLOWERED FUCHSIAS

There is not such a wide choice of heat-tolerant double-flowered fuchsia cultivars, but you should still find enough to create a good display, starting with 'Harbour Bridge', 'Nancy Lou', 'Phenomenal', 'Quasar', 'Royal Velvet', 'Shady Lady', 'Swingtime' and 'Voodoo'. 'Royal Velvet' is an excellent choice because of its beautiful red and deep purple flared double flowers and arching growth, with light to mid-green foliage. Suitable small- to medium-sized double-flowered cultivars include 'Blue Waves', 'Dollar Prinzessin', 'Heidi Ann', 'Pink Galore', 'Santa Claus' and 'Winston Churchill'. 'Heidi Ann' forms a very neat bush with its small dark green foliage and abundant flared red and lilac-purple blooms.

Top: The hardy cultivar 'Army Nurse' is a lovely semi-double with a carmine and bluish-violet flower, and grows very well in a conservatory.

Right: 'Brutus' is a wiry-growing hardy cultivar with red and purple flowers. It is excellent for producing trained shapes when grown in the conservatory.

Above: 'Heidi Ann' is a hardy shrub with small to medium sized cerise and lilac double flowers and grows well in the conservatory.

Above right: This cultivar is named 'Little Beauty' and what name could be more apt? It is highly floriferous, half hardy and very easy to grow in a conservatory.

Right: 'Nellie Nuttall' has been a 'show banker' for many years. With its plentiful semi-erect red and white flowers, it clamours for attention in the conservatory.

SINGLE AND SEMI-DOUBLE-FLOWERED FUCHSIAS

There is a much greater choice of heat-resistant single and semi-double cultivars. Good larger-flowered varieties – those with a (B) can be grown in baskets or hanging pots – include 'Amy Lye', 'Army Nurse', 'Aurora Superba', 'Bow Bells' (B), 'Brutus', 'Carmel Blue', 'Falling Stars' (B), 'Indian Maid' (B), 'Julie Horton' (B), 'Lena' (B), 'Lye's Unique', 'Mission Bells', 'Princessita' (B), 'Rufus', 'Swanley Gem' and 'Voltaire'. 'Aurora Superba' is a medium to large single with light apricot sepals and a deep orange corolla. It has lax upright growth, making it ideal as a half standard.

Small, single-flowered heat-resistant fuchsias are great for growing in pots placed around the conservatory to give points of colour. They include 'Baby Chang', 'Bambini', 'Caledonia', 'Christmas Elf', 'David', 'Derby Imp' (B), 'Fifi',

'Lindisfarne', 'Little Beauty', 'Little Jewel', 'Minirose', 'Mrs Marshall', 'Nellie Nuttall', 'Purperklokje', 'Red Rain', 'Sandboy' and 'Tom Thumb'. The pretty 'Bambini' stands out with its many very small crimson to mallow-purple flowers, while 'Sandboy' has small pink and dark mauve bell-shaped flowers with upright, bushy, short-jointed growth making an excellent small standard.

Some of the Encliandra hybrids are also heat resistant, especially 'Lottie Hobby', but 'Ariel', 'Artemis', 'Coral Baby', 'Hemsleyana', 'Marlies de Keijzer', 'Mikado' and 'Radings Mia' are well worth trying.

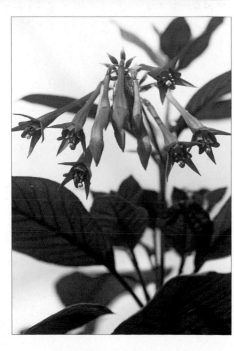

Right: 'Thalia' is one of the best-known of the Triphylla cultivars. Heat-resistant and very free-flowering, it is excellent as a striking centrepiece in the conservatory.

Greenhouse fuchsias

While it is perfectly possible to enjoy growing fuchsias without a greenhouse, you are certainly limited if you live in an area with freezing temperatures in winter. With a greenhouse, you can keep plants growing over winter, and thus grow large trained shapes such as fans, pyramids and standards, and even a climbing fuchsia if you wish, training the growth along the greenhouse ridge. You also have the perfect conditions for propagating new stock, which can be a highly rewarding process, as well as making it easy to fill your summer containers and bedding schemes with beautiful plants at very little cost, and having spares to give away.

BENEFITS OF A GREENHOUSE

One of the key features of any greenhouse is that it extends the growing season by creating a microclimate, insulating the fuchsias from the outside conditions. However, beware of overheating the greenhouse in winter because apart from the cost and environmental considerations, this causes long spindly growth when it is far better to keep your plants as compact and strong as possible.

Top: A floriferous basket hanging from a greenhouse roof, planted with the lovely fuchsia, 'Swingtime'.

Below: The author's greenhouse, with six roof-vents, large doors to allow movement of tall plants, and water butts for a convenient, environmentally friendly water supply.

TYPES OF GREENHOUSE

There are many possible types and constructions of greenhouse. You can choose from aluminium or wood and glass or plastic, with brick or glass down to the ground. If you are going to use your greenhouse for growing fuchsias, make sure it is at least 2.9m x 2.2m (10ft x 7ft), preferably bigger if you have the space. Greenhouses with sufficient height for you to stand upright close to the edges are best. If you live in an area subject to strong winds, choose one with a heavyweight frame and a good glazing system. Plastic glazing is an alternative, especially the twin-wall type, which gives better insulation in the winter and more heat protection in summer. Add additional ventilation in the form of top vents and louvres, and ensure that at least one or two of the top vents have a manual opening, preferably with a screw thread.

POSITION OF THE GREENHOUSE

Ideally, the greenhouse should run from north to south lengthwise because this will give the most even distribution of sun. If possible, arrange for the minimum natural shade in winter, and some shade from a deciduous tree in summer. Avoid placing it in a dip, which may flood in heavy rain in winter, and try to avoid the windiest parts of the garden. Different bases are available, but for the best, build from bricks or blocks

Below: A commercial greenhouse filled with clearly labelled fuchsias on staging, with more fuchsias in hanging pots suspended from the roof structure.

and pave internally with concrete slabs or brick. Part of the floor could also be a layer of gravel on weed-suppression matting.

STAGING

You will need something on which to stand your plants. Most greenhouse manufacturers will supply aluminium staging, with a choice of open slats or aluminium trays, or you can build your own in wood. Ensure the staging is at a comfortable working height, and can easily be removed if you want the floor area for larger plants.

GROWING PLANTS

There is the temptation, when you buy a splendid new greenhouse, to fill it up by purchasing new plants, accepting gifts from friends, or propagating far too many plants. Try to avoid doing this, unless you know you can give many of your plants away in early spring. As a rule of thumb, the greenhouse should be one-half full in winter at most. One way to make yourself

adhere to this rule is to partition off about one-third of the space with a plastic sheet or bubble plastic, and only heat this section in winter.

The heated greenhouse allows you to grow cultivars and species that are more tender and difficult to grow. Good examples include *F. venusta*, a beautiful climbing fuchsia with orange-red flowers and wine-red stems, and *F. triphylla*, the parent of the modern Triphylla hybrids, which is small-growing in cultivation, with orange-red flowers. Some tender varieties are quite difficult to overwinter and grow better in a heated greenhouse. Such varieties include 'Citation', a beautiful American single fuchsia with rose-pink sepals and a white flared saucer-shaped corolla, and 'Constellation', a white American double.

Remember, you can also use the greenhouse to bring containers into flower before moving them outside for your summer display and, late next autumn, you can then take them back under cover to keep them safely inside over winter.

Above: A beautiful selection of trained standards and fan fuchsias growing in a commercial greenhouse.

Below: A collection of small fuchsia plants standing on a gravel bed in autumn. Centre front is the variegated cultivar 'Tom West'.

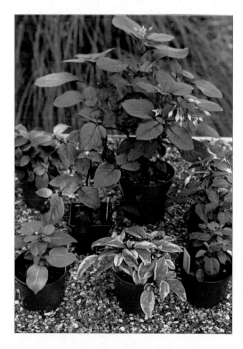

EARLY SPRING

In early spring, as the outside temperatures start to rise and the day length increases, the conditions inside the greenhouse promote rapid fuchsia growth. Make sure that you keep the plants well spaced out, turn them regularly, and pinch out the growth and pot them on as necessary. Conditions can be quite challenging at this time of year, as on bright sunny days the greenhouse can get quite hot, yet overnight frosts are still possible.

It is best to keep the greenhouse well ventilated on sunny days, and try to water or mist in the mornings, so that the plants do not sit in too much moisture overnight. When the days are warm enough and free of cold winds, the plants will benefit from a spell outside, hardening up the soft growth and keeping them growing in a compact way.

Early to mid-spring is a good time to start planting up hanging baskets, pots and containers, as many fuchsias and

companion plants start to become available from nurseries and garden centres. For the next few weeks, before you move them outside, control the watering in the greenhouse, keeping them on the dry side, so they will fill the compost (soil mix) with new roots. They will make plenty of growth and will already be in flower when moved outside in the late spring.

LATE SPRING

As the sun becomes brighter and the days longer, light shading will be necessary on the greenhouse roof and the sides receiving direct sun to prevent scorching of the young growth. Again, continue to move plants outside on suitable days to continue the hardening-up process and ensure the plants acclimatize to the outside conditions before you move them out for good. Space is often at a premium in the greenhouse at this time of year and you may need to move some plants outside permanently before they are completely

ready. If so, be prepared to protect them with fleece if there is a late frost. Plant up any remaining baskets and containers with your chosen plants, and add full shading to the greenhouse glass if the weather gets very warm, with longer sunny days.

SUMMER

Throughout the summer months, fuchsias are better growing outside, but if you wish to continue growing some plants inside, ensure that you use maximum ventilation at all times, even to the extent of removing some glass panes and replacing them with fine netting. If you are growing plants for exhibition, place the same netting over all the vents and a detachable piece over the doors, as this will help to keep bees and other insects out, and prevent damage and marking of the flowers. Keep the floor and any gravel trays wet to increase the humidity; this will also help to cool the greenhouse. However, make sure the fuchsias are not sitting in water.

Left: A collection of fuchsia standards growing in a greenhouse over the winter. They were cut back in the autumn, started to grow again and are ticking over in green leaf.

Top: Hanging baskets of fuchsias growing in a commercial greenhouse, suspended from a support rail in the roof. Note the green shading material fixed in the roof space.

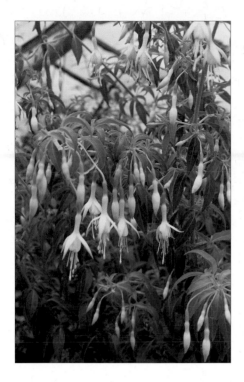

Above: A large plant of the hardy cultivar 'Hawkshead' growing in a greenhouse. It has white single flowers, which stay white in the sun, and small bright green leaves.

AUTUMN

During the late summer and early autumn, empty the greenhouse completely, clean all the glass, replacing any panes which were removed during the summer, sterilize all the benching and any other structures and check the heaters are working properly. Make sure that the whole structure is sound, replacing any cracked glass, and clean and if necessary lubricate the door slides or hinges and the vent openers. Now the greenhouse will be ready for its winter storage duties once more.

WINTER

Depending on the temperature you maintain through the winter months, the greenhouse can be used either to protect dormant plants, or to keep plants ticking over in green leaf. It is better not to overheat, since this will promote more rapid growth, which will become straggly and drawn owing to the low light levels in winter. A minimum temperature of 5°C (41°F) is ideal, not using too much energy, but protecting even the Triphylla hybrids. Keep the plants that are still in green leaf quite dry through the winter, removing any

damaged or dying leaves, and give the greenhouse some ventilation on all but the coldest days. As the days start to lengthen in spring, the plants in green leaf will start to grow fresh green growth, which is ideal for early-season cuttings. It is important to turn the plants regularly to prevent them becoming one-sided, and to pinch them out to encourage bushiness, increasing the number of potential flowering shoots.

Above: A staging table full of fuchsia plants in a commercial greenhouse, labelled and placed in groups ready for eager customers to buy. It is easy to find this environment very inspiring and tempting, but try not to buy more plants than you can actually grow.

Below: Pruned pot-grown fuchsias in green leaf, overwintering on the floor of the greenhouse underneath the staging. These plants will grow rapidly in the spring.

Ventilation, shading and heating

To grow fuchsias successfully in a greenhouse you will need to provide efficient shading and ventilation in summer, and heating and insulation in winter. The shading and ventilation prevent the temperatures becoming too high in the height of the summer. The heating will provide a minimum temperature at least a few degrees above freezing, while the insulation reduces heat loss and minimizes cold spots close to the glass. Your own requirements will very much depend on your local climate. The information on these pages relates to areas in USA weather zone 9 and below; for zone 10 and above, shading and ventilation are paramount if a greenhouse is used, while heating and insulation are less important.

HEATING

There are many different types of greenhouse heater and fuel available to the amateur grower. Probably one of the best is the electric fan heater, preferably with a remote thermostat rather than an internal type. This is the best because the fan generates a flow of air, thereby preventing stagnant zones in the greenhouse, and gives more even heating. Unfortunately, it is also usually the most expensive form of heating, because electricity is more expensive per unit of heat than other fuels.

The next best alternative is a heater running on bottled propane gas. Propane is better than butane, especially if the gas

Top: Louvre vents are an excellent way to get low-level ventilation into the greenhouse. Position them low at the opposite end to the door, or in the sides of the greenhouse.

bottles are stored outside the greenhouse where low temperature can reduce the cylinder pressure. Modern gas heaters have an accurate thermostat and a pilot light that allows the main burner to shut down when the greenhouse is warm enough. Some also have a catalytic converter to ensure the complete combustion of gas and minimize carbon monoxide production. For safety's sake, it is better to have two propane cylinders with an automatic changeover valve that will prevent the heater running out of gas in the middle of a cold night. Remember, though, that you need to exchange the empty cylinder for a full one.

A cheaper fuel option is to have mains gas professionally linked to your greenhouse. Alternatively, use an inexpensive heater that runs on paraffin, with the blue-flame type being best because they are cleaner

Above: Internal greenhouse shading blinds reduce the amount of direct sun hitting the plants during the warm summer months.

burning, though paraffin is not always available. Note that gas and paraffin heaters increase the level of carbon dioxide in the greenhouse, which aids plant growth, but they also increase the amount of water vapour, which can create ideal conditions for the fungal disease botrytis.

INSULATION

Twin-wall polycarbonate glazing gives excellent insulation without decreasing the amount of light significantly. If you are purchasing a new greenhouse, this is well worth considering. For standard greenhouses with single panes of glass, additional insulation will reduce the winter heating bills. UV stabilized bubble plastic

Left: Fuchsias standing on fired clay particles in trays inside a greenhouse. Note how the inside of the glass has been insulated with large bubble-plastic insulation.

Above: A manual greenhouse vent with a screw thread opener. This firmly holds the vent open and is almost infinitely adjustable.

Above: An adjustable automatic greenhouse vent opener allows the vents to open automatically at a pre-set temperature of your choice.

sheets with large bubbles give the best insulation, but they will reduce the light levels. The best compromise is to insulate the sides with bubble plastic and the roof with clear plastic. Ensure you do not fix insulation over the roof vents because they will still need opening in winter to prevent the accumulation of stagnant air.

SHADING

In spring and summer, shading is essential to protect the plants from too much direct sun and help keep the temperature down. There are various solutions: the simplest is to paint white shading on the outside of the glass to reflect some of the sunlight and reduce the temperature in the greenhouse. You can also buy a special type of greenhouse shading that becomes transparent when wet, but opaque when dry, so increasing the light levels on dull wet days. The best solution is to fit automatic roller blinds with shade netting on the outside of the greenhouse, which extend in sunny conditions and roll away when it is dull. Whatever you use, though, it will make the greenhouse much cooler in summer.

VENTILATION

Good ventilation is important in summer. Install the maximum number of roof vents that you can afford in the greenhouse. Use automatic openers, but you will also need two, one at either end, which are manual, to maintain ventilation on cool days. Additionally, put in louvre windows at the far end of the greenhouse, opposite the doors, below the staging level to maintain good ventilation levels. Provide extra ventilation, if needed, by removing some glass in the roof apex opposite the door and replacing it with netting. An electric fan will also keep the air moving on dull, stagnant days.

Left: Double sliding doors at the front of the greenhouse allow a large opening, thus giving excellent access and allowing easy movement of large plants through the space.

Varieties for a greenhouse

Most fuchsias are easy to grow in a greenhouse during the cooler seasons, but during the summer only heat-tolerant varieties will grow well. Provided you follow the advice concerning greenhouse ventilation, maintaining humidity and shading, then growing certain heat-tolerant fuchsias over summer is possible in all but the hottest climates. Fuchsias which stand up to these hot conditions are in the Triphylla group, in the group of species which naturally grow in very hot climates in the central parts of South America and Mexico and a number of cultivars which have inherited these characteristics. By choosing the right varieties, you can create a stunning greenhouse display.

ADDITIONAL PRECAUTIONS

The use of porous terracotta clay pots will help keep the plants' roots cool by allowing the evaporation of water through the walls of the pot, and this also helps guard against the accidental over-watering of fuchsias in hot conditions. You can further improve a fuchsia's ability to cope with heat by planting directly or sinking the pots in the greenhouse borders. This will again help keep the roots cool. However, if the daytime temperatures in your area regularly exceeds 30°C, it may be difficult to grow greenhouse fuchsias through the hottest part of the year.

SUITABLE VARIETIES

Lists of heat-tolerant fuchsias exist in books and on the internet, and those compiled in the USA, Australia and southern Europe are the most valuable.

The first group of varieties, which are very heat-tolerant, are the Triphylla and Triphylla-type cultivars. Most will grow quite well in the greenhouse over summer and flower continuously over a long period. 'Adinda', 'Billy Green', 'Bornemann's Beste', 'Coralle, 'Elfriede Ott', 'Jackqueline', 'Mary', 'Sparky', 'Thalia' and 'Traudchen Bonstedt' are among the best.

The second group contains the species, some of which are quite heat-tolerant. Try variants of *F. magellanica*, and also

Top left: The long pink Triphylla-like flowers of 'Billy Green' are very attractive. Strong, versatile and heat-resistant, this is well worth growing in the greenhouse.

Left: 'Adinda' is a small and compact-growing Triphylla. It has clusters of small salmon-pink flowers and green velvety leaves, and grows well in hot conditions.

Above: The species variant *F. magellanica* var. *gracilis* is a large graceful plant when grown outside, but will also tolerate the hot conditions inside a greenhouse quite well.

F. magellanica var. *molinae*, *F. m.* var. *aurea*, *F. m.* var. *gracilis* and *F. m.* var. *gracilis* 'Tricolor'. Others reputed to be heat-resistant are *F. arborescens*, *F. boliviana*, *F. boliviana* var. *alba*, *F. glazioviana* and *F. lycioides*.

The third heat-tolerant group contains the Encliandras and their hybrids. Many in this group grow well in hot conditions, with 'Ariel', 'Hemsleyana' and 'Lottie Hobby' highly recommended.

The fourth group contains the double-flowered cultivars, but they are the most difficult to grow in the heat because the flowers are more demanding than the singles. The following are well worth a try:

'Blue Waves', 'Dancing Flame', 'Delta's KO', 'Easter Bonnet', 'Gay Fandango', 'Happy Wedding Day', 'Harbour Bridge', 'Irene van Zoeren', 'Kevin Heinz', 'King's Ransom', 'Molesworth', 'Nancy Lou', Novella', 'Phenomenal', 'R.A.F.', 'Red Ace', 'Red Devil', 'Red Rum', 'Royal Velvet', 'Swingtime', 'Voodoo', 'White Ann' and 'Winston Churchill'.

The final group contains the single and semi-double cultivars, which are often slightly easier to grow in the heat than the doubles. Try 'Abbé Farges', 'Abundance', 'Accent', 'Achievement', 'Ambassador', 'Amigo', 'Amy Lye', 'Anna', 'Aurora Superba', 'Autumnale', 'Beauty of Exeter', 'Beauty of Swanley', 'Blands New Striped', 'Blue Sleigh Bells', 'Brutus', 'California', 'Carmel Blue', 'Checkerboard', 'City of Leicester', 'Clair de Lune', 'Derby Imp', 'Display', 'Evening Star', 'Falling Stars', 'Flash', 'Graf Witte', 'Grasmere', 'Happy Fellow', 'Hidcote Beauty', 'Ice Maiden', 'Joan Cooper', 'Joy Patmore', 'Kwintet', 'La Campanella', 'Les Hobbs', 'Little Beauty', 'Lord Byron', 'Marinka', 'Nicis Findling', 'Orange Flare', 'Papoose', 'Pixie', 'Rufus', 'Tom Thumb', 'Tom West' and 'Whiteknights Pearl'.

RED SPIDER MITE

Heat is not the only potential problem. You need to look out for greenhouse pests, particularly red spider mite, which thrives in hot dry conditions. To minimize the chances of an outbreak, keep the

greenhouse as humid as possible by regularly hose-spraying or splashing the floor. Even better, if you live in a soft water area or have an adequate supply of stored rainwater you can install a misting system to maintain consistently high humidity levels. Electronically controlled systems give bursts of misting when required by using an internal moisture or humidity sensor. This monitors the amount of water moisture in the greenhouse atmosphere, and only activates the system when required.

Above: 'R.A.F.' has beautiful large red and rose-pink double flowers and a lax habit of growth. It looks stunning hanging from the greenhouse roof.

Below left: The Encliandra cultivar 'Lottie Hobby' has vigorous and wiry growth with tiny leaves that give it a fern-like appearance, and plentiful tiny light crimson flowers.

Below: 'Dancing Flame' has a medium-sized orange and orange carmine double flower and a lax habit. It is well-suited to growing in a greenhouse basket.

Shadehouse fuchsias

In hotter climates, a shadehouse is an essential item to ensure that fuchsias will thrive through the heat of the summer months. In areas where the summer temperatures regularly reach the high 30s Celsius (over 100°F), such as Australia, New Zealand and the southern USA, fuchsias in pots will not easily survive outside in the garden. The shadehouse creates ideal natural growing conditions for fuchsias in summer, and mimics the natural conditions of some of the species that grow in shady forest margins with high cloud humidity. In the height of summer, it is also possible to provide shading for some plants growing in the ground outside the shadehouse by using netting on poles.

TYPES OF SHADEHOUSE

The oldest kind of shadehouse, still used in some parts of the world, is the lath house. The simplest kind is a box frame with strong corner posts and crosspieces, which are large enough for you to stand up inside and to hang up various containers from the roof. The roof consists of thin strips of wood (laths), typically 2.5–3 cm (1–1¼in) wide, equally spaced out. This effectively filters out approximately half the direct sunlight. The sides are open, or may be covered if protection is needed from the wind or sun. An interesting alternative, once used in California, is a pitched roof covered with closely spaced old fluorescent tubes. These disperse and diffuse the light very effectively.

The modern shadehouse is made from a tubular frame that is easy to erect and is covered with polypropylene shade netting, which is usually green. Shade netting is available in a range of sun-shading densities, with 50 per cent being the most common. It is also possible to make a wooden frame and cover it with shade netting, or to erect a pergola that can be shaded with netting in the hottest parts of the year.

USING A SHADEHOUSE

Enthusiasts may wish to use shadehouses in the far northern or southern latitudes, where the day length is very long, but the summers can vary between long periods of clear sky and equal periods of heavy cloud and rain. Here, use a cover with 30 per cent shade factor, with an additional overlaying removable top cover with 30 per cent shade factor used in the hottest spells.

When it comes to frost, shadehouses do not provide anything but the lightest protection, so do not move any plants into them until all danger of frost is past.

TYPES OF FLOOR

There are many different types of floor, but whichever one you choose it must provide a sound surface on which to stand potted fuchsias. Drainage is important in times of heavy rain, so if you use paving, lay it with

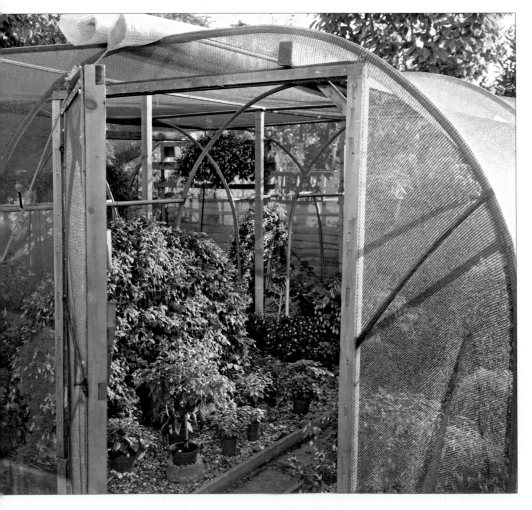

Top left: The cultivar 'Marin Glow', with its white and imperial-purple single flowers, easily bleaches in the sun, as in this picture, and benefits from a shadehouse.

Left: A view through the doorway of a shadehouse in midsummer. Inside are many pot-grown fuchsias in flower, standing on beds of moist gravel. Note the green shading material on the sides and roof.

Left: A magnificent fuchsia fan growing in a shadehouse, surrounded by other fuchsias in pots. This cultivar is 'Waveney Gem', a medium-sized single-flowered fuchsia with white sepals and a mauve corolla flushed pink. It has light green foliage and makes a vigorous lax bush. It is very adaptable, and excels as a basket plant, a small standard or a fan.

Below: A shadehouse, constructed from a wood frame and shade netting, filled with fuchsias. The central post strengthens the ridge, allowing pots and baskets to hang.

a high point in the centre sloping away to the outsides of the shadehouse. Another popular solution is to cover the floor with a heavyweight grade of weed-suppressant matting, which is porous, preventing the growth of weeds while allowing water to drain away. When it is very hot, you will need to wet the floor regularly, as you would in a greenhouse; a layer of gravel, chippings or shale will help hold moisture and maintain humidity throughout the day.

ADVANTAGES OF SHADEHOUSES
As well as heat regulation, shadehouses provide some protection from the wind, helping to stop plants from blowing over. Those made of shade netting also break up heavy drops of rain into the kind of fine mist that fuchsias love. Hot places in the world may not get much rain but, when it does rain, it is often torrential, and this is a real extra benefit.

Another advantage, for exhibitors, is that the houses limit the access of bees, which can damage and mark the flowers when they try to reach the nectar, and moths, whose caterpillars can be very destructive.

GROWING IN A SHADEHOUSE

Providing there is side protection, free-standing pot plants on the floor in a shadehouse will stay upright on all but the windiest days but taller structures, such as standards or fans, do need support to prevent them blowing over. You can use wall wires strung along one side or a vertical framework from the roof to the floor. Cement rings or other types of stand made to fit different pot sizes are another way of keeping pots upright on windy days. If the roof is high and strong enough, hanging containers, hanging baskets and pots grow exceptionally well hung from the roof, but be aware this will create extra shade for any plants below them. You must also check that there is sufficient space for turning and maintaining the pots, for wetting the floor to maintain decent humidity levels and for watering, Although the fuchsias are shaded from the sun in hot windy weather, pots will dry out very quickly and may need watering twice a day.

Also, look out for pests. While the humid conditions and the protection of the shade netting will minimize attacks from red spider mite, other pests, such as aphids, whitefly and capsid bugs, can still attack the plants. For that reason, pick the plants up when watering and thoroughly check under the leaves for any early signs of attack. Early detection makes the control of pests much easier.

FUCHSIAS FOR THE SHADEHOUSE

The shaded environment is an excellent place for growing fuchsia cultivars whose flowers change colour when exposed to direct sunlight. This phenomenon is very common with white flowers, which often tend to turn pink, such as 'Countess of Aberdeen', 'Midwinter, 'Shelford' and 'Trudi Davro'. Similarly, the shadehouse can help protect the colours of the pastel-coloured flowering fuchsias, for example 'Blush o' Dawn', 'Eleanor Clark', 'Flirtation Waltz', 'Lilian' and 'Shady Lady', where the pale

Above: A flower bud of the cultivar 'Shelford' just prior to opening. Grown in the protection of a shadehouse, blooms of 'Shelford' will maintain their pure white colour.

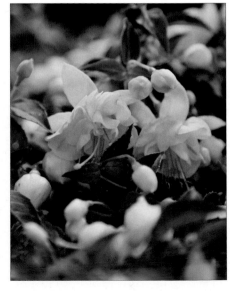

Above: 'Trudi Davro' is a lovely small white double, excellent for growing in hanging pots. The flowers should stay pure white when grown in a shadehouse.

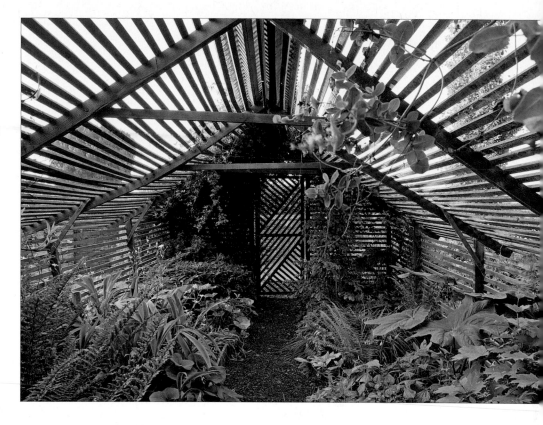

sepals become pinker and the dark corolla may bleach. Some dark-coloured fuchsia flowers also tend to bleach in the sun, while in a shadehouse they will keep their pure, deep colours – good examples are 'Golden Anniversary', 'Hot Coals', 'Marin Glow', 'Ortenburger Festival', 'Preston Guild', 'Tamworth' and 'Zulu Queen'.

Another group of fuchsias ideal for a shadehouse are the species originating from tropical cloud forests, especially those in central South America, where they have similar warm, shady conditions. Good ones include *F. boliviana* and its variants, *F. denticulata*, *F. dependens*, *F. fulgens*, *F. macrostigma*, *F. sessilifolia*, *F. splendens* and *F. venusta*. Remember, though, that many of the species can grow to a significant size and have large leaves. In latitudes more than 45 degrees north or south of the equator, the tropical species often flower best during spring and autumn, as the day length more closely matches that of their natural habitat.

You can grow Triphyllas in a shadehouse, but as most of them are happy in full sun, this is not necessary – and they can tend to grow a little long-jointed, develop too much foliage and not enough flowers. Variegated leaf cultivars can often benefit from the shelter of a shadehouse, but the leaf colours develop best in maximum light, so it is often better to find a lightly shaded outside position.

When visiting an enthusiast's shadehouse for the first time, it can be an impressive experience. You feel the change in temperature and humidity as you walk in; then comes the enthralling vision of rows of pot plants, standards and baskets, all in flower. Often it is the sight of the more unusual cultivars and species which flourish in these conditions – many of which would be difficult to grow otherwise – that inspires gardeners to invest in a shadehouse for themselves.

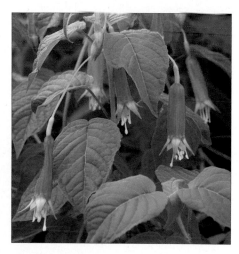

Above: *F. splendens* is easy to grow, has beautiful red and green flowers, and does very well in the shadehouse.

Left: *F. boliviana* var. *alba* has clusters of long white and red flowers and large velvety leaves, and enjoys shadehouse conditions.

GARDENING TECHNIQUES

Growing fuchsias is an enjoyable and rewarding pastime, whether you have only a few plants or whole collections of many different varieties. There are so many exciting colours, shapes and sizes of flowers and types of growth to choose from, and different ways to use them. Some fuchsias are hardy and can be grown as permanent shrubs, even in parts of the world with quite cold winters. This chapter contains tips and techniques on how to plant and grow them in this way. It also describes the best way to grow the more tender varieties. There is advice about buying and choosing fuchsias, propagating them, and growing and training them into beautiful shapes such as standards, pyramids and fans. There is information about the different types of growing medium and their suitability for growing fuchsias, and practical guidance on how to plant large containers and hanging baskets, and their subsequent care.

Left: You do not need many specialist tools to grow fuchsias. Simple basic items such as a pair of secateurs, a selection of plant pots and labels, a garden trowel and a small hoe will suffice.

Top left: There are many different types of baskets suitable for growing fuchsias. This type is a wicker construction lined with polyethylene to protect the willow.

Top middle: A large terracotta (clay) pot surrounded by fuchsias, pelargoniums and other companion plants ready for planting. This picture is from the start of a planting sequence, shown in full within this chapter.

Top right: Many sorts of different propagators are available to take fuchsia cuttings. For small quantities, homemade versions using a cover on a pot are quite suitable for windowsills.

Selecting and buying fuchsias

One of the most enjoyable parts of growing fuchsias as a hobby is the selection of new plants. The inspiration can come from seeing them in other people's gardens, or from looking at nursery catalogues. There is a tremendous sense of excitement in waiting for those first buds of your new acquisitions to open and reveal the hidden inner flower secrets. A fuchsia enthusiast should try to support the specialist fuchsia nurseries as much as possible, since this will help to keep a large range of unusual varieties in cultivation. The owners are usually enthusiasts themselves and will often be able to give very useful help and advice with problems you have, or suggestions of varieties.

ORDERING FUCHSIAS

Browse the catalogues and decide on the varieties you want to try. Most of the specialist fuchsia nurseries will accept orders for rooted cuttings or plants in small pots to be supplied in the late winter or early spring, and this is the best way to be sure you get the varieties you want. Getting together with friends, putting in and collecting a large order together, is one way to make this more economically viable.

Some growers will send an order by post, and while this is probably a good

Top: 'Display' is an excellent hardy cultivar for a beginner. It is very adaptable in its growth and is easy to grow as a standard or pyramid. It has dark foliage and almost self-coloured pink flowers with a flared corolla.

solution if you live a long way from the nursery, the best way to ensure that you start with healthy plants is to collect them yourself. Expect to come away with more plants than you ordered, though!

WHAT TO LOOK FOR

The first thing to do is to look carefully at the plant you are thinking of buying.
• Does it look strong and healthy?
• Are there any signs of disease?
• Is the growth even and balanced?

Next, look at the plant from above.
• Are the leaves growing evenly?
• Are the side shoots growing evenly? Often when the leaves are bigger on one side of the plant, the side shoots will be stronger as well.

If you want to take cuttings from the plant when you get home, pick one without the main growing tip removed (unstopped). If you are considering growing a standard, look for an unstopped plant or a rooted cutting that is growing strongly, with a straight stem.

CARING FOR NEW PLANTS

When you have bought rooted cuttings or small plants from a nursery early in the season, remember they have probably been growing in more heat than you will be able to provide. If you want to take cuttings from them, do so straight away, as these will go directly into your propagator, with no check in growth. When you bring new plants into your greenhouse, try to place them in the warmest position you can find

CHOOSING PLANTS FOR CUTTINGS

1 Look for plants with shoots pinched out evenly and growing in a balanced way. Try to choose plants not recently stopped, with growing tips.

2 This is an ideal shoot to take a tip cutting from. It is healthy, growing strongly and evenly, and there is a pair of leaves and a small growing tip.

POTTING UP STANDARD CUTTINGS

1 Choose cuttings with a balanced and even growth for growing on as a standard. You can see the healthy and well-developed root systems that will give rapid growth.

2 Pot up into 6cm (2½in) pots, centring the cutting in the pot. Keep them separate from your other plants so you remember not to pinch out the growing tips.

and gradually get them used to the growing conditions over about a week. When they are ready for potting up or potting on, move them into the next size pot and settle them in with an overhead spray, but do not soak the compost (soil mix).

LARGER PLANTS

If you do not have the facilities to raise small plants in a greenhouse early in the season, simply buy larger plants later on, and grow them on outside, following the previous guidelines for stopping and potting on. The plant cost will be higher, but there are no costs for heating.

POTTING UP ROOTED CUTTINGS

1 Pot up a rooted fuchsia cutting in a 6cm (2½in) pot, taking care not to disturb or damage the fine root system.

2 Water the fuchsia cutting in its new pot with a fine rose or an overhead spray. Use just enough water to settle the cutting in its pot.

POTTING UP MAIL-ORDER PLANTS

1 When the cuttings arrive, they should be potted up as soon as possible. If you cannot do it immediately, cut off the top of the plastic case and keep them well watered.

2 When you are ready to pot the plants up, open the plastic case. There should be a label identifying each plant. If the root balls are dry, soak them immediately.

3 Remove the elastic band and label from the plant root ball and place the cutting in a suitably sized small pot such as a 6cm (2½in). Write a plastic label with the cultivar name.

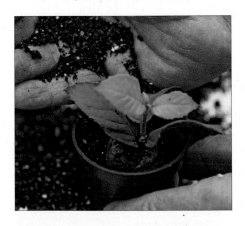

4 Complete the potting-up of the cutting by gently adding compost (soil mix) and tapping the pot to settle the contents. This cultivar is the Triphylla 'Chantry Park'.

5 Water the cuttings into their pots, using an overhead spray. Do not overwater at this time, but use enough water to settle and moisten the compost, allowing the roots to grow.

Composts and feeds

The quality of the compost (soil mix) used in containers is very important for growing fuchsias. It is the anchor for the roots and the reservoir for water and plant nutrients. Its structure is equally important, as this will allow the passage of air, vital for the health of the plants. There are many types of commercial potting compost prepared from various base materials. They contain some nutrients, but these are soon used up by strongly growing plants, especially if they are crowded into a small container, since they cannot put their roots down into the ground. It is therefore crucial to feed the plants by mixing in slow-release fertilizer granules or watering regularly with a suitable diluted liquid fertilizer.

TYPES OF COMPOST

Lawrence and Newell, two scientists at the John Innes Institute, developed the first standardized and reproducible potting composts during the 1930s. These mixes are known as John Innes formula composts, and consist of seven parts loam, three parts peat and two parts gritty sand (by volume) with increasing amounts of fertilizer to make the number one, two and three grades.

Soil-less compost (growing medium) was developed at the University of California, and is known as UC compost. It consists of 75 per cent sphagnum moss peat and 25 per cent coarse sand with

Top: A strip of fuchsia cuttings rooted in seed and cutting compost (soil mix), ready for potting up in potting compost.

added fertilizers. There have been many variations on this mixture, including the use of other additives such as vermiculite and water-retention granules. However, nowadays there is a concern about the unsustainable use of sphagnum moss peat, which can potentially destroy sites of special scientific interest. The search for substitutes has resulted in various alternatives such as coir (from coconut husks), composted bark and, more recently, composted recycled green waste.

COMPOST FOR FUCHSIAS

Fuchsias will grow well in most good-quality general-purpose composts, preferably an open free-draining mixture. In terracotta (clay) pots, mixes containing 50 per cent or more loam are best – soil-less composts

can dry out very quickly, and are difficult to re-wet when completely dry. For plastic pots, the soil-free types work well, but adding up to 20 per cent loam can be beneficial.

ADDITIVES

These are non-fertilizing materials mixed into the compost before use. Vermiculite, a thermally expanded mica, and perlite, another expanded mineral, open up the texture, and improve the drainage and water-retention abilities of the compost. Use them at a ratio of about one part vermiculite or perlite to six parts compost (by volume). Coarse sand and grit function purely as structure and drainage aids, but they will also add some weight to the compost mix, improving the stability of pot plants, especially when they dry out. Use

Above: Some different composts (soil mixes) and additives. At the back from left to right are: peat-free multi-purpose compost, loam-based compost and moss peat. At the front from left to right are: water retention granules, vermiculite and coarse grit.

Above: Some fertilizers and equipment used for growing fuchsias in the greenhouse, including a hand pressure sprayer, liquid fertilizer concentrate, slow-release fertilizer granules and a small watering can. In the background are overwintered fuchsia cuttings in 6cm (2½in) pots.

them at a ratio of about one volume part to six volume parts compost. When using multiple additives together, reduce the proportions accordingly. Water retention gel has become very popular mixed in with compost in hanging baskets, which often dry out very quickly. It will both improve the retention of water in the basket, and make re-wetting dry compost easier.

FERTILIZERS AND FEEDS

Useful supplements, fertilizers are solid materials mixed into the compost before use. Commercial compost normally contains sufficient fertilizer for a few months of growing. Feeds are liquid fertilizers, normally a liquid concentrate or soluble powder applied during watering or sprayed on as a foliar feed. Fuchsias, like all plants, need three major elements: nitrogen (N), phosphorus (P) and potassium (K) (commonly known as potash from its horticultural origin in wood ash). Nitrogen promotes leafy growth, root growth requires phosphorus, and potash promotes hardening of the wood, and flower and fruit formation. In addition, there are a number of trace elements and minor components needed for healthy growth of the plants. Fertilizers are labelled with their N:P:K contents, measured in weight per cent. For example, a high-nitrogen soluble powder feed could be 30:15:15, a balanced feed would be 20:20:20 and a high-potash feed 15:15:30.

One simple option is to use slow-release fertilizer granules. These contain concentrated fertilizer encapsulated in a polymer shell, which will not start to release the fertilizer until the compost reaches a certain temperature. The rate of release is dependent on the temperature and, to an extent, the moisture content. Alternatively, use liquid concentrate or soluble powder fertilizers mixed with water to give the correct strength. Fuchsias like a high-nitrogen feed early in the season, and a balanced feed for the rest of the season. You can use a high-potash feed at flowering time, preferably alternated with a balanced feed. Frequent feeding with a weak solution – maybe even a quarter of the recommended strength – is better than infrequent, stronger doses.

MIXING COMPOST AND ADDITIVES

1 Sift 12 parts of good-quality potting compost (soil mix) through a 5mm (¼in) sieve into a strong plastic bag.

2 After sifting, the larger lumps of hard peat, wood, bark etc. are retained in the sieve. Use this coarse material above pot crocks.

3 Add a measure (one part) of a suitable coarse grit or sand to the mixture. Here 3–5mm (⅛–¼in) Cornish Grit is used.

4 Add a measure (one part) of horticultural grade perlite or vermiculite to the mixture. This improves the drainage and texture.

5 Grip the neck of the bag to close it, leaving plenty of air space, and roll and invert the bag to mix the ingredients together.

6 The final mixture spread out in a tray. The light colours of the grit and vermiculite additives show the effective mixing.

Hybridization techniques

There are more than 10,000 recorded cultivars, of which about 5,000 are still in cultivation. Many fuchsia flower colours exist, with only yellow and deep royal blue evading the plant breeders so far, but even these may be achieved one day. Modern cultivars are created by hybridizing two fuchsias and growing the resultant seed. If a seedling looks commercially promising, new plants are produced by vegetative propagation (cuttings). The natural phenomenon of mutation known as 'sporting' has produced many other new fuchsias, including variegated-leaf cultivars such as 'Golden Marinka' from 'Marinka', and different flower colours, such as 'Lady Thumb' and 'Son of Thumb' from 'Tom Thumb'.

HISTORY OF HYBRIDIZATION

Since gardeners began their attempts at hybridization early in the 19th century, many different fuchsias have been produced, with varying shapes and sizes of leaf and flower and new flower colours. After the surge of new cultivars in the 19th century, fuchsias lost some of their popularity in the early part of the 20th century. The revival of interest in fuchsias was in part due to the formation of national fuchsia societies and the realization that the fuchsia was not just a greenhouse plant, but many varieties could also be grown in the garden as a hardy shrub.

Top: The fuchsia 'Alan Titchmarsh' is named in honour of the well-known British gardening celebrity. This bushy vigorous plant has plentiful semi-double flowers with rose sepals and a pale lilac-pink corolla.

PARTS OF THE FUCHSIA FLOWER

The fuchsia flower is formed of insect-attracting parts (including the colourful sepals and petals) and reproductive parts.

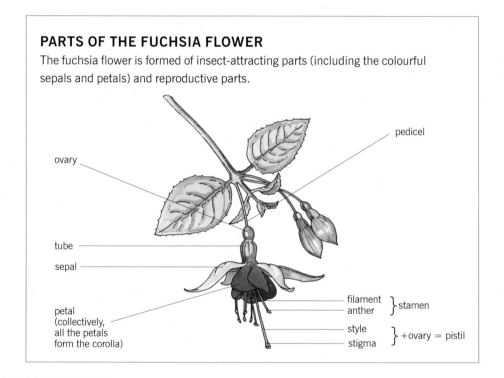

pedicel

ovary

tube

sepal

petal (collectively, all the petals form the corolla)

filament
anther } stamen

style
stigma } +ovary = pistil

HYBRIDIZING PLANTS

1 Select a suitable flower bud in the seed parent. Remove any other buds growing from the same leaf axil. Pop it open one or two days before it would normally open.

2 Emasculate the flower by carefully cutting away all the anthers (pollen-bearing organs) with scissors. Protect the flower in a polythene or muslin (cheesecloth) bag.

3 After about a week, when the stigma is receptive (sticky), pollinate the stigma by transferring pollen from the anthers of the selected male parent flower.

4 Reseal the flower in the bag to protect it from further pollen, and label. Remove the bag in 5–6 days, when the flower has died. Allow the berry to form and ripen before harvesting the seed.

In the 1930s a group of enthusiasts from the recently formed British Fuchsia Society collected 100 of the best cultivars available in Europe and took them to California at the request of the American Fuchsia Society. American growers then applied scientific methods to further hybridization and soon started to produce new cultivars with unusual colour combinations, as well as the range of large double-flowered fuchsias for which they are famous. In Europe, the focus was more on producing hardy cultivars with a better range of flower colours and sizes. In the last decade, there has been a huge increase in the production of cultivars with new and exciting flower colours and shapes.

MAKING YOUR OWN HYBRID

If you wish to produce a new fuchsia, you must first make a selected hybridization cross between two cultivars or species, or a combination of the two. The first step is to select the two separate cultivars or species to use as the pollen parent and the seed parent. Experienced hybridizers have their preferences for these, knowing the previous parentage of cultivars and the viability of their seed production. For example, the cultivars 'La Campanella' and 'String of Pearls' have been used quite extensively as seed parents. It's best to do some research, by consulting reference books and talking to other growers, before you make your choice.

GROWING ON HYBRID SEEDLINGS

Once your hybridized seeds have germinated – which may take up to six weeks, so be patient – let them grow until they are large enough to handle. Prick them out (holding them by the leaves, to avoid damaging the stems or roots) into individual pots and grow them on without stopping, potting on as necessary, or in the summer you can plant them out into a trial bed. Judge the growth habit and the flower as objectively as you can, if possible bringing in some other growers to help with the assessment.

Take cuttings from the best candidates and try growing them for a few more years. If you have anything that looks really interesting, contact one of your local fuchsia nurseries, as the growers are always interested in new cultivars.

COLLECTING AND PLANTING SEEDS

1 Carefully squash the ripe fuchsia berry in a small dish of water, breaking the skin and opening the flesh.

2 Break up the flesh as much as possible into a pulp suspended in water, releasing the seeds into the water.

3 Filter the mixture through a fine strainer, washing through the berry debris separating the pulp form the seeds.

4 Carefully pick out the fuchsia seeds and place them on a paper towel, drying them as much as possible.

5 Transfer the dried seeds into a pot or tray of good-quality seed compost, pressing them into the surface and carefully moistening.

6 Place a transparent plastic or glass cover on the pot and germinate at 15.5–18°C (60–65°F). Germination may take six weeks.

Propagating fuchsias

Taking cuttings is a really simple and rewarding way of propagating fuchsias to increase or replace stock. It is the only way to increase the stock of a specific fuchsia cultivar as plants propagated from collected seed will not come true except for the fuchsia species. You can take cuttings at almost any time of the year: soft cuttings in the late winter and spring; semi-ripe cuttings in the summer; and woody cuttings in the autumn. You can also take soft cuttings in the autumn by cutting back plants in the late summer and allowing them to shoot again. Ensure all cutting material used is short-jointed and free from any disease or infestation, and comes from strongly growing plants.

SOFT CUTTINGS

Depending on your location, climate and greenhouse conditions, take soft cuttings in the late winter or spring when plants are growing strongly. Different parts of the shoot can be used as cuttings, but it is always best to use a tip cutting, if you have

Top: A set of late summer cuttings that are well rooted and showing fresh tip growth eight weeks after planting. Spring cuttings would root in five to six weeks.

enough material. The tip cutting contains the highest concentration of natural growth hormones and it will root more quickly. It also gives a more symmetrical cutting, with the flexibility to be trained and grown on in different ways.

Before you start, ensure the parent plant is well watered and the growth is turgid (the plant has had time to take up the water). Look for growing tips where the growth is symmetrical, and cut just

below a node with a razor-sharp knife to give a cutting with two sets of leaves and a growing tip. Try to avoid handling the stem, as you could damage the delicate tissues. Remove the bottom set of leaves and immediately place the cutting into the rooting medium. Add a label with the variety name and the date, water with a fine spray and place in a propagator. You may use rooting powder, but it is not really necessary. Keep the propagator with a bottom temperature of 15.5–21°C (60–70°F), in good light, but not in direct sunlight, and the cuttings will root in 14–28 days. When rooted the cuttings take on a fresher, brighter appearance and start to make new tip growth. At this point, gradually increase the ventilation in the propagator to acclimatize the cuttings to the drier outside air and harden them off.

SEMI-RIPE CUTTINGS

In the summer, most plants are flowering and the stems have started to ripen. You can now take longer cuttings with a 'heel', the bit of bark that comes away when you tear off a whole side shoot from the parent plant. The cuttings can have up to five pairs of leaves and the growing tip. Remove all flower buds, treat the bottom node and stem with fresh rooting powder or gel, and then treat as soft cuttings.

HARDWOOD CUTTINGS

In the late summer and autumn, when the wood is ripe, you can take hardwood cuttings, again with a heel, as described for semi-ripe cuttings. Remove any flowers or

TYPES OF CUTTING

A semi-ripe cutting (left), consisting of a side shoot removed with a strip of bark from the parent stem, is similar to a hardwood cutting. On the right is a long semi-ripe cutting split into different types of cutting that could be used if propagation material is limited for an individual variety.

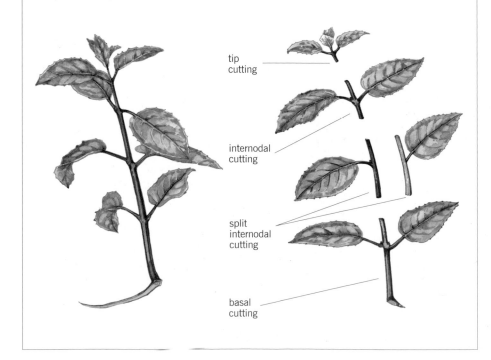

tip cutting

internodal cutting

split internodal cutting

basal cutting

buds, and treat similarly to soft cuttings. This type of cutting will also often root if inserted into sandy soil in a shady spot outside.

CUTTING COMPOST

Use commercial cutting compost (soil mix), or even better, try two parts of sifted moss peat mixed with one part of washed sharp sand or 2–3mm (½–⅛in) grit and one part of vermiculite or perlite. This gives an open, free-draining mixture with few nutrients, which will encourage rapid root formation.

PROPAGATORS

Commercial nurseries use heated propagating benches with overhead misting, and often root directly into sand. Amateur growers can rarely invest in anything quite as elaborate, but there are a number of other solutions:

- Electrically heated, gravel tray-sized propagators with vented plastic lids.
- Similar unheated ones, placed over a greenhouse heater.
- Plastic covers that fit on to seed trays or pots.
- Cut-off plastic bottles, or plastic bags fixed above pots with rubber bands.

CONTAINERS

There are many choices for cutting containers, including seed trays, plug trays and small shallow pots. Trays with individual compartments are an excellent choice. The trays with 60 small cells that fit into a standard seed tray, and split into strips of 12, are very good. They keep each cutting separate, with its own label, prevent the roots intermingling, and make

TAKING CUTTINGS

1 Using a sharp knife, remove a suitable cutting from its parent plant. A small disposable modelling knife with a retractable stainless blade, as shown here, is ideal.

2 If making your own cutting medium, mix together two parts of sifted peat moss, one part of horticultural grit or coarse sand and one part of vermiculite or perlite.

3 Fill a cell strip with cutting medium. Cut the lower leaves off the stem and insert into a prepared hole in the cutting medium. Add a label to each cell.

4 Moisten the cell strip with cuttings with an overhead spray of water, before being placed in the propagator with a bottom heat of 60°F (15.5°C).

it easier to pot up the cuttings later. If you treat them carefully, they can be reused a few times. It is easy to cut out a single cell from the strip to give away a cutting.

Below left: Some commercial and home-recycled propagators for fuchsias.

Below: Commercial propagation with heated benches, lights and misting.

Potting on

While building the structure of the plant, fuchsias need potting on into larger pots stepwise as they grow. If you allow a plant to become pot-bound, it will feel its survival is threatened and this will trigger flowering and production of seed. Potting on gradually instead of moving the plant from a small pot to a large pot will make it easier to water correctly because there is less compost (soil mix) that will stay wet and start to go stale. The roots will also use the smaller amount of new compost more efficiently rather than going straight down through the compost to the bottom of the new pot but not using the bulk of the compost until the formation of branching roots.

POTTING ON SINGLE PLANTS

As a general guideline, a rooted cutting can be potted up into a 6cm (2½in) pot. The next move could be into a 7.5cm (3in) pot, followed by a 9cm (3½in), 11cm (4¼in), 13cm (5in) and finally a 15cm (6in) pot. This sequence will give approximately the same percentage increase in compost volume at each potting-on stage. If you wish to go beyond a 15cm (6in) pot, you can continue to an 18cm (7in) pot and onwards in 5cm (2in) steps. If a plant is growing very strongly then it may be possible to miss out one pot size in the sequence, but water it very sparsely for the next two weeks, forcing the roots to search out new compost. Use of the technique shown in the step-by-step sequence will ensure that there is minimal disturbance of the root system and few air pockets, if any, in the compost.

POTTING SEVERAL PLANTS INTO A LARGE CONTAINER

Take similar care when planting up a large pot with fuchsias, or fuchsias with other container plants. In this case it will be impossible to increase the pot sizes gradually. You might use a few plants from 13cm (5in) pots and the rest from 9cm (3½in) pots. This will lead to the problems of over-potting just described, so water with great care. In other words, give enough water to settle the plants in but do not

Top: A small flowering plant of the Triphylla cultivar 'Thalia' in a terracotta (clay) pot, with a collection of other old pots.

POTTING UP TO A 6CM (2½IN) POT

1 Carefully remove the rooted cutting from its rooting cell with the minimum possible root disturbance. Note the good formation of its root system in the cell.

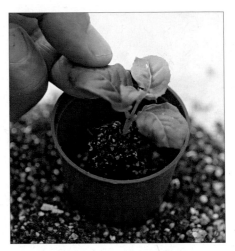

2 Add compost (soil mix) into the bottom of a clean 5cm (2in) pot, adjusting the amount to ensure the cutting is at the same level as when in the rooting cell.

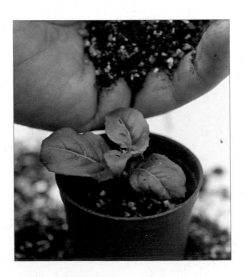

3 Add compost to fill the rest of the space in the pot, tapping it on a solid surface to ensure the contents settle and fill any voids, preventing air pockets in the pot.

4 Water in the cutting with an overhead spray and place the pot in a warm position out of draughts and direct sun until the cutting adjusts to its new surroundings.

POTTING ON TO A 7.5CM (3IN) POT

1 Add compost (soil mix) so that the smaller pot sits inside the new larger one, its top level with the rim. Fill the gap between the two pots with compost. Then carefully remove the inner pot, taking care not to disturb the compost.

2 Remove the plant from its smaller pot and drop it into the hollow, taking care not to disturb the mould.

3 Tap the new pot to settle the plant, and top up with more compost. Keep the plant moist by using an overhead spray.

Above: This quarter standard of 'Katrina Thompsen' is flowering for the first time, standing on a lawn. Note the PVC tape ties anchoring the stem firmly to the cane.

completely soak the compost. Then keep the pot as dry as possible for a period of three to four weeks in early spring, or two to three weeks in late spring, to encourage the roots to penetrate right through the pot. When the roots are short of water they will spread out in search of it. This helps reduce the problem of unused compost becoming stale because of a lack of air, and the roots will penetrate this just moist compost much quicker. Fuchsias will very quickly show when they are starting to get thirsty because the leaves become dull and slightly less turgid, and then start to droop. After this period, increase the watering and treat the plants as normal.

POTTING ON STANDARDS

Use the same techniques as described above, but remember to loosen the ties holding the main stem to the supporting cane, and push the latter down to the base of the new pot. Mixing in washed sharp sand to the top 2.5cm (1in) of compost helps to anchor the cane in the top of the pot by forming a very solid, compact but free-draining layer, and prevents it loosening as it moves in the wind.

WATERING

To keep the compost and roots healthy, it is important to use a cycle of wetting, drying out and rewetting. This cycle sucks in air to the compost every time it dries out, which is important for the health of both the roots and the compost. The gradual increase in pot size also means that the compost fills more evenly with roots using the water more quickly, thus keeping the cycle going, and allowing the plant to make the best use of the limited space. There is evidence that fuchsias grow quickest just before the roots dry out, producing larger plants more quickly.

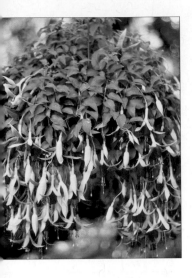

Multi-planting

An easy way of producing large fuchsia pot plants in a single season is to use 'multiple planting'. It is a common practice with commercial growers of chrysanthemums, where a number of cuttings are rooted, packed close together in one pot – producing the popular 'Pot Mums'. Multi-planting is particularly useful if you do not have the facilities for keeping fuchsias over winter. There are three main techniques, categorized by the size of the planting material used. Although the first two methods ideally need a heated greenhouse, you can also try these techniques inside a house on a bright windowsill if you have suitable plants from which to take cuttings.

MULTI-PLANTS FROM TIP CUTTINGS

The first method is to root many cuttings together in a single pot. It is the most difficult method and needs great care to prevent botrytis because of the crowding of green stems and leaves. For this reason, it is best to avoid varieties that are more prone to the disease.

Start by rooting six or seven tip cuttings in a 9cm (3½in) half pot, one in the centre and the rest equally spaced around the

Top: This cascading cultivar 'President Margaret Slater' is multi-planted in a hanging pot, its growth trailing down the pot with flowers on the ends of the branches.

edge. Alternatively, use a larger half pot and more cuttings, arranging them in concentric rings around the centre, staggering the placing of cuttings in adjacent rings to fill the pot evenly. When the cuttings have rooted and adjusted to conditions outside the propagator, stop all the cuttings at a maximum of two pairs of leaves. As the plants start to grow, remove any overlapping lower leaves with nail scissors, allowing more air into the base of the plant. If any of the cuttings do succumb to botrytis, cut them back to soil level to prevent the problem from spreading to adjacent cuttings. Continue stopping the side branches at one or two pairs of leaves,

and pot on as necessary using standard pots. Once the bottom stems have started to harden and form bark, then grow on, treating the plant in the normal way.

MULTI-PLANTS FROM ROOTED CUTTINGS

The second method involves cuttings, raised individually, ideally rooted in trays with separate compartments. Pot several of them together in a single pot, arranging them with one in the centre, then one or more rings around the outside. You can use cuttings all of the same variety, or a mixture, but if you use cuttings of different cultivars, remember that they will grow at

GROWING MULTI-PLANTS FROM TIP CUTTINGS

1 Choose a parent plant with plenty of cutting material. Take cuttings in the normal way. If the bottom leaves are large, cut them in half.

2 Fill a 9cm (3½in) pot with cutting compost (soil mix). Place one cutting in the centre and another six in a ring around the outside.

3 Add a label, water in with an overhead mist spray and place in a propagator or add a transparent cover to the pot.

different rates and there might be different degrees of self-branching with flowering at different times, especially if single, semi-double and double-flowered varieties are mixed. Pinch out the growing tips at two or three pairs of leaves, and then the resultant side branches at two pairs of leaves, potting on as necessary. Continue pinching until you achieve about 60 per cent of the size desired, then allow them to become pot bound to increase the flowering.

MULTI-PLANTS FROM LARGER PLANTS

The final method involves the use of larger plants growing in 7.5cm (3in) or 9cm (3½in) pots, and putting five or more of them into a 20cm (8in) pot with one in the centre and the rest in a circle around it. If you wish to use many more plants or want to buy plants in larger pots than 9cm, then use a correspondingly bigger pot for planting that greater size of plants in.

This method is much easier for those who do not have good propagating facilities because you can use nursery-bought plants and harden them off in your own conditions, planting them up into a large pot after the last of the frosts. With the proper attention, these pots will be spectacular in late summer. Take great care to avoid over-watering, until the plants are established, and see the earlier advice on potting up into large containers.

GROWING MULTI-PLANTS FROM ROOTED CUTTINGS

1 Part fill a 9cm (3½in) pot with compost (soil mix). Place a rooted cutting into the centre so the compost surface is just below the rim.

2 Add another four cuttings of the same variety spaced equally around the edge of the pot. Remove all the small growing tips.

3 Add compost, filling the gaps between the rooted cuttings, tapping the pot to settle them in. Water them in with an overhead spray.

4 As the individual cuttings start to grow together, remove any overlapping lower leaves. Continue to stop side shoots.

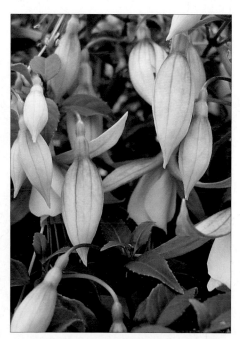

Far left: It is easy to grow an excellent multi-planted hanging pot from the single-flowered cultivar 'Hermiena'. It will reward you with prolific flowers.

Left: The beautiful pink-flushed-white flowers of the cultivar 'Shelford'. This flexible and vigorous fuchsia responds well to multi-planting.

Training shrub and bush fuchsias

Most fuchsias seen in gardens, whether in large containers or planted in the ground, are growing naturally as shrubs, and they form beautiful, graceful plants with little or no deliberate training. When a fuchsia grows from seed or from a cutting without any stopping, the natural form is rather like a Christmas tree, although this depends on how self-branching and upright the variety naturally is. In outdoor conditions, however, the central growing stem will often be damaged by the wind, frost or other physical damage, and this leads to new shoots growing up from the base to create the shrub shape. Our intervention will create the desired shape right from the beginning.

SHAPE DIFFERENCES

Though the terms 'shrub' and 'bush' are usually synonymous, for fuchsia growers a shrub has a central growth and shoots which grow up from underneath the soil around the centre, while a bush grows on a short single stem.

SHRUB TRAINING

Start with a rooted cutting. If you have taken this yourself, use one that you originally cut just below a node, since this will encourage growths from below the surface. Pot the cutting into a 6cm (2½in) pot and remove the growing tip once the cutting has grown to four pairs of leaves. This will encourage the formation of side shoots. Check the growth of the roots and when the main roots start to curl around the bottom of the pot, move it on to a 7.5cm (3in) pot, lowering the plant slightly in the pot, and water in gently. Give the plant a 90-degree turn every two to three days, or more frequently if you are growing it on a windowsill indoors.

When the resultant side shoots have grown to two pairs of leaves, stop them by pinching out the growing tips again. You often find that certain varieties will grow additional side shoots between the junction of the first side shoot and the main stem, especially at the point of removal of the main growing tip. This is a bonus, so just

Top: This shrub of 'Genii', photographed two months after the last picture in the shrub sequence (right), has now made a nice shape and is growing on outside to harden the growth and flower for the first time.

SHRUB AND BUSH STRUCTURES

In a shrub structure (left), a number of main stems grow from the ground, self-branching above to form the structure. A bush structure (right) is grown from a single central stem growing from the ground with side branches forming the structure.

STOPPING TO CREATE A SHRUB

1 Pot up a selected fuchsia cutting into a 6cm (2½in) pot and grow it on until it has four pairs of leaves and a distinct growing tip.

2 Remove the growing tip and allow the side shoots to develop. Later on, after potting, the lowest shoots will be below the soil level.

3 When the side shoots have grown to two to three pairs of leaves remove the tips again. Repeat after every one to two pairs of leaves.

Above: This large shrub fuchsia, growing in a tub as a central feature in the middle of a lawn, has been well trained to produce a dense plant with plenty of flowers.

STOPPING TO CREATE A BUSH

1 Pot up the fuchsia cutting into a 6cm (2½in) pot. Grow it on until it has five pairs of leaves and a distinct growing tip.

2 Remove the growing tip and the bottom two pairs of leaves and side shoots to leave a clear, short stem.

3 When there are two to three pairs of leaves, remove the tips again. Repeat every one to two pairs of leaves.

treat them in the same way as the other side shoots and they will add to the density and number of flowers.

Continue to pot the plant on as it grows, before hardening it off to plant in the garden as a permanent shrub. If you wish, continue to stop every one or two pairs of leaves to create a more dense, bushy and floriferous specimen plant, but remember that every stop made delays flowering by approximately three weeks.

BUSH TRAINING

A fuchsia bush grows on a single stem, which for exhibition purposes should not exceed 4cm (1½in). For garden use, this may be longer, but still not more than 7.5cm (3in). Take a fuchsia cutting and remove the lowest side shoots and leaves so that the cutting has a clear stem of 4cm (1½in) showing above the compost (soil mix) and three pairs of leaves. Place the cutting in a 6cm (2½in) pot and stop the growth by removing the growing tip. When the side shoots have started to form, stop the bottom two sets at two pairs of leaves and the upper set at one pair of leaves. Grow on as for shrub training above.

When the resultant side shoots have grown to one pair of leaves, stop them by pinching out the growing tips again. Treat all the side shoots in the same way and continue the process until the plant is in a 13cm (5in) pot, lowering the plant slightly if the basal stem has grown too long.

POTTING ON A SHRUB FROM A TERRACOTTA POT

1 Unless the plant is pot-bound, the root ball will not usually keep its shape when removed from a terracotta (clay) pot, since the surface is rougher than plastic, so it is not so easy to use the moulding technique described earlier. This shrub-trained fuchsia is ready to be potted on.

2 Add a few pieces of broken terracotta pot over the drainage hole to ensure it is not blocked, and to keep the new compost (soil mix) in the pot.

3 Add soil-based compost to the pot, covering the broken pot at the base, so that the plant will sit at the same level or slightly lower than before.

4 Place the plant in the pot and add more compost around the sides, filling all air voids and tapping the pot to settle the contents.

5 Press the compost down gently, but take care not to compact it too much. Finally, water the plant in sparingly, to settle the plant in the pot.

Growing standard fuchsias

A fuchsia grown as a standard is an excellent way to display the spectacular beauty of the flowers. To be in proportion, the head of a mature flowering standard fuchsia should be approximately one-third of the overall height, and if grown in a pot, a 1.8m (6ft) full standard needs one that is 30cm (12in) in diameter. Of the different large trained shapes, a standard fuchsia is the easiest form to grow. A lot of attention and consideration must be paid to the support cane and the ties to support the stem and head, especially in the early stages. Choose a suitable vigorous, upright variety such as 'Checkerboard', 'Display' or 'Snowcap', and follow the instructions below.

STARTING THE PROCESS

Start as early in the season as possible, or grow from a late summer/autumn cutting over the winter indoors on a windowsill, in a heated greenhouse, or in a conservatory. Either take a cutting yourself, or buy a suitable young plant from a nursery. Make sure it is unstopped, with the growing tip intact, and look for a variety

Top: A first-year full standard fuchsia 'Snowcap' placed on a lawn in a 20cm (8in) pot. The red and white flowers stand out beautifully against the green foliage and against the large *Fatsia japonica* visible in the background.

with leaves in sets of three instead of pairs as this gives an extra branch in each set in the head, allowing it to fill more quickly. If you wish to avoid the stem-growing stage, you can buy a ready-grown whip from a specialist nursery.

GROWING THE WHIP (STEM)

Pot the cutting up into a 6–7.5cm (2½–3in) pot and, looking down from above, insert a split cane as close to the main stem as possible between the leaves. Make sure the cane is straight, as this is the guide for the growing stem. As the plant begins to grow, start to remove the lowest side

shoots, which are very easy to snap out. Leave the top three sets and the growing tip in place, but do not remove the main leaves on the stem. Turn the plant one-quarter of a turn every two days (every day on a windowsill) to keep it growing evenly. As the stem starts to develop, fix it to the cane in several places using suitable ties. Check the ties regularly, because they will quickly cut into the soft stem if they are too tight.

As soon as the roots have reached the bottom of the pot and started to coil around, pot on to the next pot size. Make sure you loosen the ties and push the cane to the bottom of the new pot before re-tightening them. It is essential not to let the roots become pot-bound while growing the stem as this often initiates flower buds, which means the plant will not produce the side shoots needed to make the head. Feed regularly with a quarter-strength high-nitrogen feed, and mist the plant frequently.

STANDARD STRUCTURE

The stages of growing a standard fuchsia (from left to right). The first picture shows growing the stem – notice the leaves and top side shoots left on the plant. In the centre, the standard has nearly reached the desired height and removal of the main growing tip is imminent. The last picture shows the dormant structure of the finished standard without leaves.

FORMING THE HEAD

When the whip has reached the desired height, take out the growing tip, leaving sufficient side shoots to make the head. A guide is 2–3 sets for a mini standard, 3 sets for a quarter standard, 3–4 sets for a half standard and 4 sets for a full standard, but it will depend on the variety, and also on the stem length between the leaves. Pinch out the side shoots on the lower sets at two pairs of leaves and on the upper set at one pair of leaves. Often, additional side shoots will form at each break, especially

TRAINING A HALF STANDARD

1 Choose a young plant, ideally with leaves in sets of three, and grow it without stopping, potting on as soon as roots start to appear at the bottom of the pot.

2 Insert a split cane and tie to the stem. Remove the side shoots, leaving the top three sets. Do not remove the leaves. When flower buds appear, pinch out below them.

3 Stop the resulting sets of side shoots at two or three sets of leaves, to form the head. Do not remove the leaves from the main stem at this stage.

4 When a good, bushy head has formed, carefully remove the leaves from the main stem. Stop pinching out the growing tips, to allow the plant to flower.

CHANGING A STANDARD CANE

1 A half standard 'whip' grown from the cultivar 'John Bartlett'. After removal of the growing tip the head is forming, but the existing cane is not long enough.

2 Remove the ties to the existing cane, taking care not to damage the stem or small branches. Remove the existing cane while supporting the stem.

3 Insert a longer cane and replace the ties, ensuring the stem is straight against the cane. Pay attention to the ties supporting the developing head.

4 The standard is complete with a new cane. Note the regular ties and the length of the cane above the head. This disappears when the full head grows to its final size.

with the top set. Treat these in the same way. Stop all resulting side shoots once again at one pair of leaves, and then once more. Gradually remove the leaves from the stem and tie the standard stem in well, especially within the head itself, to prevent the risk of the whole head snapping off in the wind.

ALLOWING THE STANDARD TO FLOWER

For the final tying of the stem, PVC adhesive insulating tape is excellent, since it stretches and is waterproof. Another good alternative is green self-adhesive fabric tape. The young standard will benefit from

a spell outside to strengthen it up and form the wood necessary in the main structure. Do not pot it on again at this stage, as being root-bound helps to give more flowers. It is important to ensure any standards are well supported to prevent them being blown over and damaged.

Growing pillars and pyramids

If you want a different challenge in fuchsia training, try growing a pillar or a pyramid. These can grow to more than 3m (10ft) tall, making a very impressive sight. A pillar is simply a tall column, as the name implies, and is the easier form to grow. The shape commonly described as a pyramid is actually a cone, with the height approximately one and half times the width at the base. It is possible to grow a small one of either in a single season if you choose a fast-growing variety, but a large specimen will take three years or more. For this, you will need enough space in a heated greenhouse to keep the plant over the winter, unless you live in an area free from winter frosts.

PILLARS

The first thing to consider is how the plant should look when the pillar is completed. The aim is to make a graceful column with proportions of about 4:1 height to diameter, covered in flower. The easiest way to do this is to use the twin stem approach, described below, which will allow your pillar to grow up to 1.5m (5ft) in one season.

Take a cutting of a vigorous self-branching variety and grow it up to three pairs of leaves before removing the growing

Top: A first-year pillar grown from the fuchsia 'Katie Susan'. It will need further pruning and shaping to reach the final goal.

tip. Allow two laterals from just below the stop to form, and remove all others. Then start to train the laterals upward, supported by two canes close together or one cane with longer ties. Decide on the final height of the pillar, and grow one stem like a stretched bush to half this height, and the other like a standard to the full height. For the stretched bush side, leave all the lateral growths and stop them at one or two pairs of leaves, and for the standard side, remove all the lateral growths except the top three or four sets. Pot on as soon as the roots start to curl round the pot. As early as you can, put in the final cane, as replacing the ties becomes more difficult later.

When the bush side reaches half the final desired height, remove the growing tip and continue to stop at one or two pairs of leaves. When the standard stem reaches half the desired height, allow the laterals to stay on and pinch them at one or two pairs of leaves. From now on, stop the shoots at alternately one or two sets of leaves to maintain the shape.

When the standard stem side reaches the desired height, pinch out the growing tip, and also pinch out the laterals to complete the desired shape. Continue to pinch to build the shape. When you achieve your target plant shape, stop pinching the shoots and allow it to come into flower.

PILLAR STRUCTURE

This twin-stem pillar has been grown on two growths from a single central stem, one trained as a tall narrow bush and the other as a stretched standard to form a single structure.

GROWING A TWIN-STEM PILLAR

1 Pot up a fuchsia cutting into a 6cm (2½in) pot and grow on until it has three pairs of leaves and a growing tip. A vigorous growing culitvar is needed for this; the variety used here is 'Katie Susan'.

2 The growing tip is removed to leave two or three pairs of leaves, depending on how long you wish the main stem to be. After the stop, allow only the two side shoots from the top of the plant to grow on.

3 Continue to grow the two stems trained up the central cane, removing the side shoots of the tall standard and leaving them on the stretched bush. At half the final height, stop the bush stem.

4 From this point on, leave the side shoots on the standard side, stopping all side growths to give the desired shape. When the standard side reaches the desired height, remove the growing tip.

PYRAMIDS

When fully grown, this should look like a Christmas tree, with approximate proportions of 3:2 overall height to diameter at the base, the diameter decreasing steadily toward the top to form a pyramid or cone shape. The best growing technique for a pyramid is as a single plant, and it can take two or three years to grow.

Take a cutting of a vigorous growing variety with strong, stiff lateral growths. Grow it upward to a height of 25cm (10in) with a cane to support it, and then remove the growing tip. This stop will result in a surge of growth to the laterals, which is important for the shape. Remove the lowest pair of laterals to give a short single stem at the base. When the two new shoots start to develop from the point where you removed the growing tip, decide which has the stronger growth and remove the other. Now you will be growing the stronger shoot on up as the new leader. When it has grown 7–10cm (3–4in), stop all the laterals on the first part of the stem. The leader will have a new surge of growth. When the growth has the same number of joints as the first part of the stem, pinch out the growing tip again. However, this time remove the opposite shoot to the first stem stop, so the growth goes in the opposite direction to the previous stem and the same as the first.

Continue growing in this way, potting on, changing the support cane, adjusting ties and feeding with high-nitrogen fertilizer, alternately stopping the leader and the laterals to form the desired shape. If the laterals are growing too weakly on one side of the plant, simply lay the plant down horizontally with the weak leaders positioned vertically for a few days, and the resultant change in the flow of sap will boost the growth. Note that you will need to create special supports or hangers to do this. Grow on until the desired height is reached, then allow the pyramid to flower and enjoy the lovely display. Trim it back to retain the shape in the late summer or early autumn, and keep the plant ticking over in green leaf through the winter, as this will ensure that all parts of the structure stay alive until the next season.

PYRAMID STRUCTURE

When training a fuchsia pyramid, the alternate stopping of the leader and the branches creates the desired shape. Continue the process until you attain the desired height for the specimen.

new leader growing on the opposite side to the leader from the first stop

second stop of leader

first stop of leader

GROWING A PYRAMID

1 Start to grow the structure with a suitable cutting of a strong-growing wiry variety; in this case it is the semi-double 'Little Beauty'.

2 Grow the plant on without check, potting on as required, removing the lowest side shoots to leave a short clear stem at the base.

3 When the main stem reaches a height of 25cm (10in), remove the growing tip. Later, remove the weaker new side shoot.

4 After removing the weaker side shoot, grow the strong one as the new leader, tying into the cane and periodically stopping the side shoots.

5 When the height has doubled again, remove the tip of the leader again, but this time select the opposite growing shoot to grow on.

6 This growing structure has been allowed to flower, but in the late summer it will be trimmed to shape and overwintered in green leaf.

Growing espaliers and fans

One spectacular variation of the many shapes that you can achieve with fuchsias is a flat shape in one plane, for example an espalier or fan. The training of both shapes is to display their flowers to the front, which makes them a terrific way of brightening up a wall or fence. Fuchsias grown into these shapes require suitable winter protection in colder climates and it is best to cut them back in the late summer or early autumn, allow them to make new growth, then overwinter them in green leaf. This minimizes the chances of part of the structure suffering from die-back. Start by training an easier shape, such as a standard, before attempting either of these challenges.

ESPALIERS

A fuchsia espalier needs to be grown over a framework of canes, fixed to a wall or fence for support while the plant is outside, to prevent it being blown over. Choose a suitable variety that is vigorous and strong growing, preferably with a degree of laxness or wiriness, but strong enough to make sturdy, horizontal branches. Examples include 'Brutus', 'Phyllis' and 'Swingtime'. If you want to grow a smaller version of this shape, use small-flowered varieties such as 'Alice Hoffman' and 'Janice Ann'.

Top: A close-up photograph of the flowers and growth on a large fan of 'Lillian Annetts'. Note the density of the growth and the sheer number of double flowers produced.

Start by choosing a suitable, strong, two-leaf cutting and grow it on without stopping, removing at least every other set of side shoots, so that the laterals grow in one plane only. The natural tendency of the laterals is to grow upwards at an angle of 40–60 degrees to the main stem. With a fuchsia espalier, it is important to start training these laterals horizontally as soon as possible, while the stems are soft and green. As soon as the plant is big enough, insert a central, vertical cane and firmly attach horizontal canes to it at the level of each set of laterals, and then start to tie the laterals to it, pulling them down to the horizontal. Some angled canes pushed into the pot and tied to the horizontal canes will help keep them in the correct position.

ESPALIER STRUCTURE

An espalier is formed from a central stem and a series of strong horizontal laterals supported by a framework. The lateral side growths are tied in and carry the flowers.

TRAINING AN ESPALIER

1 Choose a vigorous-growing healthy cutting with only pairs of leaves. A three-leafed cutting cannot be used for this form as it will not grow in one plane.

2 Decide the plane of growth for the espalier. Choose the bottom set of side shoots you will use and remove every other pair as you go up the main stem.

3 Insert a cane to support the main growth and tie it up. You can now see four of the side growths that will form the espalier structure when mature.

4 Replace the main cane with a strong cane, and tie horizontal canes to it to support the growth. Tie the growths to the horizontal canes with suitable soft ties.

Pot on the moment the roots have reached the bottom of the pot, and then start feeding with high-nitrogen fertilizer to promote lots of new growth. When the plant has made six sets of laterals, remove the main growing tip, and select the strongest side shoot to continue growing upward. When the plant has reached the desired height, stop the main stem and remove any further shoots that grow from the top. Continue allowing the laterals to grow, tying them in, and pinch any side shoots from the main laterals. As the laterals grow longer, they may start to produce flowers. Allow this flowering to take place and side shoots should appear in the leaf axils once the flowers have finished.

FANS

You can grow a fan using either a single plant or three plants of the same variety. It is essential to have all the main growth and stems growing in the same plane, so it is best to pick a cutting of a strong-growing but slightly lax variety such as 'Waveney Gem'. Stop the cutting when it has made four pairs of leaves and remove the first and third sets of side shoots so that, again, all the side shoots are growing in the same plane.

Pot on as soon as roots start to coil around the bottom of the pot. Construct the support structure by inserting five to seven canes in a fan shape with the central one

FAN STRUCTURE

When beginning a fan (left), the main shoots of the initial growth should be in the same plane. Later (right), the fan growths have been stopped and the side shoots now cover more of the frame.

pointing vertically upwards, and fix horizontal canes to them to make the framework rigid. Grow the laterals to cover the framework, tying them in as necessary, and periodically stop them to increase the number of leaders covering the structure. Pull any side shoots growing towards the back through to the front, tie them in and stop them. When the main leaders are close to the edge of the frame, stop them again and allow the fan to flower.

This is the most labour-intensive structure because of the amount of pulling through and tying in of the side growths needed. The fan structure needs a lot of support to keep it in the correct shape, which is why it is best to tie the framework to a wall or fence. If you do not have much space, you can keep it small by pruning it and restricting the pot size; alternatively pot it on regularly and allow it to grow bigger from year to year, until it reaches the desired size.

TRAINING A FAN

1 Stop the cutting at three pairs of leaves. Remove the middle set of side shoots, so there are two pairs left, growing in the same plane. These will form the structure.

2 Stop the side shoots at approximately three pairs of leaves. Remove any side shoots that are not growing aligned with the plane of the fan.

3 Insert five canes to form the fan with two horizontal canes to brace the structure. Tie the growing side shoots to the cane frame, spreading them to form the fan.

4 Complete the frame structure with two more horizontal canes. This growth has reached the top of the frame and is starting to flower. Ensure you tie in the growth well.

Bonsais and fuchsia topiary

Growing fuchsias as bonsai or novelty shapes is an exciting way of training fuchsias when you have limited space. They are fiddly and intricate, but lots of fun. Bonsais take a long time to grow well – firstly, because of the length of time to get the aged woody appearance to the growth; secondly, the task of miniaturizing the growth; and thirdly, persuading the branches to take on the form you desire. Growing fuchsias as novelty shapes is easier to achieve quickly, especially when employing the quick-growing Encliandra hybrids. These will fill the frame of a three-dimensional (3D) mesh former very rapidly, but are still amenable to clipping to shape.

BONSAI FUCHSIAS

Growing fuchsias as bonsai specimens is a long-term project, as with any bonsai training. It is best to choose a variety with small, single flowers, since although the leaves are dwarfed by the training, the flowers remain the same size, and large flowers would look out of proportion. To start, you need a plant grown deliberately with a bonsai in mind or an older plant with a sound, woody structure. An older plant can be either a pot plant with a suitable shape or an old, hardy plant growing in the garden that can be dug up and used. To prepare it for its move into a bonsai container, pot it back into decreasing pot sizes over 6 months in 1cm (½in) steps. This will involve some root pruning of the tap and major roots and reducing the top growth by approximately 40 per cent, removing any unwanted laterals and leaves.

Meanwhile, shape the branches gently to the desired position with loose wire ties.

Top: A wonderful old bonsai specimen of the cultivar 'Pink Rain', with a beautiful gnarled trunk. This lax fuchsia has very pretty small pink flowers, which makes it highly suitable to bonsai.

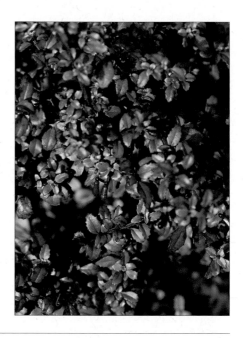

Right: 'Lottie Hobby' is an Encliandra hybrid with quite strong and vigorous wiry growth, small leaves and tiny red flowers. It is an excellent cultivar for creating topiary sculptures around a 3D wire shape.

PLANTING A BONSAI USING AN ESTABLISHED HARDY FUCHSIA

1 Dig up the plant (in this case the hardy 'Genii') while it is dormant, and prune the roots so that it fits into your bonsai container. When dormant, the plant survives this.

2 Prune the top growth back to a number of short growths. Further pruning will be needed later when growth starts. Remove any remaining old foliage.

3 Pot up in a gritty compost (soil mix) containing charcoal and blended to contain a lower level of nutrients than usual. This prevents too much rapid growth.

4 Gently water to settle the fuchsia into the container. Allow the plant to settle down for a few weeks, then start misting the wood to encourage it into growth.

TRAINING A TOPIARY SQUIRREL

1 Plant three fuchsias of the same variety (in this case 'Lottie Hobby') in a pot with a wide, stable base. Place a 3D mesh former of a squirrel over them and wire it to the pot.

2 Tease out some of the long wiry growths with a cane and move them to the desired position, filling areas of the shape that need extra growth, such as the feet and the tail.

3 Clip back the side growths that try to grow through the mesh with a pair of nail scissors. This will make them develop more side growths to fill the surface structure.

4 After some weeks, the growth reaches the top of the structure. Stop the growing tips and cut back a bit further to encourage side shoots to fill the structure at the top.

5 The growth has now filled the structure completely. Keep the structure clipped to maintain the shape but leave enough growth to enjoy the tiny flowers.

Also gradually expose the top of the uppermost roots (the nebari) by scraping away the top layer of compost (soil mix), and when inserting the fuchsia in a smaller pot, raise the height of the plant in its new container by putting more compost beneath it. When the plant is ready to move into a bonsai container, use special bonsai compost or seed compost with low nutrient levels mixed with some grit and charcoal. Prune the roots further, as necessary, and try to run the uppermost roots over a suitable smooth stone to add to the bonsai effect.

As soon as the danger of frosts has passed, grow the plant outside, protected from excessive direct sun either by artificial or natural shading. Feed with a quarter-strength balanced fertilizer once a week, keeping it moist but not saturated, and continue to shape the plant by removing large leaves and unwanted strong growth.

NOVELTY SHAPES

Commercially made wire mesh formers are readily available in many different shapes, but you can easily make one yourself if you want to try something different, with a spiral being the easiest shape. The best varieties for the job come from the Encliandra group and include 'Lottie Hobby', *F. microphylla* subsp. *hemsleyana*, *F. microphylla* subsp. *hidalgensis* and *F.* x *bacillaris*. These fuchsias have tiny leaves and grow quickly, filling and covering the structure in a season. They also have tiny flowers, and still produce them even when you clip the main shoots tightly to keep the shape. If you use a vigorous Encliandra cultivar, for example 'Lottie Hobby', it is quite possible to create a 60–100cm (2–3ft) tall figure in a season, starting from small plants in late winter or early spring.

Start by planting up to five fuchsia plants of the same variety, the number depending on the size and shape of the wire frame. Then secure the former to the pot, using wire. Ideally, you should stop the plants twice when young to initiate low branching, and they should at first be kept on the dry side to encourage rapid rooting through the pot. When the top growth reaches the edge of the wire shape, start to train and twist it along the wire, cutting back hard any growth that tries to grow straight outwards from the mesh.

If one part of the surface has a hole or a lack of growth, try to move some branches to this area, cutting back to increase branching and positioning the structure on its side for a few days if necessary, so that this part faces upright to increase the sap flow and therefore the growth. Direct the growths to fill the whole surface of the shape and keep the plants clipped regularly to maintain the shape.

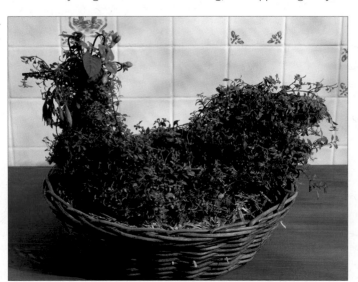

Left: A novelty chicken shape created by growing the fuchsia 'Lottie Hobby' and variegated thyme around a wire frame, bedding in moss and potting compost. Note the use of flowering tips of other fuchsias to represent the comb and wattle.

Planting in containers

Many gardens now have extensive patios, terraces and other paved or gravelled areas, and of course many have no exposed soil at all. With an imaginative choice of containers, and a careful selection of fuchsias and other plants, you can create all kinds of different moods, ambiences and garden styles in these areas. A tremendous variety of different containers in many materials and colours are available from nurseries, garden centres, DIY superstores and specialist potteries. When choosing a container, remember that fuchsias like to keep their roots cool. Porous terracotta (clay) pots are the perfect choice, as the evaporation cools them down and they also help keep the compost (soil mix) aerated.

DRAINAGE

The most important requirement for fuchsias is good drainage, because although they love moisture, they detest waterlogging of the growing medium. Therefore, it is vital to ensure the provision of good drainage holes and to increase the number or size of the holes if they are not good enough for the purpose.

To protect the pot's drainage, especially in large containers where a soil-based compost is used, it is important to add drainage material to the bottom of the container to ensure the holes stay open. An ideal way is to place curved pieces of broken clay pots over the holes, followed by a layer of stones of various sizes, broken polystyrene (Styrofoam) or similar materials. When you add the compost on top of these pieces, they will stop most of it reaching the bottom of the pot and potentially blocking the drainage holes. To further improve drainage, you can stand large clay or stone pots on special feet which raise the pot approximately 2.5cm (1in) off the ground.

PLANTING LARGE CONTAINERS

The best time to plant up large containers with fuchsias is in the spring, when the plants are growing strongly and the roots will rapidly expand and penetrate the compost. A good range of plants are

Top: Standing on steps, this large mixed pot is planted with busy Lizzie, helichrysum, pelargoniums and the fuchsias 'Coralle', 'Seventh Heaven', 'Cambridge Louie' and 'Happy Wedding Day'.

PLANTING A LARGE POT

1 Assemble all the plants you wish to use with the large pot, in this case, a terracotta (clay) bell pot. Add crocks over the drainage holes and additional material such as broken polystyrene to improve drainage.

2 Part-fill the pot with compost (soil mix) so the plants may be stood in the pot. Arrange them putting the trailing plants around the edges. Lift the plants out and replace with the same sized empty pot.

3 Add more compost to the large pot, working it around the edges of the empty pots. Remove the empty pots one by one and plant the chosen plants into their correct positions.

4 Add more potting compost to fill depressions and voids. Gently lift and drop the pot on to a soft surface to settle the contents. Water in sparingly and grow on in a sheltered area.

available in the spring, since the garden centres and nurseries expect and prepare for the demand. Plan in advance the plants you would like to use and either grow them yourself or purchase them. The actual week of planting will depend on your local climate and what extra protection, such as a greenhouse, you have available to protect from them late frosts.

You can apply the planting technique described in the pictorial sequences for the planting of any large container. Additionally, use this technique for any type of plant grown or purchased in a smaller pot when you transfer it to a larger one, as it minimizes the damage to the plants and makes it easier to fill all of the spaces with compost, not leaving any empty spaces. You can choose to add slow-release fertilizer to the compost or feed regularly with liquid fertilizers, but be careful to do either one or the other, or you may risk over-feeding or starving the plants. There is sufficient fertilizer in the new compost to last for about four to six weeks after planting, so do not start adding either type before this time has elapsed.

It is also very important to control the watering for the first weeks, keeping the container rather dry until plants have become established and made good root growth through the container. Therefore, if you are growing newly planted containers outside, take the precaution of keeping them under cover when heavy rain is likely, to prevent them becoming too wet, as this will slow down the growth.

PLANTING A CHIMNEY POT

1 Use a 'Bishop' type of chimney pot as an ideal planter. Cut a piece of heavy wire mesh to fit as a support. Add a piece of finer mesh on to the top.

2 Add a layer of coarse stone chipping to act as a bed for the compost (soil mix), to prevent it from washing through before the roots have established.

3 Add a layer of compost on to the support. Choose the plants you want to use and find empty plastic pots of the same size they are planted in.

4 Set the empty pots in evenly and add compost until it is up to the lowest parts of the cowl, working in well around the pots.

5 Knock a small plant out of its pot, lift its corresponding empty pot out and drop the plant into the empty hole. Repeat with the other plants.

6 Add more potting compost to fill any voids. Settle the contents, then water them in sparingly. Grow on in a sheltered position.

Right: An informal arrangement of terracotta (clay) urn pots piled on stones, with flowering fuchsia plants growing among them.

Far right: This large specimen fuchsia plant is growing in a decorative plastic pot and just coming into flower. Beside it is a variegated ivy, and behind it a small statue surrounded by a *Fatsia japonica*.

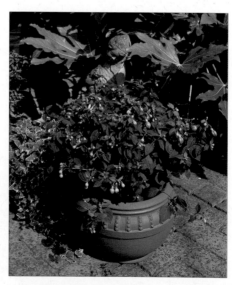

Planting in hanging baskets

Fuchsias are a natural choice for hanging baskets. The variety and profusion of fuchsia flowers and their amenable growing habits make them ideal plants in this situation, particularly the double-flowered cultivars. Fuchsias look wonderful both on their own and mixed with companion foliage and flowering plants. Look around in your own neighbourhood, or at nurseries and garden centres, at the types of fuchsia cultivars and companion plants grown in baskets. This should help you decide what combinations to try in your own baskets. Remember that they come with different habits, some have almost upright growth but big double flowers weigh down the branches, while others cascade.

BASKETS AND LINERS

There are many different types of basket to choose from, constructed from PVC wire, plastic, wicker, metal strips and other materials. The baskets usually hang by chains from a support, and it is important to ensure that these chains are strong enough to hold up a fully watered basket with a lot of plant growth, blowing about in the wind.

If you wish to have plants growing through the sides, pick an open-mesh type of basket. This type needs lining before planting: choices for the lining include sphagnum moss, pre-formed liners or plastic. The pre-formed liners are available in different sizes, and are made of many different fibres, such as coconut, jute and

Top: A mixed hanging basket planted with the fuchsias 'Ruth King', 'Golden Marinka', 'Harry Grey' and 'Auntie Jinks'.

sisal, some lined with plastic inside. A cheap solution is to make plastic liners out of empty PVC compost bags, remembering to place the black side facing outward. It is better to line the wicker type of basket with plastic, to reduce the wetting of the wicker and retain the compost (soil mix).

PLANTING

The best time to plant up a summer basket is early to mid-spring. Gather the plants you want to use and ensure they are well watered. Use a mixture of multi-purpose compost and vermiculite or perlite, as described earlier. You may want to add water-retaining gel, and/or slow-release fertilizer.

The step sequence opposite shows how to plant a basket with plants only on the upper surface; this is often all you need for

a good display, especially if you are using plants with long trailing stems around the edge, such as ivy or petunias. However, if you want to have plants coming out of the sides, you should begin by cutting small crosses in the liner. (Cutting is not necessary if the basket is only lined with moss.) Insert the plants from outside the basket, before you start filling it with compost.

GROWING ON

Once you have planted the basket, if frosts are still threatened, leave the basket in the greenhouse at night, taking it outside on suitable warm days to harden off. Keep the basket on the dry side to encourage the roots to penetrate and spread through

Below: Hanging baskets come in a wide variety of shapes and sizes. This one is a long cone-shaped wicker basket.

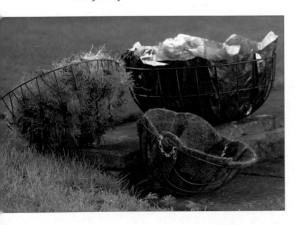

Above: A range of wire baskets displayed with different liners. Clockwise from the front: a 30cm (12in) basket with a pre-formed felt liner; a 36cm (14in) basket lined with sphagnum moss; a 40cm (16in) basket with a liner made from an old compost bag.

the compost. Turn the basket a quarter of a turn every one to two days. If you wish, you can pinch out the fuchsia growing tips one more time to increase the number of flowering shoots, but remember this will delay flowering by a few weeks. Increase the watering as the plants grow and their roots fill the basket.

When all danger of frosts has passed, hang the basket in its final position, making sure that the hook is strong and sturdy enough to take the weight. Water when necessary, remembering to increase the watering as the plants grow, the day length increases and the temperatures rise. Baskets will dry out very quickly on warm, dry and windy days, and may need watering more than once a day.

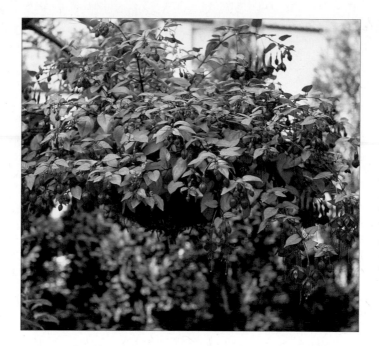

Left: A hanging basket suspended from a tree branch, planted with multiple plants of the old French cultivar 'Marinka'. This beautiful cultivar has single bright red flowers, and the sepals cup the corolla. Take care when moving this fuchsia from the greenhouse as the leaves often mark with rapid temperature changes.

PLANTING A HANGING BASKET

1 Assemble the plants you will use together with the basket and the liner or lining material and a suitable multi-purpose compost (soil mix) mixed with additives.

2 Stand the basket on a large pot to keep it upright. Line the basket using a preformed liner, cut plastic such as old compost bags, or sphagnum moss, as in this case.

3 Add the compost, pushing it well to compress the moss into the basket wire frame. Add enough compost to ensure the plants will sit at a level slightly below the basket rim.

4 Begin inserting the plants, with the largest and upright plants in the centre. Plant the trailing plants at the edge, angling them outwards.

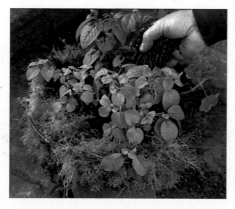

5 Add the rest of the plants and fill any voids with compost. Leave the surface higher at the edges. This will make watering easier.

6 Settle the contents and water in sparingly. The fuchsias used here were the cultivars 'Claudia', 'Postiljon' and 'Swingtime'.

Planting in borders

Fuchsias make excellent plants for all kind of borders and beds as temporary summer residents. You can use them within bedding schemes, for edging and even in the rockery. They are a great way to add extra height to the border and create an eye-catching feature. They can be used throughout the summer, then either discarded in the autumn or potted up and overwintered for use the next year, using the techniques described later. If you are growing standard fuchsias or other trained fuchsia shapes in large pots with a view to overwintering them in the greenhouse, you can sink the pots in the border, so that it is easy to lift them at the end of the season.

SOIL PREPARATION

Fuchsias are quite tolerant of different soil types, but they do not like being waterlogged and they are quite greedy feeders. They will benefit from extra organic matter, such as leaf mould, well-rotted manure, garden compost or any equivalent materials, which will improve both fertility and texture. If the soil is very heavy, you could also dig in some horticultural grit. The best time to dig over the border is in the winter or early spring, so that you can leave it a while to settle.

TEMPORARY BEDDING

Any fuchsias bedded out in a border as temporary residents should be planted normally, with the plant crown (the soil level in the pot) at ground level. If you are planting out any double-flowering types with heavy blooms where the growths are a little soft or lax, stake and tie the main branches to give some additional support. They still benefit from a good addition of organic material in the soil, but drainage is not as critical in summer as in winter. Use a good general fertilizer when planting, and

feed again during the summer following the manufacturer's instructions.

Plant out fuchsias with a sufficient distance between the plants, for them to fill up the spaces by the middle of the summer. The actual planting distance depends on the size of the plant when first planted out, and the typical growth of the variety. As an example, you might be planting out the Triphylla cultivar 'Thalia' from 12cm (5in) pots, each plant having about 20–30cm (8–12in) of growth. They will need to be spaced with about 30cm (12in) between

Top left: This half standard of the cultivar 'Thalia' is in full flower, with clusters of orange-red flowers standing out from the dark leaves. It is growing in a pot sunk into the ground and is supported against a wall with wire stays.

Left: This collection of hardy fuchsias is flowering beautifully in an oval bed in the middle of a lawn. Behind are more hardy fuchsias in a straight border at the edge of the lawn, protected by a hedge.

the centres of each plant. One of the best ways to do this if you want blocks of the same variety is in a triangular layout. Space two plants 30cm (12in) apart, and put the next one at a point halfway between and 26cm (10in) behind the first two, forming an equilateral triangle. Extend this to a three-by-three triangle with three more plants, then a four-by-four with four more and so on. Using this arrangement of plants, you can create different shapes, ensuring the plants are always the correct distance apart. Of course, if you prefer a more natural look, you can just mix and match the plants as you wish.

Small, compact-growing fuchsias are excellent for use as edging, planted as shown in the step sequence above. Fuchsias that typically only grow to 30–45cm (12–18in), such as 'Tom Thumb' and 'Happy', or fuchsias with variegated or light foliage, such as 'Tom West', 'Abigail Reine' and 'Sunray', are good choices for edging plants.

PLANTING OUT STANDARDS

Standards are very useful to raise the height of a planting scheme, but they are tender even when grown from a hardy variety, and need returning to the greenhouse for frost protection during the winter. Before

planting out, harden them up by standing them outside during the day for two weeks, then finally overnight as well for another few days, with support to prevent them from falling over. Either plant them directly into the ground or sink their pots in the ground with their rims just above soil level.

The major additional requirement when planting out standard fuchsias is to ensure proper support for the head. Tie in the trunk and head well to a strong cane; some

Above: This pretty 'Mercurius', covered with masses of flowers, is growing in a beautiful dome shape in a border of bulbs.

additional support is a good idea, especially with younger standards that have not developed heavy wood. When planting close to a wall or fence, fix some horizontal struts and tie them to the main cane, or alternatively use a strong stake behind the plant with similar horizontal struts.

PLANTING FUCHSIAS AS EDGING PLANTS

1 Compact fuchsias, especially those with a light foliage colour, make excellent edging plants. Place the plants out first to find the correct positions.

2 Dig a suitable hole the correct size for the root ball, then knock the plant out of its pot, loosen the coiled roots and place it in the hole and firm the soil around it.

3 Repeat the process for all the other plants, spacing them out in such a way they will quickly grow together and form a pretty, uniform edging to the border.

4 When they are all planted, dress the soil with a general fertilizer and hoe it in carefully around the plants. Water in with a watering can fitted with a fine rose.

Planting a hardy fuchsia bed

Permanent planting of hardy fuchsias in the garden is a wonderful way to get a superb display of flowers from early summer to late autumn, with very little maintenance needed. There is a wide range of hardy fuchsias available, most of which can grow anything from 30cm (12in) up to 1.6m (5ft) in one season in a typical Zone 8–9 climate. There is also a good range of colours, varying from the common red-and-purple, through red-and-white, pink, pink-and-white to pure white. When you are planning to create a hardy fuchsia bed, a certain amount of preparation is advisable; as usual in gardening, careful planning in advance will give better and more long-lasting results.

THE SITE

It is important to look long and hard at the area you are going to use for planting your hardy fuchsias.

- Good drainage should be at the top of your list. Waterlogged soil in the winter will kill the fuchsias, so avoid low-lying areas likely to flood. Heavy soils need improvement with organic matter and anything else to improve drainage, such as grit or sand.
- Wind exposure, especially in an area with very cold winter temperatures, will mean you can only use the hardiest varieties.
- Fuchsias prefer partial shade, but hardy ones planted in the ground will tolerate the sun quite well as long as they are watered in long dry spells. If you can provide some shade from the midday and early afternoon sun, that will help to avoid stress on hot days.

SOIL PREPARATION

The area you have chosen to plant your hardy bed needs preparation. The preparation depends on the soil type: sandy soils need extra organic material, and heavy clay types need both organic material and coarse sand and grit to improve drainage. Dig it over and remove any perennial weeds. Ideally do this in the autumn so that the area can settle and weather in the winter.

Top: A hardy fuchsia bed contrasting with the long thin stems of the purple-flowered *Verbena bonariensis* in the background.

Right: An established bed full of hardy fuchsias, their stems entwining and reaching heights of more than 2m (6ft).

PLANNING

Read the directory in this and other books, and obtain catalogues from different nurseries. In these, you will find descriptions and illustrations of different hardy fuchsias, with their flowers and colours, their growth habits and the heights to which they will grow in a typical season. Note that these are average measurements, and are based on areas where winter frosts

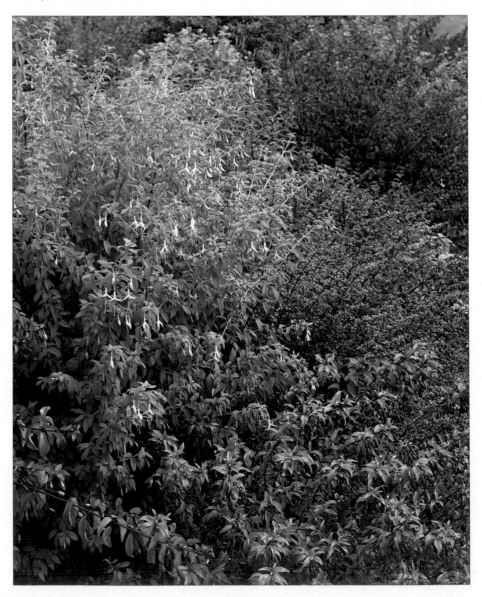

will cut them down to the ground. If you are lucky enough to live in a milder area, they will continue to grow from toward the top of the previous year's growth and will reach greater heights each year.

Make a list of the varieties you want, and plan how to plant them, thinking about the heights, colours and any other types of plants you will interplant. Generally, the larger plants should be at the back and the smaller ones at the front.

OBTAINING PLANTS

If you have a greenhouse, you can probably get some cuttings of hardy fuchsias from friends and neighbours and grow them on over the winter. If you wish to order from a nursery, do so in good time, as ideally you should have well-developed plants in

Right: This fuchsia plant of the Triphylla 'Thalia' is in full flower alongside a leafy canna, with other vividly yellow and orange flowering cannas in the background.

13–15cm (5–6in) pots by planting-out time in the late spring or early summer. Place the plants outside on suitable days in mid-spring to harden them off, and finally leave them outside in their pots for a few days before planting out.

PLANTING

First place the plants you are going to use, still in their pots, in their final positions on the bed to get the spacing correct. Mark the positions with canes and remove the plants. For each position, scoop out a shallow depression over a diameter of four to five times the pot diameter and to

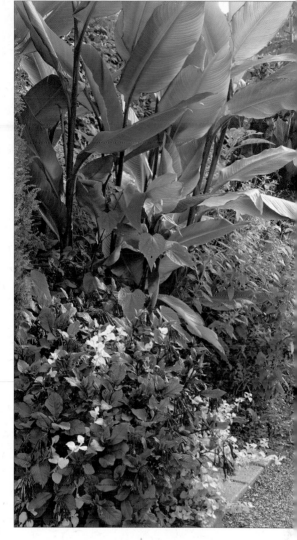

PLANTING A HARDY FUCHSIA

1 Scoop a shallow depression 65cm (26in) wide and 10cm (4in) deep. The cane shows the level of the soil surrounding the depression.

2 Dig a hole large enough at the centre to take the root ball of the plant, forking in some general fertilizer at the bottom.

3 Place the hardy fuchsia plant in the hole so that the surface of the soil around the plant is level with the base of the depression.

4 Firm the soil, then, as the plant grows through the summer, gradually pull back the soil around the plant to fill the depression.

a depth of 7.5–10cm (3–4in) at the centre. Then make a hole at the centre of the depression slightly larger than the pot, dig in some fertilizer and plant the fuchsia. The soil surface around the plant should be at the level of the bottom of the depression. Firm the soil and water the plant in well. The crown of the plant is now 7.5–10cm (3–4in) lower than the general soil level in the bed. Repeat this procedure for all the other plantings.

As the fuchsias grow and establish through the summer, gradually pull back the soil, filling the depression around each plant back to its original level, so that you cover the plant crown by 7.5–10cm (3–4in) of soil, watering in dry periods. This added protection of the crown is essential for winter survival, and the first year is the most critical. Most hardy fuchsias, if they survive the first year of planting, will probably last for many years.

Planting a fuchsia hedge

In milder areas, it is possible to grow hardy fuchsias as exotic and eye-catching hedges. Hedges of the hardy cultivar 'Riccartonii' are a beautiful sight and quite common in the south-west of England and Ireland. In gardens, these make a good dividing hedge or an attractive low hedge grown against a fence. It is not a good idea to use fuchsias as boundary hedges except in very mild areas. Grow fuchsia hedges only in parts of the garden where the average winter conditions will not kill the wood down to the ground, so that you can easily maintain the structure of the hedge. If an extreme winter does occur, it is still possible to re-grow the hedge from the base.

USING FUCHSIAS FOR HEDGES

Grow the hedge from a row of plants of the same variety, as different plants develop at different rates and it would be difficult to keep them all in shape as a hedge. Since the hedge will be in flower from midsummer until the end of the autumn, opportunities to clip and shape the hedge

Top: This low *Fuchsia magellanica* hedge, which is dripping with flower in the summer, delineates the edge of a sloping driveway from a neighbouring property.

are quite limited unless you are willing to sacrifice some flowers, so do not expect an ultra-smooth, neat surface – the result will be informal, but full of colour.

PREPARATION

Plant fuchsia hedges in a shallow trench to give the maximum protection to the crowns of the plants. You will be expecting your hedge to last for some years, so good preparation of the ground is important. Avoid any areas that are prone to waterlogging in the winter,

or provide some additional drainage by digging in a coarse horticultural grit or sharp sand, in addition to incorporating plenty of organic material such as leaf mould or rotted manure. Finish the preparation by making a shallow trench 15cm (6in) deep, and 45cm (18in) wider than the desired width of the hedge.

Below: A vigorous hardy fuchsia growing more than 2.5m (8ft) tall alongside a brick wall and over a doorway in a garden in the south-west of England. This demonstrates how high a fuchsia hedge can grow in the right conditions.

PLANTING

Decide how tall and wide you wish the hedge to be, and select a suitable variety. If you want extra thickness, you can plant in a double staggered row. The plants should be spaced about 45cm (18in) apart, unless you are making a low hedge with a dwarf variety, when a spacing of 30cm (12in) is more appropriate. Estimate how many plants you will need and add a further 10 per cent as a safety margin.

The plants need to be healthy, growing well in 13cm (5in) pots, hardened off and ready for planting in the late spring. If you cannot grow these plants yourself, order them in good time from a reputable fuchsia nursery, making it clear that you are going to use them for a hedge. They will be glad to give you advice on suitable varieties. Plant the ready plants into the trench in a row, or a staggered double row, making sure that the top of the compost (soil mix) in the pot comes level with the base of the trench. Dress the row with a suitable balanced fertilizer and water the plants in well.

GROWING ON

Grow the plants on with the absolute minimum of pruning, just trimming any wayward branches and enjoying the flowering. Water the hedge well in any dry periods and give it an occasional foliar feed to boost the growth. Gradually pull the earth back into the trench so that the crowns of the plants are 15cm (6in) below soil level.

In mid-autumn, when the growth subsides, trim the shape of the hedge by removing any long straggly growth. Protect the plants with a mulch of leaves or other organic material. During the first winter, protect the hedge with fleece in any very cold frosty periods. In the next spring, when the new growths have started to appear, remove any dead branches and give the live growth another trim to get the desired shape. It is well worth propagating or overwintering spare plants of your chosen variety ready to replace any which may have succumbed to the first winter.

Right: A *Fuchsia magellanica* hedge, bordering a path in Guernsey. It was clipped well early in the year but is now dripping with flowers, and still has a good shape.

PLANTING A HEDGE

1 When planting a hedge alongside a fence, set out the plants on the prepared soil, staggering them 30cm (12in) apart.

2 Dig a hole in the soil deeper than the depth of the pot. This ensures the crown of the plant will be well below the soil surface.

3 Knock the plant out of its pot, and loosen any long roots. Plant the fuchsia at the bottom of the hole and cover with soil.

4 Water in well, and add a mulch of composted bark or similar material to help reduce weed growth and retain moisture.

Pruning fuchsias

Fuchsias need pruning at different times of the year for various reasons. It can be simply a need to remove some wayward branches that have grown across a pathway. It may be part of re-invigorating a plant to create numerous new flowering shoots, or the pruning of a hedge after you have enjoyed the flowers through the summer. The first and most important point to consider before pruning a fuchsia is that the tools you will use – secateurs, pruners, saws and other implements – are clean and sharp. A clean cut heals more quickly and is less likely to die back or become diseased. Try to prune fuchsias when they are dormant, but when that is impossible try to ensure the soil is dry by withholding water.

REQUIRED PRUNING

Fuchsias are very amenable to hard pruning, quickly sprouting new growth. Trained structures need annual pruning to maintain the desired size and flowering density. Older plants in large pots may need some root pruning during potting down.

PRUNING PRINCIPLES

Although some of these points may be obvious, it is worth considering them before undertaking fuchsia pruning. Secateurs and other implements are – or should be – very sharp, so you should always wear gloves and exercise care when using this type of cutting equipment. Cut back fuchsias, like most shrubs, to a pair of buds so that when hard pruned, they will always shoot from close to the cut. When using bypass pruners or secateurs to cut a side branch back to the main stem, use them so the cutting blade is closest to the main stem. This sometimes means reversing them in your hand but allows a closer cut. When cutting the stems, cut them at an angle rather than horizontally, then if they do bleed the sap is more likely to drip off. Use a proprietary sealing compound if cuts are large and bleed sap profusely.

HEDGES

Fuchsia hedges should be left to grow freely through the summer and autumn, apart from the tidying of any very wayward branches, so the production of flowers continues unabated. This means you carry out most of the cutting and shaping of the hedge in the autumn and winter.

In the autumn, cut the hedge to return it to its basic height and width, leaving some extra growth to help protect it through the winter. Then in the late winter, as the buds are beginning to break, cut it back to the actual required shape, removing any damaged and diseased branches. Look carefully for any gaps, especially low down, then manipulate and prune suitable growths to fill them. In the case of a large gap at the base, consider planting another plant of the same variety later in the year.

Top left: 'Constance' is a reliable hardy cultivar, easily pruned as a standard. It has double flowers with a pink tube, green-tipped pink sepals and a rose-mauve corolla.

HARDY FUCHSIAS

All hardy fuchsias should have soft growth removed in the autumn after the frosts have blackened the foliage. This normally means removing about one-third of the growth. It helps to minimize dieback and prevents the plant loosening in the ground, blown about by the wind.

The time to prune hardy fuchsias depends on the winter conditions in your garden and which varieties you are growing. If the frosts kill the plants down to the ground each year, prune in the early spring as the fuchsias start to send shoots up from the base. Cut all of the dead stems back hard down to 5–15 cm (2–6in) of the

PRUNING CUTS

1 Use sharp secateurs to prune back a fuchsia stem as close as possible to new buds without damaging them. This ensures a minimum of dead wood, which may become diseased.

2 This is a pot plant of *F. denticulata*, pruned back hard to the new growth, which is now shooting well. When potted on, it will grow to a large shrub by the end of the summer.

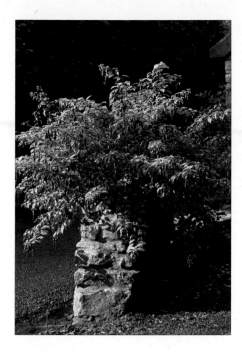

Above: A superb plant of the hardy cultivar 'Genii' in full flower, planted in a growing space created when building a stone wall. This plant is cut back hard every year and grows vigorously again.

ground and the fresh growths will make a new shrub. If the wood above ground survives through the winter, prune them when they are as dormant as possible, normally late winter, watching for excessive sap bleeding from the cuts. You can cut back hard, or very lightly, depending what size you want to maintain the plants

WARMER CLIMATES

In frost-free areas, fuchsias will grow throughout the year, without the seasonally enforced winter rest common in far northern or southern latitudes. Fuchsias growing in these conditions need pruning to give the plants a resting period. During the winter, when the plants are growing more slowly, they are pruned to tidy up the growth and invigorate the plant again by encouraging strong growth from lower down in the plant structure. In these areas, fuchsias tend to be at their best in the late spring and early summer, then will often suffer with the midsummer heat before reviving in the late summer and autumn. A light pruning in the summer tidies up the plant and creates fresh growth, giving another good flowering display in the late summer and autumn.

ROOT PRUNING A FUCHSIA

1 Cut the old growth back to a healthy pair of shoots, then prune the plant structure to get a nice evenly shaped plant.

2 Take the plant out of its pot and remove as much of the compost (soil mix) from the root ball as possible, with a cane or plant label.

3 Cut any long woody tap roots that will prevent the fuchsia from being moved into the pot of the desired size.

4 Re-pot the pruned fuchsia into the smaller pot with fresh compost, and then tap the pot on a hard surface to settle the contents.

PRUNING A HARDY FUCHSIA

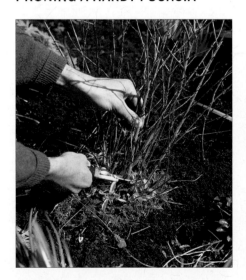

1 A hardy fuchsia has had last year's growth killed back to the ground by the winter frosts. In early spring, when the first shoots start to appear at the base, prune back to the ground.

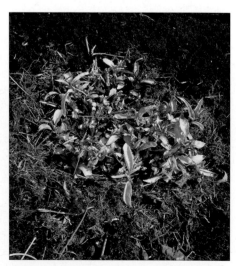

2 In a few weeks, several new shoots are growing from the base of the plant and by midsummer the plant will be flowering heavily again as a nicely shaped shrub.

Overwintering fuchsias

Gardeners living in the colder parts of the world, where there are periods of the year when the temperature is below freezing, can keep non-hardy fuchsias alive through the winter using various techniques depending on the facilities available. A lot depends on how you wish to grow fuchsias, and the type and size of your plants. A greenhouse, especially a heated one, is probably the best facility for overwintering fuchsias, but there are many other possibilities. You can use a frost-free garage or cellar, a conservatory, a spare room in the house kept cool with minimum heating, or even bury the plants in a prepared site in the garden. Any of these methods can allow fuchsias to survive cold winters.

HARDY FUCHSIAS

With the benefit of proper planting and a little extra care, hardy fuchsias will survive even quite cold winters where they are planted in the garden. The first year for a newly planted hardy fuchsia is always the most challenging, but by using the recommended planting method and pulling back the soil around the plant so the crown is 7.5–10cm (3–4in) below the surface, you will give it a good chance of survival. After the first frosts have killed the leaves, cut back the plants by about one-third to ensure removal of most of the soft growth and reduce the chances of wind-rock loosening the plant. Further, protect the crown with a layer of leaves, straw, or a similar material, and renew the coverage whenever necessary throughout the winter.

Top: Fuchsias cut back and stored underneath the staging on the floor of a frost-free greenhouse over the winter. The plants will quickly come back to life in the early spring.

Right: The view inside a heated greenhouse in the winter. Fuchsia plants are growing on the staging at the back and back left, kept in green leaf with minimum heat.

PROTECTING A HARDY FUCHSIA

1 Add a mulch of leaves or straw over the crown of a hardy fuchsia to give it some extra protection to survive the winter frosts.

2 Other mulching materials, such as moss peat, dry bracken or chipped bark, will also help to protect the plant.

PREPARING TENDER FUCHSIAS

Allowing tender fuchsias in pots to stay outside through one or two light frosts can be beneficial to help to induce dormancy. However, if you have a lot of plants, or if the weather can change suddenly in your area to severe frosty conditions, you can induce dormancy by drying and pruning.

Allow the pots to dry out as much as possible, then cut the plants back by two-thirds, remove all the remaining leaves and give the wood a spray of insecticide to kill any overwintering insects, if these have been causing problems. Leave the plants on their sides for a few days to ensure the cuts heal and avoid any sap bleeding from the cuts running down the stems and causing future dieback problems. Large mixed containers and baskets can be broken up, the plants separated and potted up, then treated in the same way. Tender plants in beds can be left until the first frosts kill the foliage, then they should be lifted, the loose soil shaken off, potted up and again treated like pot plants.

WINTER STORAGE

In a frost-free or heated greenhouse, place plants on the floor or on the staging, keeping the compost (soil mix) just slightly moist. Open the manual greenhouse vents whenever possible on warmer days to improve ventilation and decrease humidity. A fan in the greenhouse will also help stop the atmosphere becoming stagnant. The plants in a heated greenhouse will start growing new shoots in mid- to late winter, while in a frost-free greenhouse they will shoot from late winter to early spring.

Storage in an unheated greenhouse will depend on your local weather conditions. In milder areas, they might survive with just a covering of fleece on the few frosty nights, but in colder areas, they may need burying in trenches in the greenhouse border, lying them down on their sides. In areas with extremely long, cold winters, it is not possible to use an unheated greenhouse to overwinter fuchsias.

You can store plants with the compost just moist in a frost-free cellar or garage by leaving them in trays covered by fleece, or wrapped in paper and stacked on their sides in boxes. Inspect them periodically (once a month should be sufficient) to make sure they have not dried out, and remove any long white shoots from the wood to prevent them removing nutrients and vigour from the plant.

Storage in a cool conservatory or spare room is a little trickier, since the temperature will be more than 5°C (41°F) and the plants will continue to grow. Therefore, they need as much light as possible, occasional watering and regular turning. If by the spring they have made too much spindly weak growth, simply cut back this new growth quite hard before placing them back outside, where they will soon start growing normally with strong growth and short internodal joints.

OVERWINTERING A TENDER FUCHSIA

1 Dig out a tender fuchsia, planted out over the summer in a border. Take care to lift most of the main roots with the plant.

2 Clean all the loose soil off the plants and carefully pot up in dry potting compost (soil mix). Tap the pot to settle in the compost.

3 Remove the leaves and trim back the branches by one half. Spray the wood with a combined insecticide and fungicide.

4 When the spray has dried, water it sparingly and put it away in the greenhouse or other chosen storage area.

STORING POT PLANTS IN BOXES

1 After drying off pot plants that are ready for storage, wrap them up in newspaper and place them in a storage box, with the pots stacked on their sides.

2 Pack the gaps with straw or more newspaper as insulation and put the box away in a cool frost-free area over the winter. Straw is better as it allows more ventilation.

Pests and diseases

Fuchsias are quite robust and strong-growing plants, generally free from serious diseases. If you give them the right conditions and care, you should not have any problems. Slugs and snails, often among the worst pests in the garden, tend not to attack fuchsias. Keep an eye out for any signs of damage – this should be done at night in some cases, but mostly can be a part of your normal routine, especially with pot-grown plants, which you water and turn regularly. In the next pages there is a comprehensive list of the main pests and diseases that affect fuchsias, with some suggestions of techniques and treatments for keeping them under control.

APHIDS (*Aphis*)

These sap-sucking insects belonging to many different species are normally green, red or black. Adults appear in spring, under the leaves and on the stems and growing tips; heavy infestations can distort the latter. The aphids also excrete a sweet, sticky fluid (loved by ants, which sometimes 'farm' the aphids) on which small, black fungal spots known as sooty moulds can grow. Often the damage is slight and control unnecessary, but you can squash them between finger and thumb, or remove them with a jet of water. In severe cases, spray with insecticidal soap or an aphid-specific insecticide.

Top: A honeybee visiting a flower of 'Alan Titchmarsh' to collect nectar. A serious exhibitor would discourage bees because of the damage they cause to the flowers.

CAPSID BUG
(*Lygocoris pabulinus*)

This small, green, fast-moving insect can cause a lot of damage to fuchsias, especially those grown outside. They are difficult to see and as a defence mechanism, they fall to the ground and play dead. If your garden has many shrubs, hedges or overhanging trees, you are more likely to have capsid bugs. They are sap-sucking insects and make small holes in the leaves, especially in the growing tips, around which the tissue dies. Then as the growth of the leaves continues, these dead areas tear into small holes with distortion of the growing tips and loss of flower buds. This can severely delay flowering because the growth has to restart from lower leaf joints. Spray with a systemic insecticide or insecticidal soap at the first sign of damage.

ELEPHANT HAWK MOTH
(*Deilephila elpenor*)

The brown caterpillar of this impressive moth is nearly 7.5cm (3in) long, and feeds on fuchsias, *Chamerion angustifolium* (formerly *Epilobium angustifolium*) (rosebay willowherb or fireweed) or *Galium* (bedstraw). The adult feeds on nectar. It lays its eggs singly under the leaves, mainly in the months either side of midsummer, and the best control is to remove the eggs before hatching. The caterpillar feeds at night and is voracious, eating flower buds and leaves. In the day, they hide down in the plant, well camouflaged. At this stage they are hard to control, but if you find one on a specimen plant, you can move it to a fireweed, or even a less precious fuchsia that you do not mind it eating.

aphids

capsid bug

capsid bug damage

elephant hawk moth

elephant hawk moth caterpillar

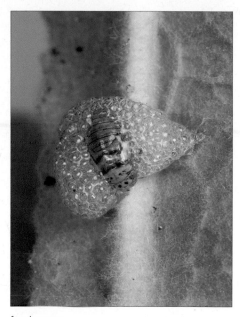

froghopper

FROGHOPPER
(*Philaenus spumarius*)

This insect, which can jump remarkable distances as an adult, is easy to recognize in its sap-sucking nymph phase, when it covers itself in a protective froth commonly known as cuckoo spit. Froghoppers do not cause serious damage but are easy to control by washing away the protective froth and killing the nymph.

FUCHSIA GALL MITE
(*Aculops fuchsiae*)

This is a very serious pest first identified in South America in the early 1970s, and in the southern USA in 1981. It was identified in France in 2003, the Channel Islands in 2006 and the first confirmed case in the UK was in 2007. It is not yet present in Australia or New Zealand. It is an eriophyoid mite 0.2–0.25mm ($\frac{1}{125}$–$\frac{1}{100}$in) long with a white to pale yellow wormlike body invisible to the naked eye. On the fuchsia, the symptoms start with a reddening of the leaves followed by thickening, fusing and galling of the growth, especially at the growing tips where growth stops. Current opinion is that large insects moving from plant to plant spread it, along with gardeners' fingers and tools. Treatments are being researched, but the best advice with severe infestations is to cut down and dispose of affected growth and spray with a suitable acaricide.

FUCHSIA RUST
(*Pucciniastrum epilobii*)

This is the most serious fungal disease affecting fuchsias. In the wild it needs both the *Chamerion angustifolium* (formerly *Epilobium angustifolium*) (rosebay willowherb or fireweed) and *Abies* (fir) to complete its life cycle, and because the former belongs to the same family as the fuchsia, it is sensible to remove it in your own garden and surroundings. The ripe spores, which can be carried by insects or on the wind, spread over large distances. The worst outbreaks tend to be in the late summer and autumn, but with a very wet spring and summer, it can be earlier. The affected leaves typically have pale or dark spots on the top, while underneath there are corresponding spots of orange pustules containing the growing fungal spores. When ripe, the spores shake off like a dust and are easily spread to other plants. As the leaves become more affected, they turn yellow and die. Once the rust becomes established, it is difficult to control. The best solution is to pick off and dispose of the infected leaves, and then spray the plant alternatively with a systemic insecticide followed by a protective fungicide. It is important to eradicate this before bringing in plants for winter storage, or the problem will persist into next year.

fuchsia gall mite

fuchsia rust

GREY MOULD
(*Botrytis cinerea*)

This fungal disease is most likely to occur in damp, stagnant conditions, and is usually at its worst over winter. The affected plant parts are covered in a grey, furry layer of fungus and the plant tissue rots. The spores have the ability to lie dormant until the right conditions occur. The best control is cleanliness, removing any diseased or dying leaves, especially those that fall into the joints between the branches and green stems. If they stay there then botrytis often sets in and migrates up the stems, killing them. In the greenhouse provide as much ventilation as possible all year round, even using fans when necessary.

RED SPIDER MITE
(*Tetranychus urticae*)

This microscopic arachnid loves the hot, dry conditions hated by fuchsias. Despite the name, only in autumn do the overwintering females take on this colour. The normal adult colour varies between white and green, with two spots on its back. Being minuscule, the mites are hard to see with the naked eye, and you are more likely to find their fine webs. The mites live on the backs of leaves and suck sap from the leaf cells, making the foliage turn brown and die. A severe infestation can result in considerable defoliation. Attacks are most likely to occur inside the

grey mould

greenhouse, but can occur outside in hot conditions. Suitable preventive measures are increasing the shading and humidity, and using a biological control or spraying with a pesticide (but not the two together). It is also important to sterilize the greenhouse in autumn because the mites will linger over winter in nooks and crannies. A new control based on a networked polymer system sprayed on to the back of the leaves works by covering the mites and eggs and killing them.

TORTRIX MOTH (*Tortricoidea*)

These small moths lay large clusters of greenish-white eggs on the underside of fuchsia leaves in spring and early summer. The small caterpillars emerge and eat about halfway through the leaf from underneath, which gradually dies. Later they move from leaf to leaf on small silk strands, and even roll up one or two leaves and live inside them. The best control is to remove the eggs before hatching, and spray with a systemic insecticide.

red spider mite

tortrix moth caterpillars

VINE WEEVIL
(*Otiorhynchus sulcatus*)

This small beetle has a dull black body 8–9mm (⅓in) long, is nocturnal and eats small, semi-circular shaped pieces out of the leaves. This is irritating rather than serious, with the real damage coming after it lays its eggs in the surface of the compost (soil mix), because the resultant white grubs (about the same size as the adult) feed on the roots. This happens from late summer through autumn and winter, into early spring. The plant will start to look distressed, with the leaves turning yellow and limp. The roots may also become slightly loose in the pot, and dormant winter plants might die if grubs remain undetected, because they can eat the entire root system. Search for the adult weevils at night with a torch and kill on sight. They are quite slow moving and frequently play dead if you find them during the daytime. They have a very hard exoskeleton and need a lot of force to squash them. You can also water in an insecticide in late summer or use composts with an insecticide included, but only use with ornamental plants, not edible crops. A biological nematode is also available.

WHITEFLY
(*Trialeurodes vaporariorum*)

Also called the 'ghostfly', this is a white 1.5mm (¹⁄₁₆in) long flying insect that lives mainly under leaves, where it sucks the

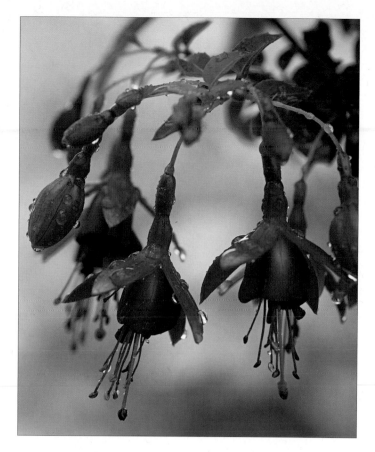

sap and leaves its scale-like nymphs. Whitefly nymphs damage the foliage, and their sugary excretions encourage the growth of sooty mould. Infestations are more likely in the greenhouse, but they can also occur outside. Growing French marigolds (*Tagetes patula*) in the greenhouse will deter the pests, but will not help if they are already present.

Check regularly under the leaves and kill any individuals you find. Yellow sticky strips trap the adults and act as an alert. When a plant is disturbed, the pests immediately fly up, resulting in mini-clouds in the case of severe infestations. Control whitefly using the predatory wasp *Encarsia formosa*, which feeds on the nymphs, or an insecticide spray, but not both.

Left: 'Tom Thumb', a dwarf-growing hardy cultivar is shown here with its red and purple single flowers dripping with water after heavy rain. When fuchsias are continuously wet, they are much more prone to fungal diseases – especially botrytis, but also rust.

vine weevil grubs and root damage

whitefly

CALENDAR
OF CARE

Fuchsias are undemanding plants, and many of the hardy varieties, once planted in the garden, will give pleasure for years with little or no attention. However, if you want to grow the more showy, non-hardy fuchsias, or to try training shapes or propagating your own plants, you will need to know what to do when, to ensure the best results.

This calendar of care describes the best time to carry out important tasks, such as encouraging dormant plants back into life, re-potting shooting plants to give them a good boost, caring for standards to make sure they will flower well from year to year, taking cuttings and planting up hanging baskets and containers, all shown season-by-season. It has tips for maintaining a hardy fuchsia bed and ways to keep fuchsias at their best through the summer with correct watering, feeding and protection of the roots from the sun, and gives details of how to prepare fuchsias for the dormant or slow-growing winter storage period.

Left: In midsummer, the stunning large double flowers of the fuchsia 'Marcus Graham' look fantastic. They have a waxy white tube, broad white sepals with a pink flush, and a full salmon-pink corolla with lighter splashes.

Top left: The striking white and deep blue single flowers of the recently released cultivar 'Geoff Oke', named in honour of the secretary of the British Fuchsia Society, make it a superb small patio pot plant.

Top middle: With a long deep pink tube, green sepals and an orangey corolla, the flowers of 'Jungle' are borne on spreading growth.

Top right: 'Ruth King' has double flowers with a pink tube and sepals and a lilac and white compact corolla, excellent for the centre of a mixed basket.

Spring care

Spring is often the most exciting time for the fuchsia grower, with many things to do and the fuchsias developing rapidly. You may be taking cuttings, re-potting plants, visiting nurseries to buy new and replacement plants, shaping and growing on fuchsias and planting up baskets and containers. Fuchsias will be growing very quickly and you can end up rushing from one project to the other, having to look after far more cultivars than you ever intended to grow. Once you are successful at taking cuttings, you may have too many healthy new plants, and it is very difficult to throw any of them away. Take heed of the advice of an experienced fuchsia grower, and stick to the plan you made in the winter.

IN THE GREENHOUSE

Throughout the early spring months, temperatures in the greenhouse can vary widely. On sunny days it can get very hot, while during the night temperatures can still drop below freezing. Some shading will be required on the inclined glass that faces the sun to prevent scorching of young plants.

Fuchsias will be growing very strongly and need pinching, potting on and turning, but don't forget that any plants needed for early flowers in the garden will take 10–12 weeks from the last pinch to begin flowering. If there are any overwintered plants that were not re-potted in the late winter, these should be done in early spring, potting down if necessary.

POTTING ON

1 Use a smaller pot inside the next-sized pot as a mould and fill the gap with potting compost (soil mix). Gently lift out the inner pot.

2 Knock the plant out of its pot and drop it into the prepared mould. Tap on the ground to settle the contents, and gently water in.

Continue to take cuttings of plants you want to propagate, especially those that you bought recently. Move plants outside on suitable days to start the hardening-off process. Start to plant up containers ready for putting out permanently when all danger of frost has passed. Grow on any plants that you are training as standards

Top left: The small red-and-purple-flowered hardy cultivar 'David' is easy to bring into flower in the spring using a greenhouse. Many other hardy single-flowered fuchsias treated in this way can be encouraged to flower early.

Left: The trailing fuchsia 'Irene Sinton' needs removal of yellowing leaves and careful watering in the spring to avoid botrytis. The large double flowers have pink sepals and a pale lilac corolla splashed with pink, with red veining on the petals.

or other shapes, remembering to re-pot them, loosen their ties and remove the side shoots or pinch them out when required to maintain the shape.

Watch the plants closely for signs of pests and diseases, since at this time of year infestations can start. Aphids, in particular, can very rapidly infest plants, and it is better to catch them early. Toward the end of the spring, as the day length gets close to the maximum, apply additional shading to reduce the temperatures in the greenhouse.

THE HARDY BORDER

If you have plants in the hardy border that you have not cut back in late winter, prune them in the early spring when conditions are good and green shoots are appearing from the base of the plant. Clean out any germinating weeds from the border, give it a dressing of a general fertilizer, and hoe a mulch of garden compost into the soil surface. If there are any inter-planted bulbs, delay the hoeing until you are sure where they are to avoid damaging the shoots. If you have any spring-flowering shrubs among the fuchsias, wait until they have finished flowering, then prune them back to the desired shape and size, remembering how much growth they will make in the summer. Watering is not normally necessary except in exceptionally dry periods. Toward the end of the spring, when all danger of frosts has passed, plant new hardy fuchsias to fill any gaps, or replace those that have not survived the winter, remembering the design.

THE GARDEN

Plant out summer bedding fuchsias that have been properly hardened off at the end of the spring when the danger of frost has passed, and bring containers outside. Be ready to protect them with fleece if there is an unseasonable cold snap.

WARMER CLIMATES

By this time in the season, the plants are growing very strongly, and may already be in flower. Staking and tying, watering, feeding and mulching permanently planted specimens are the main tasks. Shading will also be required in the greenhouse and for other

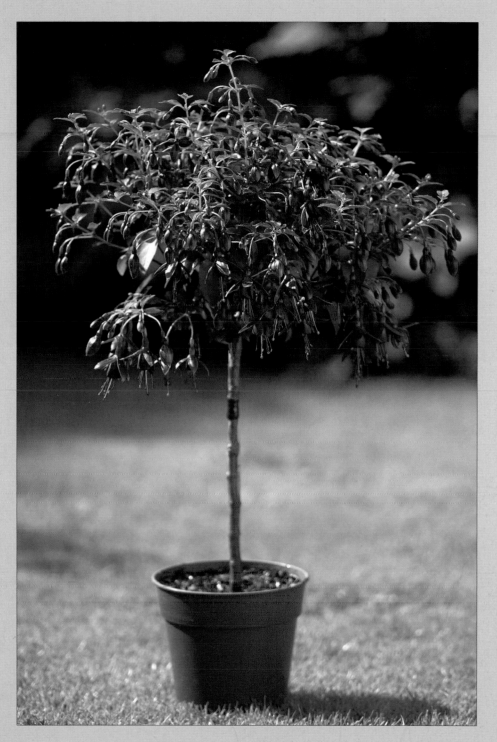

specimens planted out in exposed positions by the use of shade netting or similar protection against the strengthening sun.

THE SHADEHOUSE

This resource, which is essential in warmer climates, comes into its own at the end of the spring and allows pot plants to be grown when the temperatures regularly climb into the mid-30s Celsius (mid-90s Fahrenheit). It provides some shade from the sun, and a more humid atmosphere,

Above: Standing plants outside on mild spring days is important to harden up the growth. This miniature standard of the hardy cultivar 'Tom Thumb' has been put out in the open air on a bright day to kick-start this process.

which the fuchsias love. The care needed includes the regular watering, feeding and turning of the pot plants, watering the gravel base to increase humidity and moderate the temperature, and cleaning up any dropped leaves to avoid disease.

Summer care

Throughout the summer, fuchsias are at their peak. This is the time to take the opportunity to relax and enjoy them as much as possible. Visits to other gardens, displays and nurseries to see fuchsias in flower may give you some exciting ideas for the next season. However, you will need to carry on with some ongoing maintenance to keep your own plants at their best. The most important task is to continue with all necessary watering and feeding. The bulk of the watering and feeding applies to containers and baskets, but do not forget that the hardy border and summer bedding will need watering in long dry periods and will benefit from occasional additional foliar feeding to boost the growth.

GENERAL SUMMER TASKS

In the early summer, carry out any necessary further planting of the hardy bed, but complete this before midsummer to give the new plants the maximum time to establish before the winter. Hoe through the hardy border, or use a surface mulch to control the weeds until the fuchsias have made enough growth to suppress most of the weeds. If the border is under-planted with bulbs or inter-planted with shrubs, remove the old bulb leaves as soon as they have died down and prune any shrubs as required.

If you still have plants in the greenhouse, use maximum shading and ventilation and

Top: The lovely double flowers of 'Lillian Annetts' are a spectacular sight throughout the summer months.

keep the floors and any gravel on the benches wet to increase the humidity, but if the temperatures are regularly above 27°C (80°F) fuchsias will grow better outside or in a shadehouse.

WATERING AND FEEDING

All the plants in containers should be watered and fed regularly, and all old flowers and seedpods or berries should be removed to ensure the plants put all their energy into further flowering. Take special care with baskets, as these are most likely to dry out, especially in warm windy conditions, and are often difficult to rewet. When they are properly rewetted, there should be a steady slow dripping of water as the excess drains away. If the water

gushes through and stops draining quickly, check that the compost (soil mix) is properly wet, and if necessary take the basket down and immerse it in water until it is really soaked through.

Watering is best carried out in the early morning, and if necessary a little more in the evening, but try to avoid watering in the middle of the day, although wetting the ground around groups of containers to increase the humidity helps on the hottest days in the summer. If you have any plants in pots plunged into the borders, do not forget to water and feed these. Depending on how hot the temperatures are, fuchsias can sometimes go through a period in the hottest part of the late summer when the flowering is not very prolific, but as the days

DEADHEADING, REMOVING DEAD LEAVES AND WATERING

1 Use a pair of small nail scissors or a sharp knife to remove any dead or dying flowers to tidy up the plant. Removing these before the formation of seedpods promotes flowering.

2 Remove any seedpods (the ovaries left when the flowers fall) to ensure the plant continues to flower. If left on the plant, the seedpods will ripen to form edible (but not very tasty) berries or fruit.

3 Remove dead and dying leaves. If they fall into soft stem branches, they could cause botrytis and rot. They will often just snap off, using your fingers, or can be cut with scissors.

4 For fuchsias in pots up to 20cm (8in), a small watering can is easier to use than a large one. The flow of water is more controlled and easier to direct to the right place.

CHECKING TIES

1 Check that ties are not tight on trained shapes such as standards. If wire ties are used, this is very important, as they will cut into the growing stem and cause scarring.

2 Ties made using PVC tape are best as they hold the subject quite firmly with a wide area to spread the pressure. They also stretch slightly as the stem grows.

TAKING CUTTINGS

1 Take cuttings from the parent or stock plant, ideally cutting just below a node. If the growth is too short, take a cutting just above a node. These root nearly as well.

2 A gravel tray propagator, full of strips of cuttings in individual cells. While the top is open, check if any watering is required or any dead leaves need removing.

get shorter and the humidity returns in the mornings, there will be a second flush of heavy flowering.

TRAINED SHAPES

Any plants that you are growing into standards and other trained shapes will need continuing attention, with further stopping, tying, turning and potting on as needed. Remove any flower-buds produced.

Keep an eye out for any sign of pests and diseases and take prompt action, if necessary. The most likely pests are aphids, red spider mite, whitefly and moth caterpillars throughout the summer, and the main disease is fuchsia rust in late summer and early autumn.

SUMMER CUTTINGS

You can take cuttings in the summer, but it is often difficult to find good cutting material without buds, and the temperatures can be too high for good rooting. Reserve your efforts for new cultivars, where you will perhaps only have one plant and need to propagate some more as an insurance against losing it. Try to find a cooler area to place the cuttings in the propagator – they should be out of direct sunlight but it should not be too dark.

Right: This large fuchsia, flowering in an old ornamental pot, will need plenty of watering and feeding during the hot summer months.

Autumn care

The autumn season is a busy one with many tasks to carry out, but the timing is very dependent on the nature of the weather. This is the time to preserve your fuchsia collection by preparing your plants for the rigours of winter. There are different methods and techniques that can be used depending on the facilities you have at your disposal and the local winter climate in your area. These guidelines are written for those readers who live in areas of the world that have frost in the winter, but for those who live in frost-free areas, the autumn season means simply pruning your plants to induce a dormant period and ensure that you have a bushy plant with fresh growth for the next year.

GENERAL AUTUMN TASKS

Any pot plants that you plan to overwinter in their current pots should be treated with a proprietary vine weevil killer, unless you have used a biological control earlier in the year. Otherwise, the eggs and larvae might eat the roots over the winter. An alternative is to pot back plants before putting away for the winter, removing any vine weevil. Potting back gives the plants fresh compost and encourages new, healthy root systems. You can also do this in the winter or early spring when conditions are suitable.

Take cuttings from any plants cut back at the end of the summer when they have made new shoots, and from any other

Top: Triphylla fuchsias will flower right through the autumn until the first frosts. Continue feeding the plants in order to maintain vigorous flowering.

plants you want to keep if you can find suitable non-flowering shoots.

Clean the greenhouse and staging, then sterilize it, clean the glass and remove the shading. Put back the insulation, if necessary, and check that the heating system (if any) is in good working order.

PREPARING PLANTS FOR DORMANCY

In mid-autumn, dry out any fuchsias you wish to store in a dormant state over the winter. When they are quite dry, cut them back by about two-thirds, and remove any remaining leaves. Leave the cut stems to heal over for a few days before watering

Right: With proper care, hardy cultivars such as 'Richard John Carrington' will continue flowering well into autumn. This cultivar has single flowers of bright cerise and blue-violet.

POTTING BACK

1 Stop watering until the plant is quite dry. Knock it out of its pot, in this case a 15cm (6in) one, then remove the old potting compost (soil mix).

2 A dry, gritty compost comes away easily from the plant. It now has only a small amount of compost left on it and is ready to re-pot into a smaller pot.

3 Choose the smallest pot the plant roots will comfortably fit into, in this case an 11cm (4¼in) pot. As plants become older, some root pruning may also be required.

4 Fill the new pot with fresh potting compost. Push it down well, ensuring that you fill all the gaps, tapping the pot to help it to settle, then water in sparingly.

again. If any stems continue to bleed sap, lay the pots on their sides until the bleeding has stopped so that the sap does not run back down the stems, causing rot. Spray the remaining wood and soil surface with a combined insecticide and fungicide to kill any overwintering pests or spores.

Store the plants for the winter in the greenhouse, either on the benches if the greenhouse is cold, or on the floor under the staging if it is heated to a minimum of 5°C (41°F). If you do not have a greenhouse, store them in a frost-free shed, cellar or garage, wrapping them in paper if necessary to keep the frost away.

Trained shapes that are to be stored in a dormant state in the greenhouse can be treated in a similar way, though the pruning needs to be appropriate to the shape. Clean off all the leaves and spray the wood with a suitable treatment against red spider mite, which tends to overwinter in the bark of old specimens. Trained shapes that are to be kept in green leaf should be sprayed to kill any insects, moved into the heated greenhouse in good time before the frosts and kept ticking over. These shapes are best stored standing upright.

LATE AUTUMN TASKS

When the first frosts are threatening, break up the hanging baskets, checking for any signs of vine weevil, and cut back and pot up any plants you want to keep for the next year. These plants are also good for encouraging into growth for early cuttings in a heated greenhouse. Treat any plantings in mixed pots, troughs and containers in the same way, while specimen plants can be simply cut back and overwintered in the same pot.

When the first frosts have blackened the leaves of any non-hardy fuchsias growing in the borders that you want to keep for the following year, lift the plants, cut back the stems by one-half to two-thirds, remove the dead leaves, then pot them up and store with good ventilation for a few days, and finally place them in storage. Lastly, clear away the dead leaves and compost them unless the plants have suffered from significant fuchsia rust, in which case the leaves should be disposed of.

CUTTING BACK A HANGING POT

1 Leave the hanging pot outside, allowing exposure to a few light frosts. Bring the pot into the greenhouse to dry out before pruning.

2 Using a sharp pair of secateurs, cut off all the long growths, plus any that are crossing each other or are weak or damaged.

3 When the pruning is completed, the plants have been cut back to the edge of the pot and form a dome shape over the top of the pot.

TREATING AGAINST VINE WEEVIL

1 Carefully read the instructions before use. Pour the diluted emulsion of the proprietary treatment into a small clean watering can.

2 Apply the treatment as a soil drench to the pots. Stand the pot in a plant saucer to catch any drainage and allow it to re-absorb.

Left: This weathered terracotta (clay) pot planted with a hardy fuchsia will continue to flower well into the autumn, provided there are no early frosts. Keep feeding and removing seedpods and old flowers from the growth to help it to continue flowering vigorously.

Winter care

At this time of year, most fuchsias are stored away in their dormant state, or settled in the greenhouse, just ticking over in green leaf. It is a good time to sit back and browse through the next year's fuchsia catalogues. During the previous season, you will probably have seen and made note of fuchsia varieties you would like to try. Many nurseries now make their catalogues available on the internet, and are happy to take orders this way, or by letter or email. Order as early as possible to ensure you get your selection in good time during the next season. You may also want to tackle the more energetic task of preparing the ground for new hardy fuchsia beds or hedges when the weather is suitable.

THE HARDY BED

When frost has killed and removed the leaves from the stems in the hardy fuchsia beds, cut back any of the growth that is not woody. This is usually about the last third of the last season's growth. In very cold areas or for fuchsias you planted in the previous season, draw some soil up over the stems and add some extra winter protection in the form of dry leaves, straw or similar insulating materials.

In milder areas, the end of the winter is the time to prune fuchsias back hard as they start to make growth, before the stems are growing so strongly that they will bleed when pruned. In colder areas, this is a job for the early spring.

IN THE GREENHOUSE

For a frost-free greenhouse, maintain a minimum temperature of 1°C (34°F). For a heated greenhouse, which will keep most fuchsias ticking over in green leaf and protect more tender varieties like Triphyllas in their dormant state, keep a minimum of 5°C (41°F). It is possible to use higher temperatures, but this increases the heating cost considerably. Open the ventilation in the greenhouse on days when the weather conditions allow.

Top: 'Alf Thornley' is a lovely pink and white double-flowered bush which grows well in the greenhouse.

Right: Placing plants under the staging in a heated greenhouse in winter will keep them in green leaf. This method works well, as long as the glass extends close to ground level.

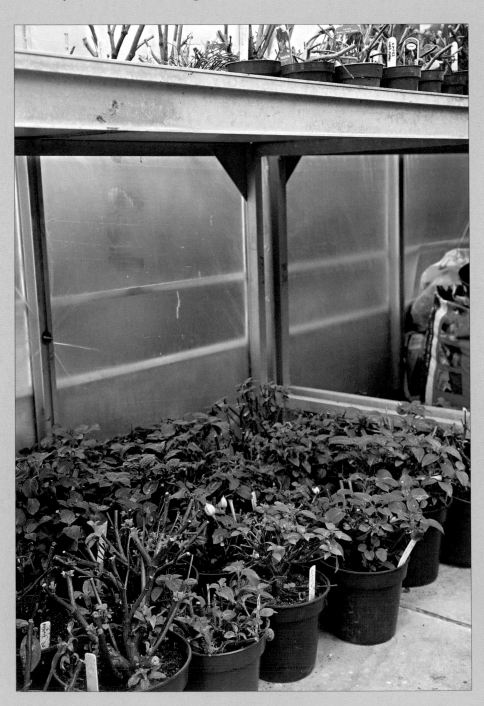

Right: Fuchsias grown from cuttings in late spring and not allowed to flower over the summer. These plants grow on in green leaf over the winter to make flourishing specimen plants the next year.

Keep watering to a minimum, and if possible water in the mornings. The plants, even the defoliated dormant ones, should be kept with the root ball just moist, although they will normally stand being dry for a few days in the winter. For the plants in green leaf, quickly remove any dead or dying leaves to minimize the chances of botrytis. Turn the plants regularly and keep an eye out for any pests and diseases, treating if necessary.

In the later part of the winter season, encourage dormant plants to start into growth by spraying the hard wood with water, which will encourage buds to break. Plants in green leaf will start to grow as the day length increases, and you can take early cuttings from these plants. These cuttings are excellent for growing standards, or for any other forms of training needing a long growth period.

Standards and other trained shapes are best kept standing upright, either as dormant plants in the frost-free greenhouse, or ticking over in green leaf in the heated greenhouse. Being upright ensures that the sap rises to the head of a standard, and will initiate the new growths needed. For a pillar, cone or pyramid, it helps to suspend the plant horizontally, and rotate it in the horizontal axis, to ensure that all the lateral growths get some period of being vertical to boost the sap flow.

DORMANT PLANTS IN STORAGE

Check any plants in dormant storage periodically. Often books will tell you to keep the plants in an area just above freezing, with a temperature of 0–4°C (32–39°F). Realistically, this is often difficult to achieve in a cold climate unless you have a cold cellar, or a garage kept frost-free. The essential point is to keep them above freezing and ensure they do not dry out.

If the temperature gets warmer for a period, dormant plants may start into growth, and when stored in the dark, produce long white straggly growths. Simply remove these. When it is warm enough to bring the plants out into the light they will start to make normal growth.

WARMER CLIMATES

If you live in an area that is free from winter frosts, induce the dormancy period by pruning to reduce the size of the plant and promote new growth from the base, which will make the plant a better shape next year.

PRUNING A FUCHSIA IN LATE WINTER

1 This 'Thalia' plant has been kept dormant through the winter, and is now starting to make new small growths.

2 Trim the wood of the branches back carefully just above the lowest strong buds, using sharp secateurs.

3 The aim is to obtain a fuchsia that is balanced in shape, with good growth from low down on the plant.

Useful addresses

GENERAL

Barbara's website
http://home.pacific.net.au/~bcooper1/fuchsia.htm
From the Blue Mountains near Sydney, Australia.

Bonsai website
http://www.bonsaigarden.net/default.html
Kath van Hanegem's site, with a lot about
fuchsias and growing bonsai fuchsias.

Dave Clark's website
http://www.fuchsiaclark.pwp.blueyonder.co.uk/
Pictures of his raisings and a lot of useful
information on fuchsia culture and hybridizing.

**Deutsche Dahlien-, Fuchsien - und
Gladiolen-Gesellschaft eV (German Dahlia,
Fuchsia and Gladioli Society)**
http://www.ddfgg.de/
A gallery of fuchsia pictures and a fuchsia
finder, all in the German language. To get to it
directly, use http://fuchsien.ddfgg.de/. There are
links to search by name, properties or breeder
(hybridizer) of 11,500 fuchsia varieties.

Eurofuchsia
http://www.eurofuchsia.org/
A European group founded in 1982 with
membership and representation from a number
of European national societies. There are links to
many of the national European fuchsia societies.

Find That Fuchsia
http://www.findthatfuchsia.info/
Website by Rick Stevens; probably the largest
list of fuchsias on the web, and some pictures.

Fuchsia Fairyland
http://www.fuchsias.tamsha.net/
Australian site of Sue and Dave from
Melbourne, with lovely pictures.

Fuchsia Magic
http://www.fuchsiamagic.com/fuchsias/
fuchsias.htm
Chris Martin's wonderful collection
of fuchsia photographs.

Fuchsias in Colour Order
http://homepage.mac.com/fuchsia/
FJ_Annex/gallery/Gallery_color.html
Japanese website with photographs organized by
flower colour. Useful for finding fuchsias with a
particular colour or identifying unknown fuchsias.

Gelderse Fuchsia Info-Site
http://www.geldersefuchsia.info/
A lot of useful information, including Dutch
winter hardiness tests and many fuchsia links,
plus tips for searching for fuchsia websites;
in Dutch/English.

Irene's website
http://www.ideboda.nl/
Interesting information and pictures;
in Dutch/English.

Jack Lamb's website
http://www.jacklamb.free-online.co.uk/
UK national collection of species.

Kenneth Nilsson's website
http://www2.dicom.se/fuchsias/
An excellent site on fuchsias in Swedish and
English, with some interesting threads on
fuchsia hardiness. This site originally hosted
the Swedish Fuchsia Society's site.

UNITED STATES

American Fuchsia Society
http://www.americanfuchsiasociety.org/
The first national society, founded in 1929. It
contains varied information and access to the AFS
registration database for fuchsia varieties online.

**Crescent City Branch of the
American Fuchsia Society**
http://ccfuchsia.net/
Contains interesting material about
gall mite-resistant fuchsias.

The Earthworks
http://www.fuchsias.net/
18034 SE 248th St, Covington,
WA 98042

Joy Creek Nursery
http://www.joycreek.com/
20300 NW Watson Rd, Scappoose,
OR 97056
Tel: +1 503 543-7474
Fax: +1 503 543-6933

Monnier's Country Gardens LLC
http://www.monnierscountrygardens.com/
17049 Mountain View LN NE Woodburn,
OR 97071
Tel: +1 503 981-3384

Northwest Fuchsia Society
http://www.nwfuchsiasociety.com/
A lot of useful information and links.

**Orange County Branch of the
National Fuchsia Society**
http://dir.gardenweb.com/directory/
ocbnfs/
Basic contact information.

Roger's Gardens
http://rogersgardens.com/Fuchsias.asp
2301 San Joaquin Hills Rd,
Corona del Mar, CA 92625
Tel: +1 949 640-5800

San Diego Fuchsia and Shade Plant Society
Secretary: Richard Hubbell,
15420 Olde Highway, 80#175,
El Cajon, CA 92021-2427
Tel: +1 619 443-3706

SW Portland Fuchsia Club
http://swportlandfuchsia.org/index.html

**Vallejo Branch of the American
Fuchsia Society**
http://westwood.fortunecity.com/rocco/83/
fuchsia1.htm

Weidner's Nursery California
http://www.weidners.com/index.html
695 Normandy Rd, Encinitas,
CA 92024
Tel: +1 760 436-2194

CANADA

British Columbia Fuchsia and Begonia Society
http://www.bcfuchsiasociety.com/

Hong's Nursery
http://www.hongs.ca/
10582 - 120th Street, Surrey,
BC, V3V 4G2
Tel: +1 604 588-3734
Email: gardens@hongs.ca

Jolly Farmer Products Inc.
http://www.jollyfarmer.com/
56 Crabbe Road, Northampton,
New Brunswick, E7N 1R6
Tel. +1 800 695 8300

Richbar Nursery Ltd
http://www.richbarnursery.com/Default.asp
3028 Red Bluff Road, Quesnel,
BC, V2J 6C6
Tel: +1 250 747-2915

UNITED KINGDOM

Bournemouth and Poole Fuchsia Society
http://www.bpfs.org.uk
A lot of useful information.

British Fuchsia Society
http://www.thebfs.org.uk/
History of the society and other information.

The Duchy of Cornwall Nursery
http://www.duchyofcornwallnursery.co.uk/
default.htm
Cott Road, Lostwithiel,
Cornwall, PL22 0HW
Tel: +44 (0)1208 872 668
Email: sales@duchyofcornwallnursery.co.uk

Gower Fuchsias
http://gower-fuchsias.co.uk/
Penclawdd Road, Penclawdd,
Swansea, SA4 3RB, Wales
Tel: +44 (0)1792 851 669
Email: sales@gower-fuchsias.co.uk

Irish Fuchsia and Pelargonium Society
Secretary: Wilfie Fisher,
54 Copeland Cresc, Comber,
Newtownards, Co. Down, BT23 5HY,
Northern Ireland
Tel: +44 (0)28 9187 2151
Email: wilfred.fisher@btinternet.com

Little Brook Fuchsias
http://www.littlebrookfuchsias.co.uk/
Index.asp
Ash Green Lane West, Ash Green,
Nr Aldershot, Hampshire, GU12 6HL
Tel: +44 (0)1252 329 731
Email: carol@littlebrookfuchsias.co.uk

Salford and Bolton Fuchsia Society
http://www.salfordboltonfuchsiasociety.co.uk/
index2.htm
A lot of useful information and links.
Look at the 'Fabulous Fuchsias' part.

Waltham Forest Fuchsia and Pelargonium Society
http://www.communigate.co.uk/london/
fuchsia/
Excellent website with society news,
articles, photos etc.

Walton Nurseries
http://www.waltonnurseries.co.uk/index.htm
Cherry Lane,
Lymm, Warrington,
Cheshire, WA13 0SY
Tel: +44 (0)1925 759 026
Email: info@WaltonNurseries.co.uk

AUSTRALIA

Australian Fuchsia Society
http://users.chariot.net.au/~jmsa/
fuchsia.htm
Society based in Adelaide, with lots of
information about fuchsias in Australia.
Look for the swan made out of fuchsia flowers.

Brenlissa Fuchsia Nursery
www.nurseriesonline.com.au/brenlissa
47 Wicklow Drive, Invermay Park, VIC 3350
Tel: +61 (0)4 3839 3578
Email: brenlissa@optusnet.com.au

Fuchsia Fantasy
75 Lillico Road, Lillico, TAS 7310
Tel: +61 (0)3 6428 2884

Jarrahdale Basket Nursery
Lot 452, Jarrahdale Rd,
Jarrahdale, WA 6124
Tel: +61 (0)8 9525 5329
Email: fuchsiajbn@bigpond.com

Metamorphosis Fuchsia Gardens
http://www2.dicom.se/fuchsias/
metamorphosis.html
226 Bellbridge Drive,
Hoppers Crossing, VIC 3029
Tel: +61 (0)3 9748 5562
Email: metphosi@netspace.net.au

NEW ZEALAND

Amberelle Fuchsias
156 Pickering Rd, RD 1, Cambridge
Tel: +64 (0)7 827 4375

Fuchsia 2000 Club
http://www.nfsnz.orconhosting.net.nz/
fu2000.htm

Maidstone Nursery
S.H.1. Otaki North
Tel: +64 (0)6 364 7013
Email: buzz@xtra.co.nz

The National Fuchsia Society of New Zealand
http://www.nfsnz.orconhosting.net.nz/index.htm
Also hosts web pages of local fuchsia groups.

SOUTH AFRICA

Western Cape Fuchsia Society
http://www.fuchsiasoc.co.za/index.htm
Information and photos.

Index

beds
  designing 40–1
  hardy, planting 134–5
  permanent 40–1
borders 50
  hardy 148
  planting 132–3
  shrub 34–5

climate change 14
composts 108–9
conservatories 88–91
containers 20, 45, 58–81
  arranging 80–1
  baskets, half 74–5
  boxes 67
  chimney pots 129
  companion plants for 63
  cottage style 45
  hanging baskets 68–71,
    81, 130–1
  mixed 62
  planting in 128–9
  pots, 60–3, 80
    chimney 78–9
    hanging 72–3
    wall 76–7
  Triphyllas for 20, 60–2
  troughs 66, 74–5
  types of 60
  urns 64–5
  window boxes 67

fuchsia
  autumn care 152–3
  bonsai, training 126–7
  bushes, training as 119
  climbing 55
  conicals 52–3, 86
  cuttings 106, 112–13,
    151
  discovery of 9
  espaliers 54, 124–5
  fan shapes 54, 87, 125
  fast-growing 20–1

feeding 109, 150–1
first hybrids 9, 10
grouping together 22–3
growing sites 18–19
history and origins 8–9
houseplants 84–7
hybridizing 14, 110–11
  history of 10–11
multi-planting 116–17
overwintering 140–1
pillars 52, 122
potting on 114–15
propagating 112–13
pruning 138–9
pyramids 52, 123
shrubs, training as
  118–19
specimen feature plants
  20–1, 22–3
species 12–13
spring care 148–9
standards 48–9, 86–7,
  115, 120–1, 133
summer bedding, for
  26–7, 28–9
summer care 150–1
topiary 54–5, 127
training 52–5, 86–7,
  118–25, 151
watering 150–1
Fuchsia
  F. 'Abbé Farges' 10,
    41, 99
  F. 'Abigail Reine' 133
  F. abrupta 12
  F. 'Abundance' 41, 99
  F. 'Accent' 99
  F. 'Achievement' 41,
    43, 51, 99
  F. 'Adinda' 28, 29,
    90, 98
  F. 'Alan Titchmarsh' 110
  F. 'Alaska' 19, 43, 62
  F. 'Alberttina' ('Albertina')
    43
  F. 'Alf Thornley' 154
  F. 'Alice Hoffman' 36,
    41, 80, 85, 124
  F. 'Alison Patricia' 30,
    31, 67
  F. alpestris 12
  F. 'Alton Water' 69
  F. 'Alwin' 27
  F. 'Ambassador' 99
  F. 'Amigo' 99
  F. 'Andenken an
    Heinrich Henkel'
    ('Heinrich Henkel') 27
  F. 'Andrew Hadfield' 37
  F. 'Anja Robbens' 28

F. 'Anna' 99
F. 'Annabel' 23, 43, 48,
  51, 54, 60, 62, 63,
  64, 67, 70, 75
F. 'Annabelle Stubbs'
  71, 73
F. 'Amy Lye' 11, 51,
  91, 99
F. apetala 9, 13
F. 'Apricot Ice' 15
F. 'Apricot Slice' 15
F. 'April' 87
F. 'Arabella' 10
F. arborescens 9, 13,
  35, 62, 90, 98
F. 'Arcadia Gold' 69
F. 'Ariel' 41, 91, 98
F. 'Army Nurse' 41, 45,
  90, 91
F. 'Art Deco' 47
F. 'Artemis' 91
F. 'Ashley and Isobel'
  71, 73
F. 'Aubergine' 46
F. 'Auntie Jinks' 37, 62,
  65, 67, 69, 70, 71,
  73, 75, 76, 130
F. 'Aurora Superba'
  91, 99
F. 'Australia Day' 15
F. 'Autumnale' 11, 26,
  27, 63, 69, 76,
  89, 99
F. 'Baby Bright' 51
F. 'Baby Chang' 87, 91
F. 'Baby Love' 43
F. 'Baby Thumb' 26,
  36, 41
F. x bacillaris 127
F. 'Bambini' 27, 87, 91
F. 'Barbara' 20, 43, 51
F. 'Barbara Norton' 69
F. 'Baroness van
  Demen' 27
F. 'Bashful' 27, 36, 41
F. 'Beacon' 22
F. 'Beacon Rosa' 22,
  41, 43, 87
F. 'Beauty of Exeter' 99
F. 'Beauty of Trowbridge'
  11, 24–5, 43
F. 'Bella Rosella' 77
F. 'Ben Jammin' 27,
  46, 47
F. 'Beranger' 41
F. 'Bertha Gadsby' 76
F. 'Bessie Kimberley'
  28, 90
F. 'Billy Green' 28, 29,
  32, 61, 63, 98

F. 'Black Country 21'
  31, 46
F. 'Black Prince'
  see F. 'Gruss aus dem
    Bodenthal'
F. 'Blacky' see
  F. 'Roesse Blacky'
F. 'Bland's New Striped'
  84, 99
F. 'Blue Beauty' 10, 45
F. 'Blue Gown' 41
F. 'Blue Sleigh Bells' 99
F. 'Blue Waves' 63, 90,
  99
F. 'Blush o' Dawn' 102
F. 'Bob Pacey' 21
F. boliviana 12, 27, 35,
  55, 90, 98
  F. b. var. alba 12,
    24, 27, 35, 90,
    98, 103
F. 'Bon Accord' 27, 30,
  31, 43
F. 'Border Queen' 17,
  19, 27, 51, 67
F. 'Bornemanns Beste'
  11, 61, 98
F. 'Bouquet' 36, 41
F. 'Bow Bells' 26, 91
F. 'Boy Marc' 28
F. 'Brenda White' 17, 34
F. 'Brian Kimberley' 61
F. 'British Stirling' 43
F. 'Brookwood Belle' 24
F. 'Brookwood Lady' 31
F. 'Brutus' 10, 41, 51,
  52, 90, 91, 99, 124
F. 'C.J. Howlett' 41
F. 'Caledonia' 10, 43, 91
F. 'California' 99
F. 'Cambridge Louie'
  49, 59, 63, 128
F. 'Camcon' 38
F. 'Canny Bob' 78
F. 'Caradella' 69, 73
F. 'Carmel Blue' 57, 79,
  91, 99
F. 'Carmen' 41
F. 'Caroline' 83
F. 'Cascade' 66, 67,
  69, 70, 71, 75, 76
F. 'Cecile' 71, 73, 75
F. 'Celia Smedley' 17,
  20, 23, 25, 27, 35,
  43, 51, 63, 64
F. 'Chang' 51, 87, 91
F. 'Chantry Park' 61,
  71, 73, 74, 76, 77,
  90, 107
F. 'Charming' 11, 41

F. 'Checkerboard' 20,
  27, 43, 51, 64,
  99, 120
F. 'Chillerton Beauty'
  41
F. 'Christmas Elf' 87, 91
F. 'Citation' 93
F. 'City of Leicester' 19,
  43, 99
F. 'Clair de Lune' 84, 99
F. 'Claudia' 76, 131
F. 'Cloth of Gold' 59, 63
F. coccinea 8, 9, 12, 84
F. x colensoi 13
F. 'Colne Fantasia' 30
F. 'Constance' 41, 138
F. 'Constellation' 19, 93
F. 'Coral Baby' 91
F. 'Coralle' ('Koralle')
  11, 16, 19, 27, 28,
  29, 32, 61, 63, 90,
  98, 128
F. 'Corallina' 45
F. corymbiflora 9
  F. c. alba 12
F. 'Cotton Candy' 43, 62
F. 'Countess of
  Aberdeen' 39, 43,
  45, 102
F. cyrtandroides 13
F. 'Daisy Bell' 76
F. 'Dancing Flame' 99
F. 'Daniel Reynolds' 78
F. 'David' 36, 41, 91
F. 'David Lockyer' 43
F. 'Dawn Fantasia' 23,
  27, 30
F. decidua 13
F. decussata 9, 12
F. 'Deep Purple' 71
F. 'Delta's KO' 99
F. 'Delta's Sara' 56, 63
F. denticulata 12, 35,
  103, 138
F. dependens 9, 103
F. 'Derby Imp' 76,
  91, 99
F. 'Devonshire
  Dumpling' 67, 69
F. 'Diana Wright' 41
F. 'Display' 87, 99,
  106, 120, 158
F. 'Doc' 27, 36
F. 'Dollar Prinzessin'
  ('Dollar Princess'/
  'Princess Dollar') 41,
  64, 66, 67, 87, 90
F. 'Dopey' 27, 36
F. 'Doreen Redfern' 43
F. 'Dorothy Handley' 47

'Display'

F. 'Drame' 10, 45
F. 'Duplex' 9
F. 'Easter Bonnet' 99
F. 'Eden Lady' 43
F. 'Eleanor Clark' 102
F. 'Elf' 36
F. 'Elfin Glade' 41
F. 'Elfriede Ott' 43, 61, 98
F. 'Emile de Wildman' 10
F. 'Emma Louise' 65, 66, 67, 71, 73, 76
F. 'Empress of Prussia' 41, 45
F. encliandra 13
F. 'Enfant Prodigue' ('Prodigue'/'Prodigy') 10, 41
F. 'Erecta Novelty' 29
F. 'Ernie' 25
F. 'Ernie Bromley' 51, 69, 75
F. 'Eruption' 28
F. 'Estelle Marie' 31, 43, 51
F. 'Europa' 11
F. 'Eva Boerg' 51, 67, 71, 88
F. 'Evening Star' 99
F. 'Evensong' 19
F. excorticata 8, 13, 47
F. 'Exmoor Gold' 41
F. 'Falling Stars' 19, 51, 91, 99
F. 'Fifi' 91
F. 'Fiona Jane' 76
F. 'Firecracker' 27, 59, 61
F. 'Flash' 99
F. 'Flirtation Waltz' 19, 39, 102
F. 'Flocon de Neige' 10
F. 'Florence Mary Abbott' 19
F. 'Flying Cloud' 14, 43
F. 'Forest King' 76
F. 'Forget-Me-Not' 10, 36
F. 'Frank Unsworth' 76
F. 'Frosted Flame' 24, 25
F. fulgens 8, 9, 13, 90, 103
F. 'Fulpila' 29
F. 'Garden News' 34, 41, 51, 63
F. garleppiana 13
F. 'Gartenmeister Bonstedt' 11, 19, 28, 29, 29, 33, 60, 63
F. 'Gay Fandango' 99
F. 'Genii' ('Jeanne') 19, 22, 23, 27, 51, 64, 118, 139
F. 'Geoff Oke' 147
F. 'Geoffrey Smith' 27

F. 'Georg Bornemann' 63
F. 'Gerharda's Aubergine' 15, 46
F. 'Giant Cascade' 55
F. glazioviana 12, 83, 90, 98
F. 'Glow' 41
F. 'Golden Anniversary' 69, 71, 73, 103
F. 'Golden Lena' 69
F. 'Golden Marinka' 59, 62, 63, 67, 69, 71, 72, 73, 75, 76, 130
F. 'Gordon Thorley' 65
F. 'Göttingen' 11
F. 'Graf Witte' 41, 99
F. 'Grandma Sinton' 43
F. 'Grasmere' 99
F. 'Greatham Mill' 41
F. 'Grumpy' 27, 36
F. 'Gruss aus dem Bodenthal' 19
F. 'Happy' 27, 36, 41, 87, 133
F. 'Happy Fellow' 99
F. 'Happy Wedding Day' 15, 23, 43, 89, 99, 128
F. 'Harbour Bridge' 90, 99
F. 'Harlow Carr' 38, 39
F. 'Harriet Lye' 11
F. 'Harry Grey' 37, 65, 67, 69, 70, 71, 73, 74, 76, 77, 130
F. 'Harvey's Reward' 31
F. 'Haute Cuisine' 19, 47, 59, 62, 67, 71, 74, 75
F. 'Hawkshead' 18, 21, 22, 35, 41, 43, 95
F. 'Hazel' 15
F. 'Heidi Ann' 41, 84, 87, 90, 91
F. hemsleyana 37, 91, 98, 127
F. 'Herald' 41
F. 'Herman de Graaff' 71
F. 'Hermiena' 71, 73, 76, 117
F. 'Hiawatha' 43
F. 'Hidcote Beauty' 43, 99
F. 'Holly's Beauty' 56, 73
F. 'Hot Coals' 103
F. 'Howlett's Hardy' 41
F. 'Ice Maiden' 99
F. 'Iceberg' 19
F. 'Impala' 39
F. 'Indian Maid' 91
F. inflata 13
F. 'Insulinde' 29, 32
F. 'Irene Sinton' 6, 8, 56, 73, 148
F. 'Irene van Zoeren' 99

F. 'Ivana van Amsterdam' 31
F. 'Jack Shahan' 51
F. 'Jack Siverns' 27, 47
F. 'Jackqueline' 98
F. 'Janice Ann' 69, 71, 74, 76, 124
F. 'Jaspers Triphywhite' 28
F. 'Jean Dawes' 76
F. 'Jeanne' *see F.* 'Genii'
F. 'Jessica Reynolds' 46
F. jimenezii 13
F. 'Joan Cooper' 99
F. 'Joan Goy' 31
F. 'Joan Pacey' 19
F. 'Joan Smith' 23
F. 'John Bartlett' 25, 31, 60, 121
F. 'Joy Patmore' 61, 63, 99
F. 'Julie Horton' 91
F. juntasensis 13
F. 'Katie Susan' 34, 122
F. 'Katrina Thompsen' 38, 51, 115
F. 'Kegworth Carnival' 43
F. 'Kevin Heinz' 99
F. 'King's Ransom' 99
F. 'Kolding Perle' 20, 35, 85
F. 'Kon Tiki' 71, 75
F. 'Koralle' *see F.* 'Coralle'
F. 'Kwintet' 43, 99
F. 'La Campanella' 65, 66, 71, 73, 76, 99, 111
F. 'Lady Bacon' 41
F. 'Lady Boothby' 55
F. 'Lady Isobel Barnett' 20, 63, 78
F. 'Lady Kathleen Spence' 19, 43
F. 'Lady Thumb' 22–3, 27, 36, 41, 64
F. 'Lancashire Lad' 25
F. 'Land van Beveren' 25, 65, 67, 71, 75
F. 'Laura' 83, 159
F. 'Len Beilby' 61
F. 'Lena' 43, 91
F. 'Leonora' 43, 63
F. 'Les Hobbs' 99
F. 'Leverkusen' 61
F. 'Liebriez' 36, 41
F. 'Lilac Lustre' 56
F. 'Lilian' 19, 43, 56, 57, 102
F. 'Lillian Annetts' 54, 124, 150
F. 'Lindisfarne' 91
F. 'Little Beauty' 53, 87, 91, 99, 123
F. 'Little Jewel' 91

F. 'London 2000' 53
F. 'Lord Byron' 99
F. 'Lottie Hobby' 37, 91, 98, 99, 126, 127
F. 'Loveliness' 11
F. 'Love's Reward' 34, 57, 66
F. loxensis 12
F. lycioides 9, 12, 90, 98
F. 'Lye's Elegance' 25
F. 'Lye's Excelsior' 11
F. 'Lye's Unique' 11, 26, 91
F. macrophylla 12
F. macrostemma 9
F. macrostigma 103
F. 'Madame Cornelissen' 11, 24, 41
F. magellanica 8, 9, 12, 14, 27, 40, 44, 98, 136, 137
F. m. alba see F. m. var. molinae
F. m. var. *aurea* 14, 44, 98
F. m. var. *gracilis* 21, 98
F. m. var. *g.* 'Tricolor' 35, 44, 98
F. m. var. *g.* 'Variegata' 21, 22, 44
F. m. var. *molinae* 21, 22, 34, 35, 40, 41, 44, 98
F. m. var. *pumila* 36, 37, 41
F. m. var. *riccartonii* 20, 21, 22, 34, 35, 44
F. m. var. *variegata* 41
F. m. var. *versicolor* 35
F. 'Maiden's Blush' *see F. m.* var. *molinae*
F. 'Mantilla' 74, 76, 90
F. 'Marcus Graham' 146–7
F. 'Margaret' 22, 35, 40, 41, 50

F. 'Margaret Brown' 16–17, 35, 41, 43
F. 'Margarite Dawson' 38, 39
F. 'Maria Landy' 67
F. 'Marilyn Olsen' 51
F. 'Marin Glow' 19, 43, 100, 103
F. 'Marinka' 64, 69, 71, 72, 75, 76, 99, 131
F. 'Marlene Gilbee' 15
F. 'Marlies de Keijzer' 91
F. 'Martin's Umbrella' 64
F. 'Mary' 11, 28, 29, 33, 61, 63, 90, 98
F. 'Mauve Lace' 41, 45
F. 'Mephisto' 43
F. 'Mercurius' 133
F. 'Meteor' 11
F. mezae 13
F. 'Micky Goult' 26, 31, 43, 67
F. microphylla 9, 13, 37
F. m. subsp. *hemsleyana see F. hemsleyana*
F. m. subsp. *hidalgensis* 127
F. 'Midwinter' 51, 53, 102
F. 'Mikado' 91
F. 'Millennium' 67, 70, 74
F. 'Miniature Jewels' 37
F. 'Minirose' 30, 31, 67, 87, 91
F. 'Mischief' 27
F. 'Miss California' 38, 39, 49, 63, 67
F. 'Mission Bells' 91
F. 'Misty Blue' 19
F. 'Molesworth' 99
F. 'Mrs Lovell Swisher' 27, 51
F. 'Mrs Marshall' 91
F. 'Mrs Popple' 21, 22, 35, 41
F. 'Mrs W.P. Wood' 35
F. 'My Little Cracker' 37
F. 'Nancy Lou' 19, 23, 38, 75, 90, 99
F. 'Natasha Sinton' 69
F. 'Nellie Nuttall' 25, 27, 31, 37, 43, 51, 91
F. 'Nettala' 43
F. 'Nice 'n' Easy' 27
F. 'Nicis Findling' 31, 99
F. 'Novella' 99
F. 'Obergartner Koch' 61
F. 'Old Somerset' 45
F. 'Olive Smith' 27, 35, 51
F. 'Orange Flare' 99
F. 'Orient Express' 29, 33, 61

'Laura'

F. 'Ortenburger Festival' 19, 103
F. 'Ostfriesland' 76
F. 'Other Fellow' 19, 26, 27, 39, 43, 63
F. 'Our Ted' 28, 33
F. 'Pabbe's Kirrevaalk' 31
F. 'Pabbe's Torreldove' 28, 47, 61
F. pallescens 12
F. 'Pan' 28
F. paniculata 13, 35
F. 'Papagena' 11
F. 'Papoose' 36, 41, 99
F. 'Paula Jane' 51, 67
F. 'Phaidra' 29
F. 'Phenomenal' 10, 20, 23, 90, 99
F. 'Phyllis' 35, 43, 124
F. 'Phyrne' 41
F. pilaloensis 13
F. 'Pinch Me' 71
F. 'Pink Bon Accord' 43
F. 'Pink Fantasia' 23, 26, 27, 29, 31, 67
F. 'Pink Galore' 90
F. 'Pink Marshmallow' 73
F. 'Pink Rain' 37, 71, 76, 126
F. 'Pixie' 99
F. 'Popsie Girl' 63, 75
F. 'Postiljon' 69, 71, 76, 131
F. 'Powder Puff' 76
F. 'President George Bartlett' 46, 47, 63
F. 'President Margaret Slater' 66, 67, 69, 71, 75, 76, 116
F. 'Preston Guild' 43, 103
F. 'Pride of the West' 55
F. 'Princessita' 25, 73, 91
F. procumbens 13, 36, 37, 40, 76
F. 'Prodigue' see F. 'Enfant Prodigue'
F. 'Prodigy' see F. 'Enfant Prodigue'

F. 'Professor Henkel' 75
F. 'Prosperity' 41
F. 'Purperklokje' 91
F. 'Purple Rain' 71
F. 'Purple Splendour' 41
F. 'Put's Folly' 39, 66, 69
F. 'Quasar' 43, 90
F. 'Queen Victoria' 9
F. 'Radings Maria' 91
F. 'R.A.F.' 99
F. 'Ratatouille' 47
F. 'Red Devil' 99
F. 'Red Imp' 36
F. 'Red Rain' 91
F. 'Red Rum' 99
F. 'Red Spider' 71
F. 'Regal' 43
F. regia 8, 12, 55
F. 'Riccartonii' see F. magellanica var. riccartonii
F. 'Richard John Carrington' 19
F. 'Rigoletto' 71
F. 'Rocket Fire' 69
F. 'Roesse Blacky' ('Blacky') 19, 65
F. 'Roesse Tethys' 31
F. 'Roger de Cooker' 28, 29, 61
F. 'Rolla' 19
F. 'Roos Breytenbach' 61
F. 'Rose Fantasia' 27, 30, 31, 51
F. 'Rose of Castile' 10, 23, 41, 45
F. 'Rose of Castile Improved' 10, 41
F. 'Rose of Denmark' 10, 23, 43
F. 'Rose Quartet' 27
F. 'Rosemarie Higham' 69
F. 'Royal Purple' 10, 55
F. 'Royal Velvet' 19, 23, 48, 62, 63, 64, 79, 90, 99
F. 'Ruby Wedding' 71, 74, 75
F. 'Rufus' 35, 41, 43, 91, 99
F. 'Ruth King' 70, 130
F. salicifolia 13
F. 'Sandboy' 87, 91
F. 'Santa Claus' 90
F. 'Santa Cruz' 22
F. 'Schneeball' 11
F. serratifolia 9,
F. sessilifolia 12, 103
F. 'Seventh Heaven' 67, 69, 70, 71, 73, 128
F. 'Shady Lady' 90, 103
F. 'Sharon Leslie' 37
F. 'Sharonelle' 36, 37
F. 'Sharpitor' 27, 35

F. 'Shelford' 38, 60, 63, 70, 74, 102, 117
F. 'Sir Matt Busby' 24, 69, 74
F. 'Sleepy' 27, 36
F. 'Sleigh Bells' 43
F. 'Sneezy' 27, 36
F. 'Snow White' 36
F. 'Snowcap' 24, 27, 35, 41, 43, 45, 51, 120
F. 'Son of Thumb' 27, 36, 41
F. 'Sophie Louise' 37, 51, 57
F. 'Sophisticated Lady' 39
F. 'Sparky' 28, 31, 33, 90, 98
F. splendens 13, 103
F. 'Stanley Cash' 43
F. 'String of Pearls' 42, 43, 111
F. 'Sunray' 26, 45, 59, 62, 63, 133
F. 'Superstar' 31, 37
F. 'Susan Green' 67, 68, 73, 75
F. 'Susan Skeen' 31
F. 'Swanley Gem' 91
F. 'Swingtime' 25, 51, 54, 59, 67, 69, 71, 74, 75, 90, 92, 99, 124, 131
F. 'Sylvia Barker' 25
F. 'Symphony' 19
F. ''t Voske' 69
F. 'Tamworth' 103
F. 'Tarra Valley' 47
F. 'Ted Sweetman' 15
F. 'Tennessee Waltz' 17, 19, 41
F. 'Thalia' 11, 17, 18, 19, 27, 28, 29, 32, 60, 61, 62, 63, 64, 90, 91, 98, 114, 132, 135, 155
F. 'Thamar' 27, 31, 67
F. 'Thornley's Hardy' 36, 41, 76
F. thymifolia 13
F. tincta 12
F. 'Ting a Ling' 19
F. 'Tinker Bell' 36
F. 'Toby Foreman' 24
F. 'Tom Thumb' 23, 26, 27, 36, 41, 45, 51, 60, 65, 87, 91, 99, 133, 149
F. 'Tom West' 26, 27, 36, 45, 59, 62, 63, 75, 87, 93, 99, 133
F. 'Trailing King' 71
F. 'Trailing Queen' 71, 76

F. 'Traudchen Bonstedt' 11, 61, 90, 98
F. triphylla 9, 11, 12, 93
F. t. flore coccinea 9
F. 'Tropic Sunset' 69
F. 'Trudi Davro' 38, 39, 71, 72, 73, 102
F. 'Tsjiep' 27
F. 'Twinny' 37, 67
F. 'University of Liverpool' 71, 75
F. 'Upward Look' 27, 30, 31
F. 'Vanessa Jackson' 71
F. 'Variegated Pink Fantasia' 27, 30, 31
F. 'Veenlust' 69
F. 'Venus Victrix' 9
F. venusta 12, 93, 103
F. 'Violet Bassett-Burr' 43
F. 'Vobeglo' 27, 31, 37
F. 'Voodoo' 90, 99
F. 'Voltaire' 10, 91
F. vulcanica 12
F. 'W.P. Wood' 41
F. 'Waldfee' 35, 41
F. 'Walsingham' 59, 69, 71
F. 'WALZ Citer' 71, 76
F. 'WALZ Jubelteen' 23, 27, 31, 49, 51, 81
F. 'Water Nymph' 24
F. 'Waveney Gem' 54, 65, 67, 71, 72, 101, 124

F. 'Wendy's Beauty' 68, 71, 73
F. 'Westminster Chimes' 37
F. 'White Ann' 99
F. 'White Joy' 43
F. 'White Pixie' 41
F. 'Whiteknights Amethyst' 41, 47
F. 'Whiteknights Cheeky' 32
F. 'Whiteknights Pearl' 99
F. 'Wilson's Pearls' 74
F. 'Winston Churchill' 57, 90, 99, 160
F. 'Wisteria' 55
F. 'Zulu Queen' 103

hedging 42–3, 136–7

paths 50
patios 50
pergolas 51
pests and diseases 142–5, 153
ponds 51

rockeries 36–7

steps 50

terraces 50

walls 50

ACKNOWLEGEMENTS

The publisher would like to thank the following for kindly allowing photography to take place in their gardens: Abbotsbury Gardens, Duchy of Cornwall Nursery, Elizabeth Coles, John Nicholass, Kath van Hanegem, The Lost Gardens of Heligan, Mike and Julie Daw, Paul and Rosemary Weekes, RHS Rosemoor, RHS Wisley, and Silver Dale Nurseries.

Thanks to Carol Gubler/British Fuchsia Society for permission to take photographs at the BFS London Show.

The publisher would also like to thank the following for allowing their photographs to be reproduced in the book (t=top, b=bottom, l=left, r=right, m=middle).

Alamy: 75tr, 77tr, 79b, 80b, 81b, 143tl, 143tm, 143tr.
Lucy Doncaster: 33tl, 151b. **Tim Ellerby:** 10m, 13br, 19m, 24tl, 24tr, 33tm, 36m, 38bl, 41b, 46bl, 46br, 54tl, 59m, 61bl, 74bl, 83m, 87tl, 90b, 91tr, 91m, 98b, 102br, 124t, 133t, 134t, 137b, 150t. **Felicity Forster:** 67b, 68m, 71bl, 74t, 76t, 81m. **Rog Frost:** 11tl. **GAP Photos:** 75tl, 102t. **Carol Gubler:** 143bl (courtesy of DEFRA). **iStockphoto:** 142bm. **Chris Martin:** 11tr. **John Nicholass:** 31t, 31br, 38br, 47tr, 48t, 49bl, 49br, 50t, 51r, 52bl, 52br, 54br, 61tr, 68b, 71bmr, 72t, 73t, 73bl, 74br, 86t, 98m, 100t, 101b, 113br, 116t, 117bl, 117br, 131t, 132t, 139tm, 139tr, 139ml, 139mr. **Photolibrary:** 23tl, 42b, 43bml (Buxus microphylla 'Faulkner'), 77b, 96m, 103t, 144br. **Steven Wooster:** 22t, 27br.

'Winston Churchill'